THE INTERDISCIPLINARY TEAM

A Handbook for the Education of Exceptional Children

Anne K. Golin
Alex J. Ducanis

AN ASPEN PUBLICATION
Aspen Systems Corporation
Rockville, Maryland
London
1981

Library of Congress Cataloging in Publication Data

Golin, Anne K.
The interdisciplinary team.

Bibliography: p. 185.
Includes index.

1. Handicapped children—Education—United
States—Handbooks, manuals, etc. 2. Teaching
teams—Handbooks, manuals, etc. 3. Interdisciplinary
approach in education—Handbooks, manuals, etc.
I. Ducanis, Alex J. II. Title. [DNLM:
1. Education of mentally retarded—Handbooks.
2. Teaching—Methods—Handbooks. LC 4625 G626i]
LC4031.G6   371.9   81-738
ISBN: 0-89443-346-6   AACR2

Copyright © 1981 by Aspen Systems Corporation

Library of Congress Catalog Card Number: 81-738
ISBN: 0-89443-346-6

Printed in the United States of America

1 2 3 4 5

To the special children

Table of Contents

v

Preface

The use of an interdisciplinary team to provide services to exceptional children is not a new approach but one that is becoming increasingly important. Teams are used not only to assess children's needs but also to provide a variety of medical, psychological, social, and educational services. This book examines the use of the team approach with exceptional children and analyzes both the benefits and the problems encountered by the interdisciplinary team in special education settings. If, as it now appears, the team approach continues as a significant aspect of the service delivery system for exceptional children and youth, then it is incumbent upon those professionals who are involved in such teams to seek an understanding of the process in which they are engaged. We hope this book will be helpful in that search.

The authors wish to recognize the excellent help they have received from Kathy Hughes and Irene Petrovich.

Chapter 1

The Team and the Exceptional Child

The use of an interdisciplinary team to provide services to exceptional children is not a new approach, but in recent years the need for collaborative efforts has become more generally recognized and accepted. Increasingly, we find that responsibility for providing services to exceptional children is shared by an interdisciplinary team of professionals. Underlying this approach is an assumption that an interdisciplinary team brings together diverse skills and expertise to provide more effective, better coordinated, and higher quality services for children. On the basis of this belief, the team approach has been adopted in a variety of settings throughout the country. Yet the implications of the team concept have not always been fully understood, and in some cases early enthusiasm has been followed by disillusionment as the difficulties inherent in the team approach became apparent.

Although the team approach has been widely heralded as a promising innovation in the delivery of services to exceptional persons, the concept seems to have generated more rhetoric than formal research, and to date an adequate theory of the team approach has not been formulated. Before an appropriate conceptual base for the team approach can be fully developed, there is a clear need for additional research on the use and effectiveness of the interdisciplinary team in working with exceptional children. A clearer understanding of the concept should improve the effectiveness of the team delivery approach.

The present volume brings together the work of several disciplines in an effort to initiate such a conceptual base. Research findings and theoretical concepts from the fields of child development, education, psychology, sociology, management, and decision sciences are integrated and applied to the team process. Existing research is supplemented by observations of teams serving exceptional children. Areas where further research is needed are identified and discussed. Throughout the book there is an attempt to help the professional become aware of the factors that have an impact upon team functioning.

In this chapter we examine what is meant by the team approach with exceptional children, see how the concept has developed, describe the characteristics of teams and the variables that affect team functioning, and, finally, provide an overview of the book.

DEFINITION OF THE INTERDISCIPLINARY TEAM

According to *Webster's Third New International Dictionary* (1976), *team* may be defined as "a number of persons associated together in work or activity as: a group of specialists or scientists functioning as a collaborative unit (the diagnostic team of psychiatrist, clinician, and social worker in a child guidance clinic)." The same source defines *teamwork* as "work done by a number of associates with usually each doing a clearly defined portion but all subordinating personal prominence to the efficiency of the whole (teamwork of a football eleven)."

Others have also emphasized collaboration as the basis of teamwork. For example, according to Rubin, Plovnick, and Fry (1975), "If the basic mission or job requires that you and others must work together and coordinate your activities with each other, then you are a team" (p. 3). Parker (1972) points out that the involvement of a number of professionals does not in itself ensure a team approach. "For a team to exist, there must be more than a variety of providers: each provider must function as a sub-unit of a whole in a synergistic relationship" (p. 9). The same point is emphasized again by Wendland and Crawford (1976). "Individuals trained in differing disciplines do not become a team by the mere process of calling themselves one, nor do they manage treatments by simply doing them. What they need is a system set up specifically to effectuate collaboration" (p. 5).

In the definitions reviewed above, the essential element seems to be collaboration or coordination of services. Therefore, for purposes of this book, the interdisciplinary team will be defined as *a functioning unit composed of individuals with varied and specialized training who coordinate their activities to provide services to children.*

In examining the team concept we find that teams have been variously described as interdisciplinary, multidisciplinary, intradisciplinary, transdisciplinary, intraprofessional, and interprofessional. The use of so many terms and the attempts to draw fine distinctions between them has at times led to confusion. When a team is composed of members of the same profession such as a number of teachers, it may appropriately be referred to as an "intraprofessional" or "intradisciplinary" team. On the other hand, a teacher, a psychologist, and a speech therapist may function together as an "interdisciplinary" or "interprofessional" team. Since in general we are dealing with differences in profession rather than differences in discipline, some prefer the use of "interprofessional." Others have suggested the use of "transdisciplinary" (Harris, 1977; Hart, 1977; McCormick & Goldman, 1979; Sirvis, 1978). However, we feel that attempts to distinguish between "interdisciplinary," "multidisciplinary," and "transdisciplinary" team approaches and the controversy that has developed around the terminology and variations in approach may be somewhat premature and unproductive. At the present time, the study of teams may best be facilitated by the use of a commonly agreed upon term to describe those teams composed of members of different disciplines or professions. Since "interdisciplinary" is the term most frequently employed in recent literature, it will be used throughout this volume.

DEVELOPMENT OF THE TEAM APPROACH

The team approach is not a recent innovation in providing services to exceptional children, although the practice has received increased attention of late. According to Ackerly (1947), "the psychiatrist, social worker, and psychologist were brought together as a full fledged team in the early 20's" (p. 191). Although the team approach was prominent in child guidance centers long before 1940, the team concept received a major impetus during World War II (Hutt, Menninger, & O'Keefe, 1947). Teamwork quickly became a "fashionable" term in rehabilitation (Whitehouse, 1951). and by the late 50's Patterson (1959) wondered whether the rehabilitation team was obsolete.

In recent years the team approach has been applied to child abuse (H. Martin, 1976; Schmitt, 1978), rehabilitation services (Crisler & Settles, 1979; Jacques, 1970; Wagner, 1977; Wile, 1970; A. J. Wilson, 1962), and exceptional children (Allen, Holm, & Schiefelbusch, 1978; Beck, 1962; Challela, 1979; Hart, 1977; Sells & West, 1976; Sirvis, 1978). An example of the application of the interdisciplinary approach to exceptional children may be found in the development of interdisciplinary clinics for the developmentally disabled in the state of Washington. A demonstration project started in 1955 as a joint effort between the University of Washington School of Medicine and the Washington State Department of Health provided a model for the establishment of additional teams. By 1976 there were eleven local child study clinics and three regional ones. Similar development has been undertaken in a number of other states (Sells & West, 1976).

Although several forces were influential in the emergence of the team approach with exceptional children, two factors seem to have been particularly significant: (1) the concept of the "whole" child; and (2) legislative mandates. Let us briefly examine how these factors have given impetus to the team approach in special education and related settings.

The Concept of the Whole Child

Whitehouse addressed the issue of the whole child in 1951 when he identified three assumptions in teamwork:

1. The human organism is dynamic and is an interacting, integrated whole.
2. Treatment must be dynamic and fluid to keep pace with the changing person and must consider all that person's needs.
3. Teamwork, an interacting partnership of professionals specializing in these needs and dealing with the person as a whole, is a valid method for meeting these requirements. (pp. 45–46)

"The whole child" may be a phrase that has become trite through overuse, but the underlying concept remains viable. It reflects the idea that the problems presented by the child are interrelated and cannot be adequately treated in isolation. The exceptional child has often been the object of categorical approaches to care and education. Yet the problems presented by any one individual may be diverse, interrelated, and not amenable to treatment by any one particular discipline. For example, the emotionally disturbed blind child may need the services of a psychiatrist, a psychologist, a mobility instructor, a teacher of the visually handicapped, a social worker, and others. Fellendorf (1975) has pointed to the need for close collaboration between educators and health care professionals.

Whether it be in the area of nutrition, upper respiratory problems, drug therapy, or in the testing of a child's hearing, it is evident that the status of a child's health and his ability to learn what the society expects him to learn at a given age, are so closely related, particularly for the exceptional child, that it is time to break down the artificial barriers between them. (p. 408)

Even when a number of problem areas are addressed, the various services provided may be fragmented and uncoordinated, resulting in confusion and apprehension on the part of the children and their families. The team approach has been developed in response to that kind of fragmentation.

External Mandates

Not only does an organization react to the needs of the client in attempting to improve the coordination of services, but it is also responsive to pressures and regulations from without. In recent years the development of the team approach has received considerable impetus from legislative mandates, state and federal government regulations, and the requirements of various third party payers. Team responsibility in assessment, diagnosis, and treatment is often seen as one way to improve the quality of service and provide for professional accountability. As a result, many organizations have moved to a team system because it was imposed from outside, rather than because of any real commitment to such an approach. Unfortunately, teams initiated *solely* because of external mandates sometimes function as teams in name only, with participants simply going through the motions rather than working toward a true coordination of services. This seems to be the case in a number of individualized education program (IEP) team meetings where most of the decisions are made before the meeting and parents are asked to approve decisions already made rather than to participate in their formulation.

However, the passage of Public Law (P.L.) 94–142 has had a great effect upon the utilization of a team approach in special education. Indeed, the development of the IEP as required by the law mandates the participation of the following:

- a representative of the public agency, other than the child's teacher, who is qualified to provide, or supervise the provision of, special education
- the child's teacher
- one or both of the child's parents
- the child, where appropriate
- other individuals at the discretion of the parent or agency.

In addition, for exceptional children who are being evaluated for the first time, the team meeting will also include a member of the evaluation team and a representative of the public agency who is familiar with the evaluation procedures and results.

Other agencies serving exceptional children are also subject to various external mandates regarding the use of a team evaluation and thus may involve a number of professionals in their assessment and treatment procedures in response to these requirements. However, in addition to these external influences, it should be noted that other factors have also affected the use of the team approach with exceptional children. For example, in some cases organizational needs seem to have played a role in the implementation of an interdisciplinary team. With greater professional specialization there has also been a significant increase in the number and variety of professionals and paraprofessionals operating with educational and other organizations. As more and more individuals become involved in providing services to a particular child, the need for clarifying the lines of communication and authority within the agency becomes increasingly acute. Otherwise the organization, like the child, may suffer negative effects from fragmentation of its services. The interdisciplinary team offers a way of organizing personnel to facilitate the exchange of pertinent information concerning the exceptional child.

CHARACTERISTICS OF THE TEAM

To clarify further the concept of the team approach, we have identified a number of general characteristics that seem to be common to interdisciplinary teams in a variety of settings. It is likely that others may disagree with some of the specific attributes that we have identified, and it may be some time before a firm consensus can be reached concerning those characteristics that are indeed common to all teams. However, this tentative set of criteria may be useful in deciding whether a specific group should be considered an interdisciplinary team.

Nine characteristics can be identified, and these may be further divided into three main categories: composition, functions, and task.

Composition

A team consists of two or more individuals. One person does not constitute a team: the nature of teamwork requires the action of two or more persons. Teams can operate with two members (such as a teacher and a counselor), three members (such as a teacher, a psychologist, and a social worker), or with larger groups. The two-member team has many of the same needs and dynamics found in larger configurations, but the interactions may be less complex than those of teams with seven or eight members.

Usually, most members of the interdisciplinary team are professionals, but nonprofessionals and paraprofessionals may also be team members. Teacher aides, child care aides, and of course the child's parents are often found to be team members. However, the interdisciplinary team will generally include at least one professional member if the group is to be considered a team.

Communication may be direct and face to face or indirect. A team may meet regularly with direct and immediate communication. However, the team concept does not necessarily exclude groups that rarely or never meet. There are instances where communication takes the form of an exchange of written reports or even telephone conversations.

There is an identifiable leader. The leadership of the team may shift due to the changing nature of the task; however, at any point in time the leadership can be identified. Leaderless groups are not teams. Some advocates of the team approach seem to suggest that teams are by definition democratic groups and are neither hierarchical nor authoritarian. This seems to be an unduly restrictive view that would rule out groups such as operating room teams, long regarded as classic examples of teamwork. Thus we do not specify the *form* that leadership might take, only that a leader is identifiable.

Functions

Teams can also be characterized by their functions or methods of operation.

Teams function both within and between organizational settings. The most common type of team is one in which there is a parent organization that provides the support system for the team's operation. Thus we may find teams functioning in schools, rehabilitation centers, and other organizations. However, teams also operate between and among organizations, with professionals from a number of agencies working together on a particular problem or a specific case. For example, the mental health team for an adolescent living in the community might include representatives from the psychiatric hospital of which the patient is a former resident, the community living facility in which the adolescent now resides, a counselor from the local community mental health center, and a teacher from the vocational training program in which the student is presently enrolled.

Roles of participants are defined. Roles of team participants are generally defined in terms of the particular professional competencies of each team member and the nature of the task to be done. Although teams differ in the extent to which roles overlap and conflict, in the clarity of the role definitions, and in the flexibility of established roles, role definition and differentiation is a team characteristic. A group in which each person can and does fill all roles is not a team.

Teams collaborate. The team is a collaborative endeavor whereby the diverse skills and expertise of team members are combined to provide solutions to specific problems. There seems to be general agreement in the team literature that such coordination of services is a definitive characteristic of teams.

There are specific protocols of operation. Each team develops certain rules of operation, certain ways of proceeding to accomplish its task. These may range from unwritten group norms of behavior to formal written procedural manuals. In either case, the protocol of operations is empirically identifiable.

Task

In addition to the above, there are certain characteristics associated with the unique task of the interdisciplinary team serving exceptional children.

The team is child centered. The child or adolescent is the focus of the team's efforts and the reason for the team's existence. While at times, it may appear that the team has been formed for the comfort and convenience of its members or the organization, the prime concern of the team is the exceptional children who are being served.

The team is task oriented. The team is primarily a task-oriented group that exists to improve the conditions of the child's life by dealing with the problems that have brought the client to the attention of the team. Whether the primary goals of the team are educational, vocational, psychological, or medical, the main focus is on the task to be completed rather than on other aspects of team functioning.

Again, these nine characteristics are suggested merely as tentative criteria to be considered in identifying a team. Other attributes could be included, and a number of other variables that may prove to be important characteristics common to all teams will be examined in later chapters.

THE TEAM SYSTEM

Any attempt to analyze the functioning of an interdisciplinary team quickly points up the need for a theoretical framework that allows us to focus on some of the major dimensions of the team concept and to organize systematically what might otherwise be considered a motley collection of isolated facts about team behavior. While much has been written about the team approach, an adequate theory of interdisciplinary teams has yet to be developed. Although it may be much too early to formulate a "theory" of interdisciplinary teamwork because more research is needed, a tentative outline of such a conceptual base may stimulate future research and theorizing. The purpose of this section is to suggest some of the major dimensions to explore as we move toward a theory of interdisciplinary teams serving exceptional children.

The operation of an interdisciplinary team is the result of a complex interaction of variables associated with the team members, the child, and the context in which the team functions. Figure 1–1 is a schematic representation of the team system and its components. The professionals on the team, the exceptional child, and the school or other organizational setting all have an impact on the goals of the team, its activities, and its outcomes. Formal and informal feedback provides information concerning outcomes to participants, with resulting changes in goals and activities. The team system serves as the core around which this book is organized.

Professionals

The team is composed of a number of professionals with different theoretical viewpoints, training, and experiences. They differ not only in the resources they bring to the group but also in role expectations, status, and the extent of their legal responsibility for the child. Among the professions often represented on

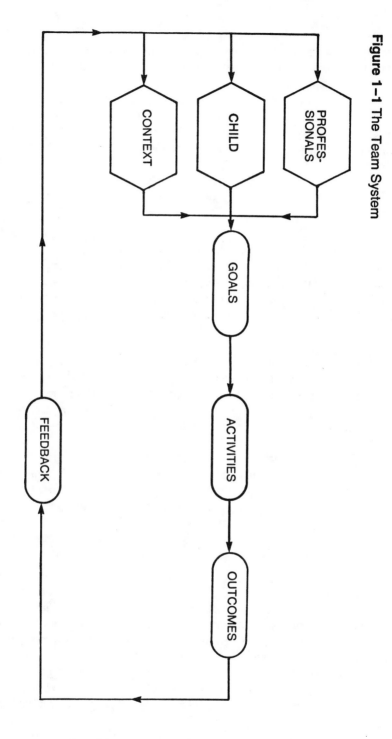

Figure 1-1 The Team System

the team are education, physical therapy, occupational therapy, social work, psychology, counseling, nursing, medicine, and various specialties within these disciplines. Each team is a unique blend of the professional and personal characteristics of its members, its effectiveness determined in large part by the dynamics of that configuration. The similarities, differences, and areas of overlap among the various professions are a source of potential conflict and misunderstanding as well as cooperation and agreement that can have considerable impact on team functioning.

Exceptional Child

The focus of the services provided by the interdisciplinary team is a child, adolescent, or family that seeks help for an educational, vocational, psychological, medical, or social problem or set of problems. For the purposes of this book, the definition used by Hobbs (1975) will be used.

> By *exceptional child* we mean a child who has been recognized and declared to be significantly different from other children on some important dimension such as intelligence, emotional stability, or ability to see or hear. We also define some children as exceptional on the basis of their status such as economically disadvantaged or delinquent. (p. 43)

The children and their families may be passive objects of the team's efforts, with their input limited to providing information to the team. Or they may be active members of the team and participants in the decision-making process. In any case, the child is a crucial component of the team system, and ultimately it is he or she who benefits from the team's effectiveness or suffers from its inadequacies.

Context

The team's context is the organizational setting in which it operates, the network of services of which it is a part, and the social system in which it is located. Schools, rehabilitation centers, hospitals, and other agencies provide particular organizational structures that markedly affect the operation of the team. The size and type of organization, its referral and treatment policies, and its communication channels and administrative structure are some of the variables making up the organizational context that is important for a full understanding of the team.

Goals

Goals are objects or aims that give direction to the team. In order to operate effectively, there must be agreement among team members regarding the direction of their efforts. In practice, however, each professional member of the team may have a particular conception of the team goals; the organization in which the team functions may have formally specified particular goals for the team; and the child's family may have certain goals to be met by the team. Thus the team goals may be quite diverse or even contradictory. Furthermore, unless the team members perceive some congruence between their individual goals and the goals of the team, they may quickly lose interest in participating in the team, with a consequent decrease in team effectiveness. If there is not some minimal sense of shared direction, the team is likely quite literally to fall apart.

Activities

The team's activities are what it does and how it goes about doing it. Activities include the task-related actions of team participants—diagnostic and assessment activities, decision making, conducting case conferences, and writing reports. The specific nature of these activities is determined by the professionals involved, the problems presented by the clients, the organizational context in which the activities are carried out, and the goals of the team. In addition, the team engages in a number of activities designed to improve or maintain the functioning of the group, including the development of a system of norms, the establishment of communication networks, and other forms of interaction. These team-maintenance activities are important for the smooth operation of the team.

Outcomes

Outcomes are those events that occur as a result of the team's activities. A child may or may not show the progress that was anticipated by the team or may show the expected progress in some areas but not in others. Whether outcomes are positive or negative, they provide some measure of the team's effectiveness. They also provide feedback that may lead to modification of the team's activities or a change in its goals. While many of the outcomes are related to the child, there are also outcomes that are related to the participants or to the organization. All of the outcomes are important in the evaluation of the team and its impact.

This book will examine the components of the team system, and some of the ways in which the team approach has been used with exceptional children. The dynamics of the interdisciplinary team and the roles of parents as team members will be explored. Finally, some of the problems in teamwork and ways of improving team performance will be delineated.

Chapter 2

The Child

The children who are served by interdisciplinary teams display a wide variety of medical, psychological, and educational problems. Collaborative efforts are frequently required because no single profession encompasses sufficient knowledge to deal adequately with the complex problems presented by exceptional children. The team approach provides a way to integrate the skills and knowledge of several specialists to better address sets of interrelated problems in these children. One purpose of the team is to avoid or reduce the fragmentation of services that too often occurs when several professionals are working with the same child. This chapter examines some of the issues associated with providing services for exceptional children, explores the problems presented by these children, and gives examples of the various approaches that have been used to provide services to them.

MAJOR ISSUES

Special educational provisions for children with various sensory impairments and mental and physical handicaps are usually traced to the early work of men such as Itard, Sequin, Gallaudet, Howe, and Braille (Hewett & Forness, 1977; Reynolds & Birch, 1977; Tarver, 1977). Begun in the nineteenth century with the development of techniques for working with blind and deaf individuals, and with Itard's educational intervention with the Wild Boy of Aveyron, special educational services were broadened in the twentieth century to include more mildly handicapped children.

Initially it seemed obvious that diagnosis of specific disorders, such as deafness or mental retardation, was necessary in order to identify the special needs of the child and to provide appropriate remediation. However, as the negative aspects of categorical labeling became more evident, there was a shift toward noncategorical approaches to providing educational and other services to exceptional children.

Labeling

The stigmatizing effects of popular labels such as "emotionally disturbed" or "mentally retarded" have been discussed by a number of authors (Bartel & Guskin, 1980; Mercer, 1973). According to deviance theory, labeling produces negative reactions to labeled individuals and lowered expectations of their performance (Becker, 1963; Freidson, 1966; Rains, Kitsuse, Duster, & Freidson, 1975). For example, the child who is labeled as mentally retarded is expected to perform in a manner consistent with the label and may respond to these expectations by lowered performance. In this way, a self-perpetuating circle of labeling and underachievement may be established. The negative attitudes of peers and others to such labels adds to the devaluation of the individual and may result in a process of self-labeling that is particularly destructive. Such devaluation is often reinforced by efforts of fund-raising agencies to seek public support of their cause through appeals to pity and guilt. Advertising for funds may inadvertently contribute to the stigmatizing of handicapped children by emphasizing the ways in which children with physical or mental disabilities are different from normal "healthy" children.

For many exceptional children the more serious handicap is not the disability itself but the social handicap associated with it. In reference to physical disabilities, Meyerson (1971) has pointed out that "disability is not an objective *thing in a person* but a social value judgment" (p.11). In this sense disability is a socially defined phenomenon. As Meyerson sees it, society produces a disability by creating a culture in which certain tools are required. A physical disability, then, exists only when the individual lacks an adequate physical tool or skill and when the culture perceives this lack as making the person less able than his peers. If the skill is not differentiated or required by a certain culture, then its impairment cannot be a disability.

Mercer (1973) has examined the labeling of retarded children. According to Mercer, retardation can be viewed from a *clinical* perspective or a *social system* perspective. The clinical approach views mental retardation as a handicapping condition that exists in the individual and is diagnosed by professionals using assessment instruments. The clinical perspective may involve either a pathological (medical) model or a statistical model. The pathological model focuses on the conditions which interfere with physiological functions, while the statistical focuses on the child's deviation from the norm. Mercer describes how a behavioral score on a test (a low IQ score) becomes associated with biological functions and "statistical abnormality is equated with biological pathology" (Mercer, 1973, p. 6). Once children are so labeled, there is a tendency to regard mental retardation as an "attribute of the individual." On the other hand, from the social system perspective, retardation is viewed as an "acquired social status." The retarded child is one who has the *status* of a mental retardate in one or more social systems, rather than a *condition* of retardation.

One of the most serious objections to the labeling of children as mentally retarded revolves around the misuse of intelligence tests with children of minority racial and ethnic groups. Mercer (1973), for example, found disproportionate numbers of black and Mexican-American children placed in special education classes in Riverside, California. Similar findings by others, along with court cases such as *Diana v. State Board of Education* (1970) and *Larry P. v. Wilson Riles* (1972), focused attention on the inappropriate placement of Mexican-American and black students on the basis of inaccurate and inappropriate testing procedures. Based on her research in this area, Mercer (1975) has advocated a multicultural pluralistic approach to assessment of a child's performance as a means of avoiding many of the problems associated with classification.

Diagnostic and classification systems used in the assessment of psychological and educational problems are often based on those used in medical science. The purpose of such systems as used in medicine generally is to be able to describe the etiology, prognosis, and appropriate treatment of a particular disease. When the patient appears with a set of complaints or symptoms, the physician hopes to identify the underlying disorder (such as appendicitis), to recognize its etiology and prognosis, and, if possible, to proceed with an appropriate treatment. However, the medical model of diagnosis is not necessarily appropriate for dealing with other kinds of problems, such as learning disorders or disruptive behavior. Furthermore, the categories used to classify exceptional children are based on different kinds of symptoms. While some categories, such as hearing impaired, visually handicapped, and crippled, may reflect physiological deviations, others, such as mental retardation, learning disabilities, and emotional disturbance, reflect deviations in *behavior*. Labels based on these categories tend to be ill defined and may be of little help in educational planning for these children. Some of the categories include such a heterogeneous group of children that the label conveys little of significance as far as treatment approaches are concerned. But, once the label has been applied, it may be used to explain the child's deviant behavior—for example, a teacher may say that Johnny has gotten into trouble "because he is retarded" or "because he has a learning disability," as though the label accounted for his behavior. One complaint has been that psychologists sometimes give a battery of tests to a child in order to come up with the appropriate label and then behave as if the problem is solved. Thus, much of the criticism of labeling of exceptional children is related to the fact that the label itself may not be very helpful in decisions about intervention strategies.

The negative consequences of labeling, along with questions raised about the validity of IQ tests and other assessment instruments often used as the basis for labeling, were among the considerations that led to major changes in public policy regarding exceptional children. The passage of P.L. 94–142 reflected the concern of parents and professionals about the labeling and consequent segregation of exceptional children in special classrooms. This legislation has had significant impact not only upon special educators but upon all professionals who provide services to exceptional children.

Public Law 94–142

P.L. 94–142, The Education for All Handicapped Children Act of 1975, defines handicapped children as

> those evaluated as being mentally retarded, hard of hearing, deaf, speech impaired, visually handicapped, seriously emotionally disturbed, orthopedically impaired, other health impaired, deaf-blind, multi-handicapped, or as having specific learning disabilities who because of those impairments need special education and related services.

These are the children who are covered under the provisions of the federal legislation.

According to this legislation, all handicapped children must be provided with an appropriate educational program in the least restrictive environment. Since many handicapped children were previously either unserved or inappropriately served, P.L. 94–142 has had a significant effect upon the quantity and quality of services offered to exceptional children and has been referred to as "the most important piece of educational legislation in this country's history" (Corrigan, 1978, p. 10).

Not all exceptional children are included in the provisions of P.L. 94–142. Children who are mildly emotionally disturbed, socially maladjusted, or gifted and talented are not covered under the federal mandate, although they may be included through state or local school district policy (Kauffman, 1980; Raiser & Van Nagel, 1980). Nevertheless, the federal legislation clearly recognizes the rights of the handicapped children covered in the law to an appropriate educational program. They can no longer be denied access to a free public education.

The law is the culmination of several years of actions in the courts and state and federal legislatures that Abeson and Zettel (1977) have referred to as a "quiet revolution." Stemming from the civil rights movement of the 1960s and major court cases in Pennsylvania, the District of Columbia, and elsewhere, the law stipulates that all handicapped children between the ages of 3 and 21 will receive a free appropriate public education in the least restrictive environment. The law provides for the right to nondiscriminatory testing, for a written IEP, and for due process procedures for handicapped children and their parents.

To ensure nondiscriminatory testing, the law requires that tests be administered in the child's native language, by trained personnel, and that they be used to assess specific educational needs rather than giving a single general intelligence test. It also stipulates that decisions should not be based on only one assessment procedure and that the assessment should be conducted by a multidisciplinary team including a teacher or other expert in the child's disability area.

The written IEP must include a statement of the child's present performance level; a statement of annual goals (including short-term objectives); a statement of the educational services to be provided and of the extent of the child's participation in regular educational programs; dates for initiation of services and their anticipated duration; and evaluation criteria for each objective. The IEP is to be developed in a meeting of the teacher, parents, and a representative of the local education agency or intermediate unit. The child may also be involved in the IEP meeting where appropriate.

Specific aspects of P.L. 94–142 will be considered further at various points in this book.

SERVICES FOR THE EXCEPTIONAL CHILD

Children who require special services of one kind or another run the gamut from profoundly retarded to gifted and talented. In addition to children with sensory impairments, mental handicaps, and various emotional and learning disorders, there are also those children who are victims of child abuse and neglect, those with drug or alcohol problems, and juvenile delinquents. Teams designed to serve such children are likely to include special education teachers, regular classroom teachers, administrators, physical and occupational therapists, social workers, psychologists, speech therapists, physicians, counselors, and nurses. The exact composition of the team is determined by the problems presented by the child, the professional expertise required to address those problems, and the organizational setting in which the interaction occurs. Each child presents a unique set of problems that serves to define the task of the team and determine which professionals are needed to adequately meet the child's needs. For example, a profoundly handicapped child will require services from an interdisciplinary team of professionals that are very different from the services provided by an IEP team for a mildly handicapped child in a regular classroom.

To illustrate some of the types of problems posed by exceptional children and the kinds of teams that might be used to address those problems, we will look at some hypothetical children and the teams that might serve them. The first case study is a young autistic child seen in a child development clinic.

Case Study 1.

Three-year-old Elizabeth R. is the only child of a couple in their early 30s. The father is an engineer and the mother an interior decorator. The parents waited until they were established financially and professionally before having children, and they have had a difficult time coping with Elizabeth's disability. Consequently, they have decided to forego having other children.

They brought Elizabeth to the clinic when she was seven months of age, because she did not seem to be responding normally to her environment or to them. At first they thought perhaps she had a hearing problem, because she was often unresponsive to her mother's voice or other sounds around her. However, this was ruled out by audiometric testing.

The child study team who evaluated Elizabeth included a pediatrician, a pediatric resident, a psychiatrist, a psychologist, a speech and hearing specialist, a nurse, and a preschool teacher. After assessment, she was placed in the center's preschool program for autistic children and a behavior modification program was instituted. Elizabeth's program is carefully monitored by the teacher, several aides, the psychologist, and other members of the treatment team. In the meantime, her parents have been meeting with the social worker and with a local parents' group to learn how to deal more effectively with Elizabeth's behavior at home and to reinforce the progress she is making at the clinic school.

A different kind of team is required by the young woman in the next case study.

Case Study 2.

Sally S. is a 13-year-old junior high school student who attends a public school near her home in a large midwestern city. Sally is an attractive and gregarious girl who has many friends and is active in a number of after-school clubs. She has an older brother and sister, who seem to relate well to Sally although they do not spend a lot of time with her since they attend high school. Her father is a lawyer and her mother is a homemaker.

At school, Sally has been evaluated by an educational planning team that includes her regular classroom teacher, the school psychologist, the principal, and an itinerant teacher of the visually handicapped who meets twice a week with Sally. Sally's parents have attended two IEP team meetings for planning her educational program. Her special education teacher has referred Sally to local volunteers for tape recording of some of her textbooks and for transcribing some of her assignments into Braille. However, Sally is becoming sufficiently proficient with the Optacon (which converts regular printed material to tactual stimuli that she can "read" with her finger) so that she can now read her own assignments, although this takes a considerable amount of time.

Sally still has some problems in orientation and mobility, and her teacher is concerned that she relies too much on her friends and siblings to help her get around. The itinerant teacher has asked for a mobility specialist to work with Sally for a few weeks to improve her mobility skills and increase her independence. The mobility instructor will also help Sally in her orientation to the large high school she will be attending next fall. Her regular classroom teacher sees no other serious problem for Sally in adjusting to a new environment, and her itinerant teacher will continue to work with her at the high school, as well as to orient appropriate high school personnel to Sally's special needs.

The next case illustrates a very different set of problems requiring yet another kind of team.

Case Study 3.

Johnny B., a ten-year-old urban youngster was recently arrested for stealing an automobile, along with his older brother Jim and his brother's friend. According to Johnny the boys only borrowed the car for a short "joy ride." However, his brother's friend, who had boasted about how well he could drive, ran the stolen car into a fence after only a couple of blocks. The police caught them before they could get away, and Johnny and his brother have been at the detention home for about two weeks. The brother's friend was quickly released to his parents' custody, but the authorities have been reluctant to let Johnny and Jim return to their home because of their mother's drinking. The boys' father deserted the family three years ago, and the mother says she cannot control the boys any longer and does not want them in the home.

Both boys have been chronically truant from school and have had previous minor incidents with the police. Johnny is described in his school records as "of average intelligence but functioning well below his potential, particularly in reading and math. It seems likely that Johnny has a learning disability that is interfering with his school performance, but his lack of motivation, high rate of absenteeism, and uncooperative attitude during testing make an accurate assessment difficult."

At the present time, Johnny is receiving services from several child care workers and the medical staff at the detention center, a social worker and a psychologist working for the courts, and a teacher, a teacher's aide, and a school counselor provided by the local school district. Close collaboration of medical, psychological, social, and educational services is necessary if Johnny is to be placed in an appropriate residential setting and provided with the continuing supportive services that he requires. If the professionals involved do not coordinate their activities, Johnny may not receive all the help that he needs and may be subject to inconsistent and even conflicting decisions.

From these examples, we can see that the team and its membership are defined by the nature of the problems presented by the child and by the organizational context in which the team operates. Interdisciplinary teams are as diverse as the exceptional children they serve and the organizations with which they are affiliated.

These hypothetical cases illustrate some of the ways interdisciplinary teams can be used to meet the special needs of children with many different kinds of problems. Very seldom do exceptional children present a single problem. Instead, they are likely to present a cluster of interrelated medical, psychological, educational, and social problems. Each of these aspects may need to be addressed by appropriate professional personnel if the child's needs are to be adequately met.

Thus the exceptional child and the family can be viewed as the focus of a network of medical, psychological, educational, and social services within the community. This system is illustrated in Figure 2–1. The interdisciplinary team is composed of representatives of these various services who attend to specific aspects of the child's functioning.

Medical Aspects

The exceptional child often presents one or more physical problems that require the attention of a physician or other health professional. The medical and physical problems of the exceptional child include a number of specific sensory and physical handicapping conditions. The child may have a visual handicap, hearing impairment, neurological involvement, a chronic disease, an orthopedic disorder, or a birth defect such as cleft palate or spina bifida. Severe congenital impairments are usually identified at birth or shortly thereafter, but milder handicaps may not be recognized until later.

Health Professionals

The number and severity of the physical problems will determine who should be involved in assessment and treatment of the child. For example, Urban (1975) suggests that management teams working with hearing impaired children should include "audiologists, educators, mental health professionals, otolaryngologists, pediatricians, and speech and language pathologists" (p. 17). In addition, other professionals may be asked to join such teams when needed. These include "geneticists, neurologists, pedodontists, plastic surgeons, radiologists, and urologists" (p. 18).

Often the pediatrician or family practitioner is the first health professional to have contact with the exceptional child and the child's family. The child may be seen for a routine physical examination or because the parents have observed

Figure 2-1 Service Network for the Exceptional Child

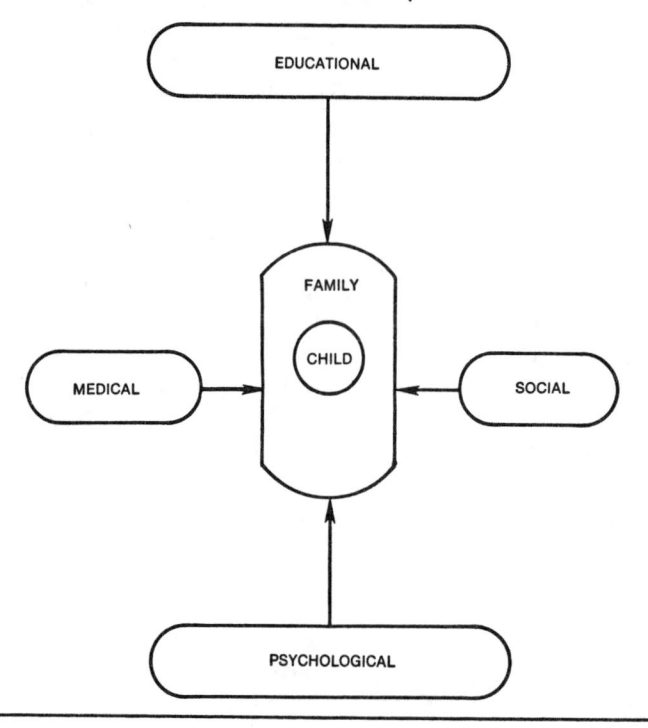

certain irregularities or a general lack of responsiveness. If specific problems are identified, the child may be referred to an appropriate medical specialist for followup of the presenting symptoms.

The extent of medical services provided the child varies with the type and severity of the condition. For many children with physical disabilities, the medical problem is no longer a major one. After the original trauma, infection, or other medical crisis has been treated, the resulting sensory or physical impairment may be more of a psychological or educational problem than a medical one. Chronic diseases such as diabetes, asthma, or juvenile arthritis may involve continued treatment. Other disorders, such as spinal cord injuries, may necessitate a close monitoring of the child's condition because of the danger of recurring infections or decubitus ulcers. Still other physically handicapping conditions may require no more than routine physical examinations and treatment of usual childhood disorders.

While the pediatrician and physicians in other specialty areas are most likely to be involved with the physical and medical aspects of the handicapped child, other allied health professionals may also work with the child. Nurses may provide a number of services in relation to the child; dental services may be provided by one or more dental specialists; speech pathologists may provide remedial training for speech and language problems; and dieticians, occupational therapists, medical technologists, and respiratory therapists may also provide specific services to the child.

Physical therapists and physical therapy assistants provide services to relieve pain and restore maximum physical functioning in children with orthopedic, neurological, or related disorders. The physical therapist may also help the classroom teacher in the physical management of the child. For example, as Mullins (1979) indicates:

> Proper positioning of a cerebral palsied child is very important in order to prevent contractures, to save the teacher from unnecessary effort, and to place the child in the very best attitude for learning. Techniques will be worked out in consultation with an orthopedist, who may be doing surgery on the child, and the physical therapist who is an invaluable aid to the teacher. The PT [physical therapist] can demonstrate, for example, how to tie the child in the wheelchair or regular chair. . . . The PT [physical therapist] or perhaps the occupational therapist may help the teacher adapt educational materials for the student. (p. 163)

The variety of health professionals who may be called upon to provide services to an exceptional child is quite extensive, and the need for coordination of care in such cases is obvious. As Wilson (1970) points out, "A practitioner is less and less commonly a solo agent providing comprehensive aid; instead a coordinated team of health professionals is engaged in a joint approach to medical risks" (p. 23). It is important that the medical and health-related professionals coordinate their activities, not only with each other, but also with the other services being provided by psychologists, educators, and social service agencies in the community.

The Sick Role

A major contribution has been made to our understanding of the child's medical problems by the concept of the sick "role," articulated by Talcott Parsons in 1951. Illness is described by Parsons as a "state of disturbance in the 'normal' functioning of the total human individual, including both the state of the organism as a biological system and of his personal and social adjustments. It is thus partly biologically and partly socially defined" (Parsons, 1951b, p. 431). Thus the behavior of the ill person is not only a medical issue but also a social-psychological event. Parson's analysis deals with the doctor-patient relationship, but this approach has many implications for the other helping professions.

Parsons contends that being sick is not simply a "condition" but a *social role*, the test of this being "the existence of a set of institutionalized expectations and the corresponding sentiments and sanctions" (p. 436). Parsons describes these role expectations in some detail.

> There seem to be four aspects of the institutionalized expectation sys-
> tem relative to the sick role. First, is the exception from normal social
> role responsibilities, which of course is relative to the nature and
> severity of the illness. . . . The second closely related aspect is the
> institutionalized definition that the sick person cannot be expected by
> "pulling himself together" to get well by an act of decision or will.
> . . . He can't "help it." . . . The third element is the definition of
> the state of being ill as itself undesirable with its obligation to want
> to "get well." . . . Finally, the fourth closely related element is the
> obligation—in proportion to the severity of the condition, of course—
> to seek *technically competent* help, namely, in the most usual case,
> that of a physician and to *cooperate* with him in the process of trying
> to get well. It is here, of course, that the role of the sick person as
> patient becomes articulated with that of the physician in a comple-
> mentary role structure. (Parsons, 1951b, pp. 436–437)

So the sick role, as conceived by Parsons, carries with it the right to be exempt from the usual social responsibilities and recognition that the individual is not responsible for his illness. Sick persons can stay home from work, refuse to drive the nursery school carpool, or miss school—with a clear recognition by all that it is "not their fault." Along with these privileges are two obligations: to wish to recover and to seek competent help. Sick persons are not supposed to enjoy the role too much; the "secondary gain" or positive byproducts of being sick are restricted, and patients are supposed to try to get better.

Although the sick role is in some ways a deviant role, it differs from other forms of deviance in that the "sick person is not regarded as 'responsible' for his condition, 'he can't help it.' He may, of course, have carelessly exposed himself to danger of accident, but then once injured he cannot, for instance, mend a fractured leg by 'will power'" (Parsons, 1951b, p. 440).

Parsons and Fox (1952) compared the role relationships of doctor and patient with those of parent and child, indicating the similarities between the dependence of the child and the position of the sick person. Assuming that "the role of the physician in the more general sense, is psychotherapeutic" (p. 40), Parsons and Fox identify four major aspects of therapy that have relevance for the profes-sional's role.

1. *Permissiveness.* Patients are allowed to express their feelings, wishes, and
   fantasies.

2. *Support.* This involves "accepting [the patient] as a bona fide member of the therapeutic system because he is deemed worth helping" (p. 40). This permissive-supportive approach is balanced by two methods used to control the patient's behavior.
3. *Denial of reciprocity.* The doctor "will adhere scrupulously to a professional attitude" (p. 40) and does not reciprocate the emotional responsiveness of the patient. This allows physicians to maintain an "asymmetrical" relationship in which they are clearly in charge. Professional neutrality and distance are used to maintain the professional's superior position vis-à-vis the patient.
4. *Conditional rewards.* The physician "introduces conditional rewards (of which his approval is probably the most important) for the patient's good work in the therapeutic situation" (p. 44).

Thus, the doctor motivates the patient to become well and rewards efforts in that direction; this is the basis of the physician's leverage with the patient. Since, according to Parsons, the sick role is a temporary form of deviance in which the affected individual is unable to fulfill normal social roles, there are pressures on the patient to return to a nondeviant state. The role of the therapist then is to ensure that the patient gives up the deviant sick role and resumes the responsibilities that have been temporarily set aside. Since both of these roles are too important to be left to chance, they have become institutionalized with reciprocal expectation on the part of the two players. In this sense the doctor and his patient can be viewed as a social system.

Segall (1976) reviews 20 years of research on Parson's concept of the sick role and concludes that "the extent to which this theoretical model contributes to a greater understanding of the way in which the sick person actually thinks, feels and behaves still awaits empirical verification" (p. 168). The Parsonian concept, according to Segall, is best illustrated by "temporary, acute physical illness," and evidence suggests that the sick role is affected by social, cultural, and personal factors as well as by the nature of the illness.

In a more recent restatement of his concept of the sick role (1975), Parsons points out that he had never intended to restrict the concept of the sick role to "deviant behavior" or to acute illness. Nor did he mean to imply that the role of the patient is completely passive. Indeed, with less acute illness, the active participation of the client may be substantial. However, Parsons contends, the patient-physician relationship is basically an asymmetrical one since "there must be a built-in institutionalized superiority of the professional roles [compared with lay roles], grounded in responsibility, competence, and occupational concern" (Parsons, 1975, p. 271). He views the relationship between the full-time career professional and the lay person (client) as inherently asymmetrical and hierarchical with respect to issues concerning health and illness, in the same way that there is a built-in asymmetry between professor and student or lawyer and client.

When the patient is a child, Parsons (1951a) notes "certain features of the role of sick adult must be altered, particularly with respect to the levels of responsibility which can be imputed to the child" (p. 457). Therefore "third parties, notably parents, must play a particularly important part in the situation. It is common for pediatricians, when they refer to 'my patient,' often to mean the mother rather than the sick child" (p. 457).

Several authors (Freidson, 1961; Gallagher, 1976; Gordon, 1966; Segall, 1976, & Wilson, 1970) have raised questions about the Parsonian model. In particular, critics have noted that, while Parsons gives the major role to the physician, a wide variety of health professionals may be involved in the delivery of services (Gallagher, 1976; Wilson, 1970). Furthermore, they contend that the model may not account for certain kinds of treatment patterns, such as those involved in chronic illness or disability or with preventative medicine. However, the asymmetrical relationship between physician and patient described in such detail by Parsons seems to have some applicability to the relationship between the team and the child. Not only the physician but other members of the team are likely to interact with the child patient in what is essentially an asymmetrical relationship.

The Medical Model

For many educators, psychologists, and other members of the interdisciplinary team, the medical model is an inappropriate paradigm for the treatment of exceptional children. Kauffman and Hallahan (1974) have summarized the arguments of many of the critics of the medical model in psychology and special education, who

> object to its use on the grounds that it leads to the following untenable assumptions:
> 1. Maladaptive behavior is conceptualized as a symptom of "underlying" pathology.
> 2. The primary function of the therapeutic agent is to determine the true etiology of the problem, correctly classify the disorder, and offer treatment appropriate for the specific nosological variety.
> 3. Treatment of the symptom itself rather than the underlying problem is both dangerous and fruitless: the "real" pathology will remain and ultimately reveal itself in some other symptom, possibly more insidious than the first.
> 4. Behavioral pathology is seen as only the reflection of a disease process which infects the mental apparatus and inexorably draws its victim towards the abyss of mental illness.

5. Special educators must view learning and behavior difficulties as symptoms of more fundamental problems which must be resolved before educational intervention can be successful. (Kauffman & Hallahan, 1974, p. 97)

Kauffman and Hallahan suggest that these interpretations of the medical model do not accurately represent the conceptual models actually used in medical practice and that in fact a diagnostic-prescriptive process may be helpful in special education. They suggest that there are several aspects of medical treatment that may be applicable.

1. The necessity of treatment is based on empirical data.
2. Priorities are established for assessment and treatment.
3. Treatment effects are evaluated empirically.
4. Beneficial treatment may be offered even in the absence of knowledge of etiology or understanding of the therapeutic mechanism, although etiologies are sought and known etiologies may imply specific treatments.
5. The need for prosthesis, prophylaxis, and therapy is recognized.
6. Ecological variables are considered. (p. 99)

Misconceptions of the views of other professionals, such as those identified by Kauffman and Hallahan regarding the perceptions of psychologists and special educators concerning the physician's role and the medical model, are likely to give rise to misunderstanding among professionals on the interdisciplinary team.

Psychological Development

Regardless of the child's physical condition and possible medical problems, there are important psychological aspects which also need to be addressed in understanding the exceptional child. Psychological development is an important factor determining the child's behavior in a variety of situations, and the psychological development of exceptional children has been addressed in detail by a number of authors (Cruickshank, 1980; Mordock, 1975; Wynn & O'Connor, 1979). Attention is usually focused on the cognitive, social-emotional, and behavioral aspects of development.

Since there is as yet no comprehensive, generally agreed upon theory of child development that accounts for the many and varied aspects of the child's mental and emotional growth, it is necessary to examine different theories that focus on different aspects of development. Thus psychologists, counselors, child development specialists, and others who are concerned with the psychological development of the child may approach the child from quite varied points of view, depending upon their particular theoretical orientation and training. We will briefly review some of the important aspects of psychological development in terms of two of the major theoretical approaches.

Cognitive development

One of the most widely recognized approaches to understanding the cognitive development of children is that of Jean Piaget (1926, 1952; Piaget & Inhelder, 1969). Piaget describes the process whereby a newborn infant, unaware of the world around him and equipped with only a few built-in reflexes, develops the complex cognitive structure of an adult. He conceptualizes cognitive development in terms of the changing cognitive structures of the child as the ready-made "schemata" of the infant, combined and integrated into more and more complex behaviors. Cognitive development arises from four major factors (Piaget & Inhelder, 1969):

1. maturation of the child's nervous system;
2. physical experience with the surrounding environment;
3. social interaction and social transmission manifested through language and education;
4. conjuncture of these three factors through a process of "equilibration" as the child strives to maintain a mental equilibrium between assimilation of the environment and accommodation to the environment.

Piaget is often referred to as a "genetic epistomologist" because his primary interest is in how the child learns and acquires knowledge rather than in child development itself. How new knowledge is assimilated with existing mental structures and how the structures change to accommodate new knowledge are described in detail by Piaget. All children, according to Piaget, move through an invariant sequence of the stages of cognitive development. Although bright children may develop more quickly than others and retarded children more slowly, the progression from stage to stage is similar for all. He is less interested in individual differences than in describing the stages of cognitive development that are universal.

While Piaget does not focus upon the particular learning characteristics of exceptional children, psychologists and other professionals working with such children find Piaget's model a useful one in assessing and understanding the cognitive development of many children. A number of authors (Furth, 1966; Inhelder, 1968; Robinson & Robinson, 1976; Woodward, 1963; Wynne & O'Connor, 1979) have addressed the implications of Piaget's theories for exceptional children. In general, it appears that although exceptional children will show the same sequence of cognitive stages as other children, differences in the *rate* of development may reflect some of the specific problems of the sensory, motor, or mental deficits of exceptional children.

Briefly, the four stages described by Piaget include:

1. *Sensory-motor period.* The child from birth to about seven years of age demonstrates intelligence primarily through sensory perceptions and motor activities. The infant at birth is helpless and unaware of the world; by the age of two the child has become a social organism, able to anticipate coming events.

2. *Preoperational period.* Between the ages of two and seven, the child must bridge the gap between the sensory-motor activities of infancy and the mental activities of the school child. The child learns to represent objects and events internally, to use language, and to think prelogically, but the child's thought is determined by immediate perception and is egocentric.

3. *Concrete Operations.* While the preoperational child is stimulus bound, the child who has reached the period of concrete operations (from 7 to 11 years of age) is free of the pull of immediate experience and can operate logically on concrete objects. The child is able to use language to speed up thoughts, which no longer need to be tied to physical performance. Although children at this stage can think logically, they cannot go beyond their own concrete experience and deal with abstractions.

4. *Formal Operations.* During the period of formal operations, which begins to emerge around the ages of 10 or 11, the child can follow the *form* of reasoning and thus can begin to function in the area of abstract verbal problems in addition to the concrete situations of the previous period. At this point the child "becomes capable of reasoning correctly about propositions he does not believe, or at least not yet; that is, propositions that he considers pure hypotheses" (Piaget & Inhelder, 1969, p. 132). This is the beginning of formal or hypothetico-deductive thinking.

Piaget's theories explain that the thinking of children differs from that of adults in substantial and identifiable ways that are qualitative as well as quantitative. The young child cannot think like an adult because he does not have the mental structures and operations to think like an adult.

Although the primary focus of Piaget's research and writing is on cognitive development, he does not ignore affective or emotional development:

> There is no behavior pattern however intellectual which does not involve affective factors as motives; but, reciprocally, there can be no affective states without the intervention of perceptions or comprehensions which constitute their cognitive structure. Behavior is therefore of a piece. . . . The two aspects, affective and cognitive, are at the same time inseparable and irreducible. (Piaget & Inhelder, 1969, p. 158)

Social-emotional development

While Piaget is correct in pointing out the interrelatedness of cognitive and emotional development, some theorists have chosen to focus more closely on the latter. Eric Erikson, for example, has described human development in terms of a series of stages he calls "the eight ages of man." Erikson bases his conceptualization upon two assumptions:

1. Human personality develops according to the child's readiness to be aware of and to interact within a growing social radius.
2. Society is structured so as not only to invite this series of interactions but to structure their rate and sequence.

For Erikson, human development consists of a series of alternative basic attitudes (such as "trust" or "mistrust"), a series of crises or critical steps that are universal turning points in psychological development. Influenced by the social anthropologists, Erikson moves beyond traditional psychoanalytic theory to a more general view of the child's social-cultural environment and how the child is molded by society.

Each individual moves through five stages from birth to adulthood.

1. *Basic trust vs. mistrust.* During the first year or two of life, bodily experience is of utmost importance. Consistent physical comfort, love, and nurturance produce a sense of trust in the infant. "The infant's first social achievement, then, is his willingness to let the mother out of sight without undue anxiety or rage, because she has become an inner certainty as well as an outer predictability. Such consistency, continuity, and sameness of experience provide a rudimentary sense of ego identity" (Erikson, 1963, p. 247).
2. *Autonomy vs. shame and doubt.* The learning of self-control during this stage is exemplified by the toilet training experience. The major question is whether the child develops a sense of autonomy and self-control or a continued dependence and lack of self-control that produces doubt and shame. Parents need to provide a reassuring firmness that protects children against being overwhelmed by situations they cannot yet control while allowing them to "stand on their own feet."
3. *Initiative vs. guilt.* Between the ages of three and five or six, the child "is eager and able to make things cooperatively, to combine with other children for the purpose of constructing and planning, and he is willing to profit from teachers and to emulate ideal prototypes" (p. 258). The child is establishing an identity and moving out into a wider world. The

danger is that children will develop such a strong sense of guilt that they will be immobilized and unable to develop true initiative.

4. *Industry vs. inferiority.* During the school-age years the child becomes a producer who wins recognition through work. Children at this stage are learning the technology of their society, through schools and other training experiences. Failure at this time leads to a sense of inadequacy and inferiority and an inability to identify with the "tool users" of the society.

5. *Identity vs. role confusion.* This stage marks the end of childhood and the advent of adolescence. Because of the marked physiological changes during this period, the sense of identity and continuity previously acquired is questioned again. Many of the behaviors characteristic of adolescents, such as their cliquishness and intolerance for those who are different, reflect a defense against a sense of identity confusion.

As the adolescent moves into adulthood, new challenges emerge: developing an intimate and loving relationship (intimacy vs. isolation), establishing a family (generating vs. stagnation), and acquiring a mature sense of ego integration (ego integrity vs. despair). Thus, Erikson puts childhood into the broader perspective of an individual's total life. He looks not only at the past but also at the future of the child.

Erikson's view of childhood is a comprehensive one that provides a useful framework for understanding the dynamics of exceptional children. There are a number of ways in which the specific handicaps of the child may affect the resolution of the crises posed by Erikson, and those who are working with exceptional children need to remain sensitive to the unique problems associated with each handicap as well as the general framework of psychological development. Erikson emphasizes the importance of successful resolution of the crisis at one stage if the child is to be able to cope adequately with those of succeeding stages. Psychological problems arise when the child is unable to resolve a developmental crisis and move on with confidence to the next stage. Resolution of the crisis associated with a particular stage leads to ego growth, while a failure to resolve the crisis can lead to a continued lack of trust, obsessiveness, guilt, and other negative emotions that interfere with the child's ability to cope with the world around him. Thus, a variety of psychological ills may result from the child's early experiences and the parent-child interaction.

While there are many other theories related to psychological development, those of Piaget and Erikson touch on a number of the significant factors that affect the child and that may in part determine the kinds of services needed by an exceptional child. Emotionally disturbed children may present problems to be dealt with by psychiatrists, psychologists, play therapists, child development specialists, and other professionals involved in the assessment and treatment process. The neurotic child, the autistic child, and the child with psychosomatic disorders each have certain unique needs that must be addressed by various members of the team. The child may be treated with play therapy, individual psychotherapy, family therapy, behavior modification, placement in a residential treatment setting, or some combination of treatments.

Social Factors

In addition to the psychological and medical aspects of the child's condition, there are several social factors to be considered in an overall assessment of the child. The social environment in which the child lives is a crucial element in the child's adjustment and ability to handle stress.

The family, of course, is a major part of the social environment of the young child. As the child grows older and moves into a larger social radius, friends, school, and the community come to play a more significant role in the child's life. But, initially, it is the family that represents the external world to the infant and young child, and many of the feelings and attitudes shaped by the family relationships will generalize to the world at large.

For the exceptional child, the family may play an even more important role in the child's interaction with the environment because of the increased dependence of many handicapped children. For the deaf child, the visually handicapped child, or the orthopedically impaired child, the parents will play a crucial role by helping the child reach out to the environment. The family of the exceptional child will be discussed more fully in Chapter 7.

The ecological system of the child

A number of authors have addressed the interaction of the exceptional child and the environment in terms of an ecological approach (Gallagher, 1980; Hobbs, 1966, 1975; Rhodes, 1967; Thomas & Marshall, 1977). According to Hobbs (1975): "Ecology is the study of the balance of forces among organisms and environments. Human ecology is the study of the dynamic relationship between the individual and his unique set of environmental circumstances at a particular period of time" (p. 113). With such an approach, the focus is on the reciprocal relationships between the child and the environment. Changes in one part of the system lead to changes in other parts. Problems reside not only in the child alone, but "in the ecological system of which the child is an integral part" (Hobbs, 1975, pp. 113–114). The system is seen as a dynamic one that is constantly changing.

Thomas and Marshall (1977) demonstrate the use of the ecological model in the clinical evaluation and coordination of services in a medically based multidisciplinary program for handicapped children. They describe the relationships between various parts of the system.

The system's habitats are connected with the child and each other so that modification in any one area causes a shift in the other spheres. For example, an increase in the frequency and/or severity of a child's seizures will require diversification of his medical regimen (perhaps further tests or medication change), his educational program (even if merely reduction of stress through a decrease in the length of time spent in his studies at any one period), his recreational program (perhaps a change in the types of activities), and his family (the child's mother may need to spend more time with him to accomplish the other modifications and less time with other family members). (Thomas & Marshall, 1977, p. 17)

Hobbs (1966) has described the application of the ecological model to the treatment of emotionally disturbed children. Developed as an alternative to the more traditional hospital-based psychiatric unit often used to treat such children, Project Re-Ed was designed to involve the child's home, neighborhood, school, agency, and community in the treatment process. Instead of treating only the child, the ecological approach attempts to improve the small social system of which the child is a part. The family, the school, the neighborhood, and the community are all part of the ecological unit, and improvement can come from smaller changes in several components.

Although Project Re-Ed served emotionally disturbed children, Hobbs contends that the ecological systems approach is also useful in working with physically handicapped children as well. "In fact, a systems analysis is especially valuable in conceptualizing the problem of a blind child or a child with epilepsy or with a chronic and debilitating cardiac condition. . . . The greater the handicap, physical or other, the greater the need for intervention strategies to be based on a systems analysis of the problem" (Hobbs, 1975, p. 115).

The ecological model offers a different way of viewing the assessment, classification, and treatment of exceptional children. By focusing attention on the system rather than on the child alone, the ecological approach seeks the involvement of members of the family, the school, and the community in a cooperative endeavor aimed at improving the functioning of the whole system. Exactly who will be involved in this process depends upon the needs of the child and the major components of the child's ecological unit, but participants may include social workers, parents, clergymen, playground or recreation workers, and others who are part of the child's social environment. One or more social service or family service agencies may be involved as well, or these services may be provided through the hospital, school, or clinic with major responsibility for the child's treatment. Other support services in the community—volunteer agencies, such as the Muscular Dystrophy Association or the Association of Retarded Citizens, and alternative living arrangements, such as group homes—may also be involved.

Educational Aspects

The final component included in Figure 2–1 is the educational service provided to the exceptional child. While special educational programs have been the predominant source of educational services to handicapped children, many exceptional children, including gifted or delinquent children, have not always been included in special education programs. P.L. 94–142 has also led to changes in the traditional approaches to special education services since more and more exceptional children are being served in regular classrooms.

The specific kinds of educational programs offered depend upon the physical and psychological problems of the child as well as the specific educational limitations. The range of educational programs includes hospital- or residence-based programs, special schools, special classes in regular schools, regular class placement with a supplementary resource room or itinerant teacher, and regular class placement without additional services. P. L. 94–142 indicates that

> to the maximum extent appropriate, handicapped children, including children in public or private institutions or other care facilities, are educated with children who are not handicapped, and that special classes, separate schooling, or other removal of handicapped children from the regular educational environment occurs only when the nature or severity of the handicap is such that education in regular classes with the use of supplementary aids and services cannot be achieved satisfactorily. (P. L. 94–142, Sec. 612, 5, B, 1975)

This provision, that handicapped children must be educated in the "least restrictive environment," suggests that placement should be related to the educational needs of the child rather than based on categorical labels. The IEP for each child spells out the annual goals and objectives, the instructional plan for meeting those objectives, and how the child's progress and the program will be evaluated. Ideally, the regular classroom teacher and the special educator will work together to plan and implement the child's educational program. Furthermore, it is important that other school personnel, such as the school psychologist, counselors, administrators, and others who provide services to the child, coordinate their activities with that of the teachers who have daily responsibility for the child's program. They may be involved in the evaluation team and/or the IEP team along with the parents and perhaps the child himself.

The special education teacher may have a special class or a resource room within a regular school or serve as an itinerant teacher across several schools. The teacher may focus primarily on academic skills or may teach preacademic and self-help skills, communication, and social skills, depending on the educational needs of the child and the severity of the impairment. The teacher may serve as a consultant to the regular classroom teacher to help identify ways of modifying the curriculum and the classroom environment to accommodate the exceptional child.

A variety of models are available to the educator as foundations for the development of instructional programs. Although many approaches have been developed to provide help in working with children with specific disabilities, such as learning disabilities or hearing impairment, growing recognition of the common educational needs of children across disability categories has led to greater attention to approaches and procedures that are applicable to a variety of children. Two approaches that have some general application to the teaching of exceptional children are Bloom's *taxonomy of educational objectives* and the principles of *behavior modification*.

Educational Objectives

One important step in providing educational service to exceptional children is the identification of specific educational objectives. Much impetus was given to this process by the work of Benjamin Bloom (1956) and his colleagues in developing a taxonomy of educational objectives. The cognitive and affective objectives they have described provide a framework to the educator who is developing curriculum or planning instructional programs for specific children.

Educational objectives in the *cognitive domain* which have been identified include the following categories:

- *Knowledge* is the recall of information, facts, principles, and theories. All that is necessary is that the material be remembered, although some modifications may be called for. The whole cognitive domain is arranged as a hierarchy, and knowledge is seen as the lowest of the categories. All the other classifications involve the use of knowledge.
- *Comprehension* is the understanding of material and can involve translation, interpretation, and extrapolation or prediction. It is the lowest level of understanding.
- *Application* is a higher level of understanding than comprehension since the student must be able to use methods, principles, theories, etc., in new situations.
- *Analysis* is breaking down ideas into component elements so as to understand the relationships, organization, or structures of the material.
- *Synthesis* is the integration of various elements into a new pattern or structure.
- *Evaluation* is the highest level in the cognitive hierarchy because it involves all of the previous abilities. This category refers to both quantitative and qualitative judgments of the value of specific material as compared with some criterion. The criterion may be internal or external and defined by the student or given to him.

The taxonomy spells out specific educational objectives falling in each category. Because of the hierarchical nature of the taxonomy, the teacher is encouraged to move beyond mere knowledge objectives and to focus on higher level cognitive processes. This is particularly important in planning the educational program for gifted children but also has application to planning for other exceptional children.

The affective domain described by Krathwohl, Bloom, and Masia (1964) provides a framework for developing educational objectives concerning interests, attitudes, and values. The categories included in the affective domain are *receiving* (attending), *responding, valuing, organizing,* and *characterizing by a value or value complex.* Setting goals for affective education generally raises more problems than developing educational objectives in the cognitive domain. Ethical questions regarding the teaching of values and the role of the school in affective education are often raised by parents and educators and have led to a greater hesitation on the part of educators to specify affective goals.

Behavior Modification

Special education has borrowed heavily from research and theory in psychology and other social sciences. One of the most significant contributions of psychology to education has been in the area of learning theories and principles of behavioral analysis. Techniques of behavior modification or behavior management have been adopted in a variety of special education settings and used with many different kinds of educational problems and disabilities.

Based upon Skinner's principles of operant conditioning, behavior modification techniques utilize reinforcement conditions to shape the behaviors of the child or adult. In general, the goals of behavioral approaches include reducing or eliminating inappropriate and maladaptive behaviors and initiating, maintaining, and increasing appropriate and adaptive responses. Thus, behavior modification has been used to reduce rocking behavior in blind children (Caetano & Kauffman, 1975), to shape a "generosity" response in severely retarded children (Wiesen, Hartley, Richardson, & Roske, 1967), to toilet train the retarded (Foxx & Azrin, 1973), to extinguish self-destructive behavior in retarded children (Lovaas & Simmons, 1969), and to teach speech to autistic children (Hewett, 1965). Bijou (1973) has emphasized an individualized approach with a basic instructional strategy that can be applied to different children in different settings. Bijou's model includes specifying the target behaviors, evaluating the child's entering behaviors, planning and implementing the educational program, assessing the child's progress and changing the program in light of the child's progress, and maintaining or generalizing the new behaviors.

In general, behavior modification programs seek to change the frequency of certain responses (decreasing maladaptive responses and increasing adaptive ones) by arranging reinforcements (rewards or punishments) that are contingent upon the target behavior. Kalish (1977) summarizes the four steps in operant conditioning as follows:

1. Behavior to be changed must be specified in concrete, observable terms . . . .
2. Initial base-line measurements of relevant behaviors are recorded for ultimate comparison with subsequent behavior changes.
3. Response-reinforcement contingencies are established.
4. Reinforcement is applied in a consistent, immediate, and appropriate fashion. (p. 466)

Behavioral principles have been applied to teaching exceptional children by a number of authors (Gardner, 1977; Haring, 1978; Haring & Phillips, 1972; Hewett, 1968; Lovitt, 1976) and to the development of instructional technologies (Gagne, 1977; Glaser, 1963).

Behavioral approaches in education vary from the simple application of reinforcement principles to modify the behavior of one or two children in a classroom to the development of a classroom management system designed to affect the behavior of all the children in that class. In its most elaborate form, the behavior modification approach is seen in the token economy systems employed in some institutions. Complex systems of reinforcement using tokens that can be cashed in for rewards of varying value have been established in a number of settings with psychiatric patients, retarded populations, and delinquents, among others. Such systems require the cooperation of all the institutional personnel if they are to work effectively.

There are many other models available to the educator in working with exceptional children. Each disability area has developed certain approaches that seem to be particularly applicable to the problems of children with that specific handicap. Many of the approaches that have become important in education, such as the behavioral approach, have been borrowed from psychology or other disciplines and adapted to educational problems.

Since much of the child's time is spent in the classroom situation, the role of the teacher is a crucial one in determining the success of the team's efforts. Whether the child is the responsibility of a regular classroom teacher or of a special educator, the approach adopted by the teacher may significantly affect the results achieved by the team.

Coordinating Services

If the team members are operating with different frames of reference, such as those described above, it will be difficult to integrate the various approaches into a coordinated and consistent treatment plan. If some team members emphasize that the problem is essentially a medical one—that is, the problem is *in* the child—then their approach may be to focus on changing the child to adapt better to the environmental setting in which he or she must operate. Other team members may perceive the problem as an environmental one, *outside* the child, best alleviated by controlling the environment so as to better meet the needs of the child. Unless these differences in approach are openly addressed and negotiated among the members of the team, the team's efforts may be inconsistent and even contradictory at times. Such underlying differences in the professional's perceptions of the problems presented by the children being served may be reflected in disagreements about the goals and objectives of treatment. As a consequence, the planning process is likely to be fragmented and poorly coordinated.

Not only the professional but also the nonprofessional staff may need to be involved in the discussion of approaches and theoretical frameworks to be used with the children being served by the team. Aides and other staff members may play an important role in implementing the plans developed by the team, but unless they are ready to support the particular approach that has been decided upon, the treatment plans of the professionals may never be fully carried out. In a token economy system, for example, it is necessary that all those who are involved in implementing the system and awarding the reinforcements be fully acquainted with the procedures and the rationale behind them. Often the failure of a newly initiated behavioral modification system in an institution or school can be traced to the failure of the staff to follow through with the procedures because of a lack of understanding of the new methods or the reasons behind them. Inservice programs alone may not provide the opportunity for staff to discuss expected problems and to correct their misperceptions about the new approach.

Professionals often receive little training in the viewpoints of other professionals and the approaches they may take in their work. A lack of understanding of the services offered by other professionals on the team and the differences in approaches among professionals can lead to serious difficulties in an interdisciplinary team. The next chapter addresses some of the differences in the professions that may affect team functioning.

Chapter 3

The Professions

The professionals who constitute the human service teams that work with exceptional children possess varied skills and knowledge that, in part, define their role on the team. However, the term "professional" generally implies more than occupational competence. A number of factors interact to create a unique professional identity.

Paradoxically, professionalization has both facilitated and impeded the de-. velopment and operation of the interdisciplinary team. The rapid expansion of knowledge in the disciplines and the greater availability of different modalities of care have been accompanied by a dramatic increase in specialization and even subspecialization. These changes have led to a division of labor wherein educators and other human service professionals have delegated certain aspects of care to other workers, who have themselves then aspired to, and in some cases attained, the title of "professional." These new professionals have in turn delegated some of their duties to other subprofessional workers. Of course, in such a system there is a good chance that the child may receive services that are fragmented and uncoordinated. Recognition of this possibility is one of the reasons behind the development of the team approach. At the same time, there are aspects of professional status and of the professions themselves that may militate against the optimal functioning of the interdisciplinary team.

In this chapter we will explore those characteristics of the professions that seem to have an impact upon team function—namely, the nature of a profession, the way in which professions have developed, and the relationship between the team approach and the professionalization process.

THE NATURE OF A PROFESSION

Originally, "profession" referred to the act of professing, and, according to Hughes (1965), "professionals *profess*. They profess to know better than others the nature of certain matters, and to know better than their clients what ails them or their affairs. This is the essence of the professional idea and the professional claim. From it flow many consequences" (p. 2).

While many would agree with Hughes that knowledge is one of the attributes characteristic of a profession, there is a surprising lack of consensus about what constitutes a profession. For example, Cogan (1953), following a comprehensive review of the definitions of a profession, concludes that "no broad acceptance of any authoritative definition has been observed" (p. 47).

One of the earliest attempts to define a profession was that of Abraham Flexner (1915), whose classic paper is cited and whose ideas have reappeared in many of the later definitions. Flexner proposed six criteria characterizing a profession: a profession is characterized by *intellectual activities*, based on *science and learning*, used for *practical purposes*, which can be *taught*, is *organized internally*, and is *altruistic*. The professions were seen by Flexner as morally superior to other occupations, and he notes that "what matters most is professional spirit. . . [since, when] accepted professions are prosecuted at a mercenary or selfish level, law and medicine are ethically no better than trades" (p. 90).

It is this sense of altruism or "professional spirit" that has traditionally set the professions not only apart from but also above other methods of earning a living. Professional work is seen as an end in itself, not merely a means to an end (Greenwood, 1957). Such lofty status serves as a significant incentive for those individuals who hope to become members of the professions and for those occupational groups that are striving toward professionalization.

Much of the confusion and ambiguity associated with "profession" arises from the popular usages of the term. For example, "professional" is sometimes distinguished from "amateur" on the basis of receiving payment for services. It is in this sense that a tennis player, a singer, and a plumber might all be called "professional" even though these occupations differ greatly from the original professional groups (doctors, lawyers, and the clergy).

The difficulties inherent in reaching consensus on the definition of a term that is both a social science concept and a popular expression has led Becker (1962) to take a "radically sociological" viewpoint,

> regarding professions simply as those occupations which have been fortunate enough in the politics of today's work world to gain and maintain possession of that honorific title. On this view, there is no such thing as the "true" profession and no set of characteristics necessarily associated with the title. There are only those work groups which are commonly regarded as professions and those which are not. (p. 33)

In contrast to a functional viewpoint of the professions, Bucher and Strauss (1961) outline what they call a *process* approach.

> Functionalism sees a profession largely as a relatively homogeneous community whose members share identity, values, definitions of role, and interests. . . . In actuality, the assumption of relative homogeneity within the professions may not be entirely useful; there are many identities, many values, and many interests. (pp. 325–326)

They propose rather, that a profession can be viewed as a "loose amalgamation of segments which are in movement" (p. 333), and they examine the diversities, cleavages, and emerging specializations within the field of medicine.

Sussman (1966) proposes that "the core characteristics of a profession are: *service orientation* and a *body of theoretical knowledge*, with *autonomy of the work group* as a by-product of the two" (p. 184). By "service orientation," Sussman refers not only to the notion of altruistic motivation rather than self-interest but also to the idea that "the community defines the need for the service and accords it varying prestige, status, and power" (p. 184). The second characteristic, a body of theoretical knowledge, refers to abstract information usually acquired during a long period of training. Because of the professional's specialized knowledge and service orientation, the community generally sanctions a greater degree of autonomy for the professional than for members of other occupations. Since professionals possess unique knowledge and skills, they alone are considered capable of judging what is best for the client. As Greenwood (1957) puts it, "the client's subordination to professional authority invests the professional with a monopoly of judgment. When an occupation strives toward professionalization, one of its aspirations is to acquire this monopoly" (p. 48). This greater degree of freedom or autonomy usually necessitates a code of ethics regulating the behavior of members of the profession. However, several recent trends, including the rise of "consumerism," a more knowledgeable public, and increasing governmental intervention, seem to be eroding some of the autonomy of the professions.

In addition to these core characteristics, there are a number of other traits associated with professionalism (Goode, 1960; Sussman, 1966). For example, through various professional associations and organizations, a profession is generally able to set standards of ethics and training and to establish criteria for admission to the profession. The profession also "engages in organizational and legislative activities leading to certification and licensure, the legitimization of power and the perpetuation of autonomy" (Sussman, 1966, p. 184).

Although a profession may be identified in this fashion, a number of writers (Goode, 1960; Greenwood, 1957; Sussman, 1966) have pointed out that it may be more reasonable to regard professionalization as a continuum rather than as an all-or-none phenomenon. In this view, an occupation may be regarded as *more* or *less* professional depending on how closely it meets certain adopted criteria. It is to be expected, then, that any particular field of service will be staffed by a diversity of occupational groups of varying degrees of professionalization and that the development and movement of such groups will have major impact on the delivery of services and on the human service team.

THE DEVELOPMENT OF A PROFESSION

Professionalization, and the increased prestige and status associated with it, is the goal of the members of many occupational groups. This is true of those occupations loosely referred to as the health or human service professions. In moving from a nonprofessional or paraprofessional status to that of a "true" profession, these occupations pass through several more or less distinct stages of professionalization, as illustrated in Table 3–1. Along the way, changes can be seen in the social context, in the role definition, and in the knowledge base of the emerging profession. The process begins with the recognition of an unmet social need in Stage I and culminates in Stage IV in external recognition of the autonomy of the profession, the development of a system of professional norms and values, and a growing body of knowledge leading to further specialization within the profession.

As the knowledge base of any profession grows, there is a tendency for individuals to specialize in a particular area. The specialty then goes through a developmental process similar to that of the parent profession, until the new profession gains recognition within the parent profession as well as from the outside community. This process has been illustrated in the health professions whenever physicians have attempted to use others to extend the services provided to patients. Some of these paraprofessional groups have moved through the various stages of professionalization and are now claiming full professional status in their own right. These new professions have in turn spawned additional paraprofessionals. An unfortunate side effect of this is that in some professions a rather rigid hierarchical system has been instituted, precluding the development of any rational career ladder.

An important aspect of professionalization is the basic assumption that those who are "higher" in the system possess all of the knowledge and skills of those lower in the hierarchy. When this assumption can no longer be defended, the subordinate group begins the move toward professionalization. Such situations are often fraught with acrimony and rancor and may lead to inter- and intra-professional strife and rivalry. Typically, each profession becomes more protective of its domain and of its portion of the knowledge base. This occurs both horizontally and vertically. Horizontally, the need for specialization caused by

Table 3-1 Stages of Professionalization

Stage	Social Context	Role Definition	Knowledge Base
I.	Social demand or need to be filled.	Undifferentiated attempts to fill need. Anyone may try (and does).	No unique body of knowledge.
II.	Recognition by society that some fill this need better than others.	Differentiation — some people or group fill need.	Development of a body of knowledge unique to filling needs.
III.	Outside recognition of special group.	Self-recognition and development of means of recognition of who is in group and who is not.	Development of means of induction into group, transmission of knowledge, values, and skills.
IV.	Outside recognition of the right to control group membership.	Regulation of group membership.	Increasing knowledge leading to specialization within role.

an increase in the knowledge base creates a split between two or more groups of equal status, such as radiologists and anesthesiologists. Vertically, differentiation occurs when one group delegates duties to another group, based upon the aforementioned assumption that the first group is master of the complete knowledge base of the second group. Eventually, those considered lower in the hierarchy begin to assert that their knowledge base is indeed specialized and that the higher group is not privy to it.

The medical profession in particular sometimes has difficulty maintaining control of what were vertically subordinate groups. As members of the parent profession, physicians perceive themselves as having the ultimate moral, legal, and ethical responsibility for the welfare of the client but see their authority being diffused and eroded as their knowledge base is spread among a number of other professions and paraprofessional groups.

As new professions emerge, there is a tendency to delegate the more routine tasks to lower levels of workers. Thus the human service occupations take the form of a pyramid that grows from the bottom and at the same time widens its base. Figure 3–1 shows this hierarchical pyramid with some illustrative occupational groups.

A Case Study of Professionalization

The process by which an occupational group evolves into a profession may be illustrated by a brief review of the development of special education. While the purpose here is not to trace the full history of the development of this profession, an examination of some of the characteristics of its evolution may serve to illustrate that professions move through various stages of development, and to show the ways in which professions continually seek to define and redefine their role in relation to the client and to other professions.

Figure 3–1 Hierarchical Relationships in the Professions

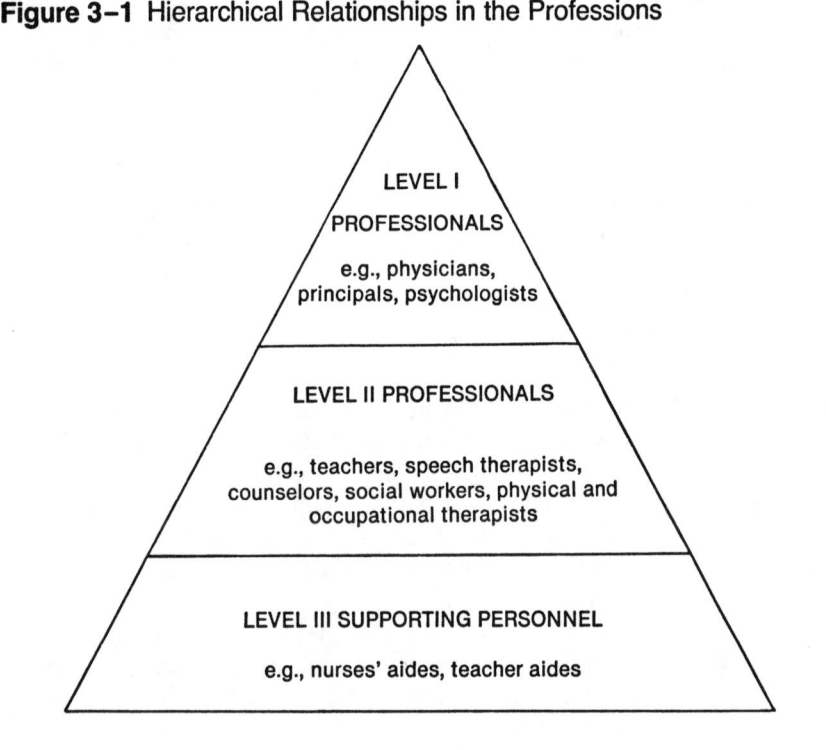

LEVEL I
PROFESSIONALS
e.g., physicians,
principals, psychologists

LEVEL II PROFESSIONALS

e.g., teachers, speech therapists,
counselors, social workers, physical and
occupational therapists

LEVEL III SUPPORTING PERSONNEL

e.g., nurses' aides, teacher aides

It must be recognized that in the early stages of the development of a profession, that is, Stage I in Table 3-1, where "anyone may try (and does)" to meet the social needs, there may be widely diverging viewpoints on the nature of the problem that is being addressed as well as the nature of the care or treatment to be employed with the client.

The child in need of help is often not difficult to identify; however, the labeling and categorization of such children has led to long and often acrimonious debates among those who would care for them. Children with physical disabilities, such as the hearing impaired and those with visual handicaps, became the object of concern of a number of individuals and groups at a rather early date.

As has been mentioned earlier, many persons in the field of special education view the work of Jean Itard with Victor, the Wild Boy of Aveyron, as one of the first identifiable precursors of the profession of special education. Others might hold that the roots of the profession are in the work of people like Jacob Rodrigues Periere, who pioneered in the teaching of the deaf. The work of such individuals led to the initiation of the development of a body of knowledge unique to filling the special needs of the handicapped. By the mid 1800s, a number of persons might be identified by the public as having expertise in the care, treatment, and education of children with special needs. Among these individuals are included Edward Seguin, Thomas Hopkins Gallaudet, and Samuel Gridley Howe. During the period from the mid 1800s to early 1900s, there is an initial attempt to develop training programs for persons who would be or were working with the handicapped. For example, Connor (1976) says,

> according to Walin (1914), the University of Pennsylvania offered a three course sequence in 1897 in the education of the mentally retarded. Soon after, New York University initiated a course, "Education of Defectives," and Teachers College, Columbia University offered "The Psychology and Education of Exceptional Children" in 1906 and 1908 respectively. (p. 369)

With reference again to Table 3-1, it may be seen that the profession has advanced by this time to Stage III. Further evidence of this may be found in the development of professional associations. The Proceedings of the 1898 National Education Association lists Alexander Graham Bell as one of the participants in the section concerned with "the deaf, blind, and mentally defective" (National Education Association, 1898).

One of the major forces in the development of the profession of special education was the Council on Exceptional Children (CEC) in the early 1920s. Within a decade, this organization began the publication of a journal and the work of organizing a number of disparate groups to seek some common goals.

Some would hold that the groups are still disparate and that, while the CEC may be the umbrella organization, the prime professional organization of many special educators is one of the more specialized organizations involved with specific categories, such as mental retardation or visual handicaps. Many of these other associations were also being developed during the same period with the consequent problems of overlap and rivalry.

The first half of the twentieth century has seen the continued development of the field through the establishment of standards, certification requirements, and accreditation mechanisms, and the development of a more clear perception of self-identity. In the latter half of the twentieth century, the development of a greater concern for the rights of all persons has led to an even greater need for professionalization. Whether this will occur or not is a matter of conjecture. When we look more closely at the field, we see that there are still a number of seemingly distinct specialties within the profession, as well as other groups who work with the same children on the same problems. Differences in philosophy or in theoretical approach divide the field in several instances. This poses a problem that is not unique to professions who serve the needs of the exceptional child; however, the problem must be directly addressed in order that the child may receive appropriate services.

In terms of the characteristics described by Sussman (1966), discussed earlier in this chapter, special education clearly demonstrates a strong service orientation. It also has a body of theoretical knowledge, although some might question the uniqueness of that knowledge. It is also clear that society recognizes the need for such services. Special education has engaged in several of the activities that Sussman has called professional *traits*: development of a professional association or, in this case, associations, legislative activities, development of standards of training and admission to the profession, publication of professional journals, and a code of ethics.

What is unclear at this time is the answer to the question as to whether special education is indeed a profession or a loose amalgam of a number of different professions. For this reason, it is all the more important that those who serve the needs of the exceptional child focus upon the welfare of the client and that the differences among the various approaches to specific problems be explored by an interdisciplinary team.

INTERNAL CONTROL OF PROFESSIONS

Many of the professions represented on the interdisciplinary team are presently in a state of flux. Some are moving toward greater professionalization, some seem to be losing prestige and power, and others are plagued by internal dissension and fragmentation as a result of increased specialization within the field.

The role expectations and actual behavior of the individual team member will be greatly influenced by the stability or conflict within the profession. Indeed, conflict within the emerging or changing profession can have a marked impact on the operation of the team itself. Therefore, we will briefly examine some of the sources of conflict that may affect the team and how this conflict is controlled by the professions.

According to Parsons (1959), there are two main types of professional groups: those formed in the workplace by the employing organization (for example, a school or a hospital) and those formed by individuals. Of the two, it is the latter that plays the major role in professionalization and deals with intraprofessional conflict.

> The main thrust toward professionalization by marginal occupations comes through the association organized by leaders of the field. Its major activities are to provide the conditions for all its members to function as professionals, serving the society, increasingly utilizing a growing body of theoretical knowledge and obtaining a payoff in prestige and financial rewards. (Sussman, 1966, p. 191)

We have already seen the role played by the CEC and other associations in the professionalization of special education. Often the professional association will establish an official journal or some other mechanism for communicating with members, promoting the profession, and exerting control over professional activities.

More generally, the profession's attempt to establish an identity and to draw boundaries between itself and other professions or specialties may serve as an integrative force within the emerging profession. At the same time, there may be a number of factors leading to fragmentation and conflict within the group. As Goode (1960) puts it, "no occupation, then, becomes a profession without a struggle" (p. 902). The external conflict with other professions has often been noted. "If a new occupation claims the right to solve a problem which formerly was solved by another, that claim is an accusation of incompetence and the outraged counteraccusation is, of course, 'encroachment'" (Goode, 1960, p. 902). Goode also illustrates this point with the conflict between two emerging professional specialties, clinical psychology and psychiatry, a battle that has continued over a period of several years.

External threats by other professions are not infrequent, but in some cases such *interprofessional* conflict can lead to a pulling together of disparate interests within the threatened group and a submerging of internal differences, at least temporarily. On the other hand, *intraprofessional* conflicts precipitated by professionalization are less obvious and often overlooked, but these may actually be much more disruptive to the emerging profession than external threats.

As long as the professional organization serves primarily to provide mutual support and help in solving the typical problems members face in carrying out their professional duties, then its effect will be primarily an integrative one. However, as the push for professionalization grows stronger, the membership may be far from unanimous in their support of these efforts, and "reactionaries" within the profession may become more vocal in their opposition to the proposed changes.

As the group moves toward further professionalization, the association usually includes among its goals: increasing the length and difficulty of professional preparation, raising standards for admission to training programs, and establishing licensure and/or certification requirements. However, these goals may not be supported by all members of the professional organization. As Sussman (1966) points out, the rank and file may not move as quickly as the leaders of the emerging professions. Furthermore, the move to raise standards may be thought to imply some degree of incompetence among the present ranks, and the establishment of new and more rigid requirements for membership may be seen by older members as a threat. Although "grandfathering" provisions are often included to reduce resistance to change, such arrangements may be seen as leading to a kind of second-class citizenship within the profession. While some attempts may be made to upgrade the less qualified members, Sussman indicates that the price of professionalization may be to award status and prestige to some who are "undeserving" with the hope that they will quickly leave the field.

For many members, the promise of greater economic rewards, prestige, and power serves as a strong incentive, and the majority of the membership may give full support to the association's moves toward professionalization. However, according to Bucher and Strauss (1961), "associations are not everybody's association but represent one segment of a particular alliance of segments" of the profession (p. 33). The various segments within a profession (or even within a specialty within a profession) may differ in terms of perceived mission, work activities, methodology and techniques, relationships with clients, sense of colleagueship, interests, and associations. This diversity may not be apparent to outsiders, who respond to the public image projected by the professional association and its leaders. Yet this public image may only reflect the power of particular segments within the organization, rather than represent the unified position of the total membership (Bucher & Strauss, 1961).

For individual team members, the political machinations within the professional association may have little meaning except as they influence professional roles or how others perceive those roles. However, insofar as the conflicts within the profession make roles ambiguous and provide a misleading view of responsibilities, they may interfere with how team members function, both with the child and with other team members. If the profession has not adequately conveyed an appropriate image to outsiders, individual members may find it necessary to spend an inordinate amount of time clarifying their role on the team. It should be noted, however, that a certain amount of role "flexibility" is desirable for effective team functioning; overly rigid definition of professional roles may prohibit "give and take" and fail to provide opportunities for role negotiation that can be important to the smooth functioning of the team. If the professional association is too restrictive in its regulation of the professional activities of its members, professionals may find serious conflicts between their roles as team members and the role expectations of the professional association.

EXTERNAL CONTROL OF PROFESSIONS

While a great deal has been written about the autonomy of the professions and their ability to regulate themselves, professions differ in how much professional autonomy is exercised and who decides how much autonomy is allowed. Close examination reveals that there is a great deal of variation in the degree of external control exerted upon the professions.

External controls are exercised in a number of ways, including governmental licensure and regulation. The professional associations attempt to exert control within the profession by certification and disciplinary procedures. However, the associations may also attempt to exert control over the practice of other professions, particularly when one profession sees its prerogatives eroded or usurped by another. Another means of external control is the accreditation of educational programs by external agencies. Individual organizations and institutions maintain control over who may practice or provide services and thus also exert some control over the professions.

Such controls have clear implications for the operation of the interdisciplinary team, since they have impact on who does what, who is responsible for supervision, and the scope and limits of a particular profession. Interestingly, the impetus for external recognition and control has often come from within the particular professional group, as when a number of health professions requested that the American Medical Association assume responsibility for the approval of their educational programs.

Some of the factors that may lead a profession to seek governmental regulation through licensure and certification or similar statutes are:

- an inability to prevent those who are considered unqualified from practicing.
- the need to define and protect the scope of practice on a statutory basis.
- the need for legal status to assure recognition for purposes such as third party payment requirements or federal funding programs for student support.

Each of these factors may influence the way professionals interact in an interdisciplinary team. For example, if unqualified persons are using the title of a particular unlicensed profession, the integrity of that profession may be questioned by members of other professions on the team, causing qualified members of the unlicensed profession to lose status within the team. The competence of all practitioners of that profession is called into question since there is no way to judge whether in fact the individual is a professional or a charlatan.

A second important factor is the apparent need to define legally the boundaries of the profession. This has two purposes: to ensure that these areas of professional practice will not be encroached upon by other professions and to retain exclusive rights to as many professional prerogatives as possible. An example of action on the part of one profession to prevent what was believed to be an encroachment, and reaction to it, is found in Lieberman (1980).

> Around 1972 The American Speech and Hearing Association (ASHA) requested a meeting with representatives of the field of learning disabilities to discuss the fact that learning disabilities personnel were muscling in on jobs previously held by speech and language therapists. There was some consternation on the part of ASHA (and rightfully so) that speech personnel were losing jobs to learning disabilities teachers. (p. 15)

He goes on to detail a struggle for territory between and among a number of professions who deal with the learning disabled child. He examines professionals such as reading specialists, occupational therapists, and optometrists in relation to their claim upon the professional territory of the teacher of the learning disabled. He also points out that

> Nowhere is there a more critical area for decision making than territoriality. With the proliferation of all kinds of specialized personnel in public school buildings, territoriality has arisen as a major socio-cultural factor in the delivery of services to children. There was a time when a graduate degree in a particular field defined the parameters of one's potential capabilities in a particular job. This is no longer the case, especially as it pertains to the field of learning disabilities. Not only is everyone involved due to the multidisciplinary nature of the disorder; everyone claims that they are able to perform teaching functions that everyone else can. . . . the territoriality issue surfaces in the form of who does what to whom. (p. 18)

It is interesting that in the same issue of the *Journal of Learning Disabilities* in which the Lieberman article appears, Lyon concludes an empirical study of the differences of perceptions of the medical evaluation of learning disabled children by pediatricians and teachers of learning disabled children by observing that these differences

> may undermine the effectiveness of communication between the two groups. If the goal of an interdisciplinary approach is to succeed, it is necessary that cooperating professionals learn more about learning disabilities and understand their own and each other's contributions, limitations, and opinions. (Lyon, 1980, pp. 23–24)

While the example used here is taken from the field of learning disabilities, it is not difficult to produce examples from other disciplines (Goode, 1960; Quick, 1976).

The task of defining professional boundaries will continue no doubt for a long time and is necessarily a continual one if the professions are to remain vital and not stagnate. Such definitions in the past have been surrounded with rancor and argument and will probably continue to be so in the future.

Another example of an attempt to define and retain a professional prerogative is seen in a statement about speech pathologists and audiologists who sought licensure in a particular state.

> An attorney general's opinion concerning an individual who was not a physician and who advertised speech and hearing therapy stated that therapy could be considered a medical sub-specialty and that the person offering therapy probably should be a physician or an individual working under the direct supervision of a physician. (Nicolais, 1976, p. 22)

Speech pathologists considered it to be an infringement upon their assumed right to work on a *referral* basis without postreferral supervision by a physician, so they sought legal status to clarify the issue. The question of who may perform or prescribe therapy and under what type of supervision is a critical one for the team. As more and more specialties are developed and the knowledge base grows, it becomes impossible for one person to master all of that knowledge or even any major part of it. In the case of the attorney general's opinion given above, is it possible for *any physician* to monitor the work of a speech pathologist or audiologist or is it necessary for that person to be a master of that area? As the scope of human services and health care are redefined to include the total individual, it becomes increasingly unlikely that *any one* person will be able to monitor that care adequately.

The third reason for seeking governmental sanction is that of legal recognition as a profession. In a sense this ensures that when legislation is drafted the profession will be taken into account. For example, when government grants or fellowships are made available, it is much more likely that those professional areas already sanctioned will receive a share of such support. This "official" recognition confers a certain status on the profession and lends a certain aura of protection to the client, who assumes that some responsible party (in this case the government) is overseeing the operation of that profession.

Another type of external control is exercised through the process of accrediting the institutions that educate persons for the profession.

BECOMING A PROFESSIONAL

Up to now our discussion has focused on the professions themselves, rather than on the individuals who make up those groups. Now let us look briefly at the socialization process whereby the individual acquires the skills and roles of the profession and at the same time adopts its norms and values. As Vollmer and Mills (1966) point out, "becoming a professional is a gradual process—it doesn't happen all at once" (p. 87). It is a process that begins long before the candidate is admitted to a professional school and long before a final career choice is made. Attitudes toward specific professions may originate in childhood, shaped by real-life experiences with teachers, doctors, dentists, and so forth, and also by what the child reads, sees, or hears concerning these roles. These early attitudes may be unspoken or even unconscious and are usually modified by later experience and information, but nonetheless the early impressions will have an impact on the eventual career choice.

At the point of admission to a professional school, the student may have an unrealistic, perhaps even romanticized notion of what the professional role entails. Thus an important function of professional training is to initiate trainees into the "culture" of the profession and to develop in them a more realistic expectation of the role to be played. The student gradually becomes aware of the explicit and implicit norms that govern the behavior of members of the profession and may adopt as role models those professionals whose skills he or she particularly admires.

Professional training is long and expensive. This fact alone has shaped the composition of the professions in the United States. Until recent years, children from families of moderate means were often unable to stay in school long enough to complete professional training. Expensive education was beyond their reach. Despite recent attempts to increase the proportion of low-income and minority students in professional training programs and to provide financial assistance for such students, the older, well-established professions have not altered much in composition.

Typically, as an occupational group moves toward greater professionalization, there is an increase in the length of training. Usually this involves requiring more prerequisites and more coursework and internship-type experiences. However, unless the profession can offer sufficient gains in status and economic incentives, the training period cannot be unduly lengthened (Hughes, 1965).

Admission

Increased selectivity in admissions, like length of training, is another sign of greater professionalization. The better-established professions that offer greater prestige and potential economic rewards are likely to attract large numbers of persons wishing to enter their ranks. Thus they can also maintain the highest standards of selectivity. These standards are likely to be upheld not only by the faculty of the training institution but also by the professional association, since greater selectivity further increases the status of the profession. In those professions of highest prestige, criteria not necessary or relevant to the development of needed skills may be used to screen applicants. Minority groups have long been familiar with the "hidden" criteria that sometimes underly the admissions process. Often women found admission to medical or law schools difficult because, as they were told, they lacked the "motivation" of men and would "leave the field" to keep house and raise children.

Professions of lower status have traditionally been unable to maintain the stringent requirements of law and medicine, not because these fields were less crucial to meeting social or individual needs, but because the fewer numbers of applications in relation to places available did not allow for such selectivity. On the other hand, the shorter periods of training in the less prestigious professions meant less initial expense, and apprentice professionals could more quickly begin to regain a return on their educational investment. Thus professions such as teaching and social work became an avenue of social mobility for students of moderate income, for women, and for minority groups.

In some instances, outside sources play a role in "professionalizing" an occupation by providing training funds or scholarships to attract promising candidates into an area of personnel shortage. The federal government has played a major role in the upgrading of a number of professions by making available to students federal stipends for professional training and by providing training monies to the university for faculty support and associated expenses. In this manner, universities were offered incentives to provide training programs in areas that Congress felt to be of high priority, and at the same time students who might not have otherwise considered it were encouraged by the available support to enter professional training. The governmental agency administering the federal grant monies also provided guidelines for such program components as curricular content and admission standards and developed the procedures for program review. Eventually, the federal funds are decreased and the university is expected to take over the bulk of the expense of the program so that federal funds could be moved to other programs designed to meet newly emerging needs.

One of the difficulties faced by professional schools is the collection of data by which to validate admission criteria. Often the university faculty members with major responsibility for admission decisions have neither the time nor the financial resources to test out the predictions that an admissions decision implies. In effect, the acceptance of an applicant into a professional program involves two predictions:

1. This candidate will successfully complete the training program.
2. The applicant will be a successful practitioner of the profession.

Leaving aside for the moment the ambiguities and methodological difficulties inherent in the term "successful," we can see that the more closely the training program simulates professional practice, the easier it is to predict the successful student will become a successful professional. Of course, it is not unusual to find brilliant and talented students who fail to live up to the promise of their training days when they enter the "real" world. However, it is the difficulty in measuring "success" that poses the greatest problems for faculty admission committees. Too often they seize upon whatever "hard" data happens to be available (such as grade point average or test scores) because they cannot, with the resources available, carefully judge the actual effectiveness of their graduates as professionals.

Socialization

The socialization process does not necessarily end with the granting of a professional degree. As noted earlier, the more established the profession and the higher its status, the longer the period of apprenticeship. In medicine, for example, internships, residencies, and specialized training extend long past the traditional four years of medical school. The development of a private practice and referral system and acceptance into a major hospital as a staff member are part of the long-term process of establishing a medical career.

The Level II professions in Figure 3–1, such as teaching or social work, may require considerably shorter periods of preparation. However, in these professions, too, receiving a degree and getting a job is only the beginning. As many new professionals can attest, it may take many months or even years of experience before one earns full acceptance as a member of the profession. Teachers, for example, may be awarded only temporary certification until further education and/or experience is acquired. Full acceptance as a professional is based not only on proven skill and expertise in the tools of the profession but also in many cases on how well the initiate carries out role expectations.

We have mentioned that the choice of a professional career is determined in part by attitudes toward that career formed early in life. It should be noted that such a choice also depends on the individual's self-image; the career chosen is likely to be one not markedly inconsistent with the individual's self-concept. Where there is a significant discrepancy between one's view of the professional role and the image of oneself, the socialization process will involve a major alteration in one or both of these perceptions. Even when one feels that the chosen career is a "natural" one, the individual's professional education will involve a gradual internalization of "a professional image which becomes a significant aspect of the self-concept" (Vollmer & Mills, 1966, p. 98). The internalization of new roles and changes in self-image have several implications for professional education:

- Such changes take time and cannot be unduly rushed.
- Self-concept depends not only on internal reactions but also on the reactions of others.
- An opportunity to "practice" the role is necessary.

Changes in self-concept require an arena in which to test out new skills and perceptions and to receive confirmation from others. To a great extent, we feel like a professional when others behave toward us as though we are a professional. This generally happens when the student is placed in a field training situation and is expected to play a professional role. As children and coworkers begin to respond to the student with acceptance and respect, the student plays the role with increasing confidence and authority. Thus he is encouraged to "try on" the professional role under the watchful eye of a supervisor who is likely to focus not only on the development of specific skills but also on the professional image the student projects. The student learns to *act* like a professional as well as to *be* one.

During the process of socialization, the would-be professional may find that the new role is not always congruent with previous roles, and the trainee may begin to experience role conflict. Expectations of others may be such that they demand mutually exclusive behaviors, and the student is forced either to compromise certain roles or to abandon them altogether. Conflicts between private and public responsibilities are obvious and not unusual, as when the busy teacher compromises his or her role as spouse or parent in order to meet professional obligations.

Equally important, although less obvious, are the conflicts between the various professional roles the individual is expected to fill. For example, the apprentice professional may be expected to demonstrate the responsibility and autonomy of a professional but at the same time play the role of student in interactions with supervisors and teachers. This inconsistency may interfere with performance in both roles. Such conflicts are not limited to students; established professionals also experience role conflicts and find themselves forced to establish priorities in their activities in order to resolve real or potential conflicts in expectations. In a later chapter we will examine the conflicts between one's roles as a professional and as a team member—conflicts that seem to be inherent in the team approach.

Some conflicts seem inherent in the nature of the profession itself, and a great deal of time and effort may be spent in attempts to clarify role expectations for the profession as a whole. The conflict of the "scientist-professional" model in clinical psychology has absorbed that profession for over twenty years without clear resolution. Clinical training programs, internship facilities, professional organizations, and individual psychologists have all felt the impact of the conflict between the roles of scientist-researcher and professional practitioner. University professors often experience similar conflicts with regard to expectations stemming from their roles in teaching, scholarly activity, and public service. Since the reward system for professional activities, in terms of status and money, is presumably tied to effective performance in expected roles, the conflict can be a very real one for the individual. Because establishing oneself in a professional career is a long-range endeavor, the young professional is often forced to make decisions regarding role priorities rather early in his or her career, although the results of those decisions may not become clear for some time.

Among the roles in which the professional is expected to engage are those involving interaction with members of other professional groups. One aspect of the role of the teacher, for example, is to help implement individual education plans. The activities of the special education teacher must often be coordinated with those of the school psychologist and the regular classroom teacher. Human service professionals in general must learn what to expect of other members of the team and how to fill their own roles appropriately and effectively. One must be sensitive to differences in status and power associated with various role positions.

PROFESSIONAL STATUS

One of the factors that affects the way in which professionals interact on the team is status. It is important here to differentiate between *individual status*, which may be conferred upon a team member for various reasons related to her or his performance on the team, and *professional status*, which is accorded individuals because of their professional identification. Before we look briefly at the concept of status and the relative status positions of some of the human service professions represented on the interdisciplinary team, it should be noted that most studies of professional status have used populations of lay persons to

Chapter 4

Organizational Setting

The professionals who constitute the interdisciplinary team are generally members of some human service organization such as a school, community mental health center, rehabilitation agency, or hospital. This chapter explores some types of organizations and the impact of organization settings upon the functioning of the team.

In one sense, the nature of the organization defines the team, its members, its tasks, and, to some extent, the place and time of its interaction. Thus how the team operates is markedly influenced by its organizational setting. Some of the characteristics of an organization that influence the functioning of the team are the type of organization and its goals, the structure, the locus of authority and control, and the organization's norms and values. Such characteristics are influential no matter what type of institution is involved.

When one thinks of providing services to children, it is normal to think of the school as being one of the prime organizations involved. While this is indeed the case in many instances, it should not be forgotten that the school is only one of a large number of agencies that are involved with the welfare of the child and adolescent. Thus, we must go beyond single institutions when we look at the impact of the organization on the team.

CHARACTERISTICS OF ORGANIZATIONS

The type of institution in which the team operates can be a major factor in determining the clientele served, what programs are offered, and the staff people hired (Coe, 1970). In these and other ways, the type of institution has a significant impact on the type of team that operates within its walls and the way that team is structured and functions.

While there has been a great deal written concerning the place of organizational theory and organizational development in human service institutions, it would seem that as yet there is no entirely adequate basis for organizational analysis and development in what Drucker termed the "Third Sector" (i.e., service organizations). Indeed, Drucker (1978) in regard to such organizations says:

> Both the businessman and the civil servant tend to underrate the difficulty of managing service institutions. The businessman thinks it's all a matter of being efficient, the civil servant thinks it's all a matter of having the right procedures and controls. Both are wrong—service institutions are more complex than either businesses or government agencies—as we are painfully finding out in our attempts to make the hospital a little more manageable (no one to my knowledge has yet tried to do this with the university).
>
> Indeed we know far too little about managing the service institution—it is simply too recent a phenomenon. But we do know that it needs to be managed. And we do know that defining what its task is and what it should not be is the most essential step in making the service institutions of the Third Sector manageable, managed, and performing.

It is, however, possible to look at some of the characteristics of human service organizations and see how they may relate to team functioning. In doing so, we must remember that the dominant organizational pattern in Western society is *bureaucratic*. The bureaucratic organization is hierarchical, with power and authority concentrated at higher levels in the organization. As Kingdon (1973) puts it:

> formal rules and scalar authority, or hierarchy, bear the main burden of socially integrating our organizations and mobilizing our resources. . . . individuals in our organizations relinquish their power to be the scalar authority of officials who are then charged with the responsibility for establishing formal rules controlling resource allocation and socially integrating the organization. (pp. 1–2)

In addition to a hierarchical authority structure undergirded by a system of rules and procedures, bureaucratic organizations generally are characterized by a differentiation of tasks performed by individuals and by subunits of the organization.

The fact is, the ways in which human service institutions are organized have a major influence on the operation of the team. All human service organizations have a number of attributes in common, all of which have some impact on the interdisciplinary team.

The organization *exists in a social context* and interacts with that context in both a proactive and reactive manner. It is therefore an open system receiving input from the environment and in turn generating some form of output. Development of the organization is based on some *identified human need*. Such needs may change over a period of time. Indeed, the organization that does not undergo modification in accord with changing human needs will cease to exist. Most often, organizations do modify their activities to address changing needs, although this change may lag well behind the identification of new needs.

The organization is based on some *belief* or *theory* of the nature of man, the nature of society, or the nature of the universe; it may also be based on a specific theory that conditions its structure, goals, and activities. *Resources* and *energy* are utilized by organizations to produce some *believed social good*.

To accomplish that social good, organizations will adopt, utilize, or exhibit some of the following characteristics: explicit or implicit goals and objectives, patterns of authority and decision making, communication, rewards and sanctions, norms and values. They are composed of and address specific populations with roles and membership within the organization. They occupy space. They employ various processes and technologies in achieving their outcomes.

Goals and Objectives

When goals are set by a superordinate authority, they may differ from the goals of any one team member or the team as a whole. For example, when case loads are set at higher levels than the team considers consistent with adequate client care, the team goals of "effective" client care are in conflict with a goal of "efficient" care on the part of an authority structure.

Perrow (1961) discusses two kinds of goals in a complex organization. First are the *official goals*, which are

> general purposes of the organization as put forth in the charter, annual reports, public statements by key executives and other authoritative pronouncements. . . . The official goal of a hospital may be to promote the health of the community through curing the ill, and sometimes through preventing illness, teaching, and conducting research. (p. 855)

Such goals are often deliberately vague and abstract, and in order to understand organizational behavior adequately, it is necessary to examine a second type of goal—what Perrow calls *operative goals*. As the name suggests, operative goals are the operating policies of the organization; "they tell us what the organization is actually trying to do, regardless of what the official goals say are the aims" (p. 855).

Even when operative goals are quite clear, it does not necessarily mean that the goals of the team or of any team member will coincide with the goals of the parent organization. For example, this may be true of the goals of the *school* as it is conceived in American (United States) society. Goals of the school as perceived by various constituencies have varied considerably between and among constituencies from time period to time period. Whether the goals were seen as individual, in leading to upward social mobility, or social, in helping to integrate a diverse population, there has been one basic trend which reflects an almost universally accepted goal for the educational institutions in the United States: the education of greater and greater portions of the population at higher and higher levels. While this may seem to some so self-evident that it need not be mentioned, it is nonetheless of profound importance when we examine how such a movement relates to the need for teamwork in providing the services necessary to meet such a goal.

The passage of P. L. 94–142 is but another manifestation of the movement toward educational opportunity for all at the highest level they can obtain. This ideal is based upon the belief that the quality of life of the individual and the quality of the society is enhanced when all children have access to an education appropriate to their needs in an environment that places the least restrictions upon them. In order to fulfill such a goal, the inclusion in the program of the typical school of a more diverse group of professionals has become necessary. This in turn has created the need to reexamine the way in which professionals interact in the school setting in relationship to the individual student. It is self-evident that the professions, differing as they do in their expertise and the way in which they view their responsibility to the child, may have goals which differ from the overall organizational goal, either in content or emphasis. For example, individual classroom teachers who view the children placed in their classes due to the effect of P. L. 94–142 as an added burden may not have the same commitment to teamwork or to those children as teachers who agree in principle, and work in practice, to implement the intent of the law.

It may be seen that when the goals of the team or of some team members differ significantly from those of the organization, there may be a negative impact on the functioning of the team. Similarly, when the team as a whole questions the organizational goals, team functions in terms of those goals may be greatly impaired. As a result the team disintegrates or begins to develop its own set of goals, which may be at variance with those of the parent organization.

Authority and Control

The locus of authority may condition how the team functions since the authority structure determines the overall goals of the organization and how those goals are to be achieved. For example, let us examine the school system as typical of those agencies providing service to children. In a sense, when we speak of authority and decision making in the schools, we are talking about control. In the United States, the issue of control of school systems has become quite complex with local, state, and federal involvement through the legislative, judicial, and executive branches of government. Traditionally, the schools have been controlled at the local level by boards of lay persons selected by the community. By and large this has worked to the advantage of education in the United States and is looked upon as a positive influence in the structure of the schools and of society generally.

However, there are instances in which the control of the schools by lay persons may not have resulted in the best possible education of the students. Among notable examples are the attempts by members of lay boards to resist efforts to desegregate the schools. In some instances, of course, such resistance may have had roots in an honest difference of opinion as to how best to accomplish the task of desegregation, but often it seems to have reflected primarily resistance to such changes. There seems to be a parallel in the public schools between the situation concerning desegregation and that involving mainstreaming children with certain handicaps. There is, of course, a certain difference, in that very few people would openly admit to a prejudice toward physically or mentally handicapped children, in contrast to individuals who would demonstrate against those who are racially different. The resistance, therefore, is often not as overt but takes more subtle forms. As we have seen, the attitudes of professionals are also subjected to vagaries from fads and misperceptions current during any particular time period as well as the pressures of the particular social milieu in which they are operating.

Does this mean, then, that lay control should be wrested from the hands of the public as it has been in the case of medical treatment? It may be that the advent of the team system will provide a means to reintegrate the public, the parent, and the child so that both the individual and society are better served. Too often both the professional and the public have been at odds concerning the "best" ways of proceeding. The team approach presents one method for a resolution of this dilemma.

Schools are instruments of society and as such are asked to carry out the will of that society. In addition, the schools are also looked upon as instrumental in helping the individual reach individual goals. These different roles are not always compatible in a situation in which there are insufficient resources to meet all goals.

Thus, control of an organization is likely to be a complex compromise of internal and external forces characterized by a multitude of conflicting values, goals, and priorities. As the power structure shifts in response to changing pressures within the agency and outside it, goals and priorities will also shift, with corresponding changes in "what people do" within the agency.

Lines of Communication

As the knowledge base of human service organizations has expanded, there has been an increased need for additional types of professionals—and consequently an increase in the division of labor and the degree of specialization. In bureaucratic organizations this has been equated with more efficient use of personnel. But such specialization has in many instances led to such fragmentation that no one is really taking care of the child as a total person. The development of the team approach may indeed be a direct response to this situation.

The division of labor and the separation of function within the organization have brought concomitant problems in communication. Most organizations are set up in a way that is in natural conflict with the team approach. There seems to be an almost slavish adherence to the notion that individuals with similar functions should be housed and administered as units. Among the factors that tend to reinforce such a structure are the need to identify with a particular professional group who speak the same language, an unfamiliarity with the other professions, and the need to house certain types of equipment together (e.g., vocational education, physical therapy, etc.).

The communication system also tends to reinforce the development of units along professional lines. For example, the organizational chart for a general hospital typically shows each service (e.g., nursing, social work, occupational therapy) as a separate unit reporting to the administrator of the hospital. A similar situation can be found in many large human service organizations such as schools and rehabilitation centers where the psychologist reports to the chief of psychology, the special educator to the head of that division, the regular teacher to a supervisor, and so forth. What is immediately apparent is that, under this system, use of the team approach may lead to some confusion in lines of communication and authority.

When each professional is responsible both to a team and to a functional unit, there is the distinct possibility that there may be divided and therefore, in some cases, ineffective leadership and authority. This has the effect of blurring lines of communication and increasing the possibility of confusion and conflict. The result is reduced efficiency in services.

Thus we can see the crux of this particular problem: the team consists of individuals who believe they owe their primary allegiance and responsibility to a functionally organized unit or department, while the secondary group (i.e., the team) only provides a convenient battleground upon which interprofessional and interdepartmental wars are fought. In a dispute between a "team leader" and a department head, it is not difficult to see where the individual professional will probably stand, particularly if decisions about promotions and salary rest with the departmental unit.

Processes

Large organizations in general attempt to rationalize their operations by adopting standard procedures. These are the rules by which the institution deals both with its clientele and with its internal operations. Over a period of time these rules tend to become solidified and are codified in procedure manuals and similar publications. Unfortunately, such systems of rules are seldom child centered but instead tend to focus on the organization and its internal needs. Schools, for example, historically have not been places where the team approach has found much favor. True, team teaching produced some words of approbation for a time, especially when outside funding was available. But by and large the team concept has had little direct impact upon practices in the elementary and secondary schools of the United States. Even where teams are said to be functioning there is often little evidence that they fit even the most gratuitous definition of a team. In large part this has been true due to the traditional organizational patterns utilized in the school systems of the nation. These patterns are reinforced by the patterns of funding and staffing that have developed over many years and by the manner in which both teachers and administrators are selected and prepared.

No matter what the rhetoric has been, the predominant pattern of service delivery to students in the elementary school has been one of the individual teacher doing it all (with the exception of art, music, and gym). The teacher at the secondary level specializes in one or more subject areas. Various attempts have been made to rearrange schools to make them more efficient, principally through emulation of business or industrial models. However, the central organizational structure seems to endure.

For example, Moran (1978), in writing about how assessment procedures are to be scheduled in the classroom, comments that the "teacher will need some assistance from peer or parent volunteers, paid aides, or administrators. . . . if a school has no pool of assistants, a teacher might enlist the aid of the principal in requesting parent volunteers or older students who could be released from class during library time or independent work time" (p. 38). This, of course, is an appropriate approach to a problem faced by teachers who are attempting to fulfill their responsibilities in a professional manner. However, the mere fact that the teacher must in a sense ask the help of "volunteers" in order to discharge a mandated task speaks to the problems that are posed in many schools when the question of the team approach is raised. That is to say, if teachers cannot be replaced in the classroom for that time that is to be used for assessment procedures, how might one expect that they would be replaced for IEP meetings and other team activities? This is another way that the staffing patterns and organizational structure of the school may have impact on the team approach. This should be taken, not as a criticism of the excellent work and the dedication of the numerous volunteers who do help in the schools, but rather as a question concerning the way in which schools are organized in relation to a concept that has a great deal of merit but nonetheless poses problems to the traditional organizational pattern.

Another example comes from an interview with a veteran teacher who spoke about the difficulties encountered in attempting to develop IEPs. She said:

> They are incredibly hard to schedule. You have to have a liaison person, that is, an administrator, present, and the parent, and a time when you are free from your classroom. Administrators are difficult to get because of their other commitments—parents who want to be present when the IEP is developed often call shortly before the meeting and wish to reschedule. . . . Not all the people that should be involved are involved; for example, in the field of the emotionally disturbed, it would be helpful to have a social worker available but there is simply not the staff . . . An IEP is meant to be a total programming for a child, but all those who will be dealing with the child rarely come together. . . . One teacher may be dealing with as many as 20 different children and the time required to schedule and take part in that many meetings may be substantial.

Thus we can see that the processes and organization of an institution may not, in effect, articulate team efforts.

Rewards, Sanctions, Norms, and Values

The manner in which the individual is held accountable to the organization influences behavior. In bureaucratic organizations, rewards and sanctions are applied in terms that are not always consonant with the avowed goals of the organization. For example, in universities much is said about the virtues of excellent teaching, but promotions are based for the most part on research and publication. Similarly, if the organization mouths pious platitudes about the virtue of working in teams but bases its actual reward structure on individual achievement with a disciplinary context, teamwork may be much less valued.

Support for this contention is found in a study by Geigle-Bentz, who concludes that the "opinions of interdisciplinary health care team members toward the team approach, communication, democracy, leadership roles are not consistent with those suggested in the health care literature" (Geigle-Bentz, 1975, p. 118). In other words, in a study of what team members actually thought about the team approach, it was found that their opinions varied markedly from those normally found in what people write about teams.

The reward structure may be such that teamwork goes relatively unnoticed. If promotions, pay raises, and similar rewards are based on recognition by disciplinary units of the organization, most staffers will make their greatest efforts in these areas. In addition to the extrinsic reward system, there may also exist an intrinsic system that ties in with departmental disciplinary organization rather than with the team structure. Such systems often are reinforced by their congruence with the values and norms of the various professions.

Memberships and Roles

The organization defines who will be a member of a team and what role that individual will play on the team. Definitions may be informal or very highly structured, with written descriptions of the job and the necessary qualifications for membership. Since these descriptions are generally written in terms of the formal or operative goals of the organization, they may not accurately reflect the roles actually played by the various team members as a whole.

It is readily seen that individual and/or team orientations to professional roles may be in conflict with bureaucratically prescribed functions. Such conflict may lead to attendant problems in defining team functions and subsequent loss of team and organizational effectiveness. If, indeed, one of the characteristics of a profession is autonomous action and self-regulation, this is at odds with bureaucratic organizational structure.

Spatial Relationships

Physical location is an important aspect of how the organization influences team functioning. If, for example, a team is housed in one office with adjoining desks, it is more likely that informal interaction will take place than if team members are housed in separate offices in different wings of the building. Similarly, the spatial arrangements for conferences and other meetings can have great bearing on how the team members interact. This problem may be exacerbated when some members of the team are physically separated from the remainder of the group, those who are itinerant and serve several schools or agencies, for example. In such instances there may be great difficulty in assuring adequate communication between and among team members.

INTERORGANIZATIONAL RELATIONSHIPS

In addition to the influence of intraorganizational characteristics on the teams, forces generated by interorganizational relationships also have impact on team functioning.

The relationships between organizations have been examined by Levine and White (1972). Although interorganizational relationships have continued to grow in complexity since their study was conducted, many of their findings and interpretations seem relevant to other settings and other times. They investigated the interaction of 22 health organizations in a medium-sized New England community. Included in the 22 agencies were 5 hospitals, 3 governmental organizations (health, welfare, and schools), and 14 voluntary agencies. Since no agency has unlimited resources, health organizations usually limit their functions to those they can handle expertly. This being the case, most agencies find it is necessary to exchange resources or elements with other organizations. "The need for a sufficient number of clients, for example, is often more efficiently met through exchange with other organizations than through independent case finding procedures" (Levine and White, 1972, p. 587).

The researchers identify three main types of elements exchanged between health agencies: *referral* of clients; *services* of professionals, volunteers, and other personnel; and *other resources* including equipment, funds, and information. Thus patients may be sent from one agency to another for additional services; a professional from the second agency may provide these services and the first agency will pay the second for these services. It was found that interorganizational exchange was determined by the functions of the interacting organizations as well as by prestige, leadership, and other factors.

Exchange, however, is only one factor in interorganizational relationships. Competition for scarce resources, whether from public or private sources, often affects the way in which institutions interrelate. Such competitive situations often discourage teamwork when members of the team are from different organizations. For example, one institution's need for patients to fill beds may reduce the chances that a client will be transferred to another institution where more adequate care might be given.

Organizational Problems

Throughout this chapter, we have examined the impact of bureaucratic organization on the team. It is apparent the adaptation of the bureaucratic model has not been as successful in the human service sector as it was in the early stages of industrialization in the business sector. The worker-organization relationship does not seem to be the same in industry and in human service institutions. In fact, continued attempts to impose more bureaucratic structures on human service organizations often lead to frustration and dysfunction in terms of client service.

A number of authors, including Drucker (1978) and Weisbord (1976), have pointed to differences between the models of organization in industry and in the human service field. One obvious source of conflict comes from the interaction of the professional and the organization. Taken at its simplest level, the professional is by definition autonomous, while organizations have as their main function the "direction and control of human behavior." Organizations are largely predicated on the idea that rational division of tasks is an appropriate way to maximize the delivery of services. In practice, the professional in the human service organization may function as a caregiver one moment, as a teacher or student the next moment, and as a researcher during the next. The tasks are complex and at times defy rational division. Indeed the development of the team approach may have been in large part due to an inappropriate application of the principle of division of tasks. Fragmentation of care has often resulted, to the detriment of the child.

One development in special education which may help to alleviate some of the fragmentation in educational and other services to children with special needs is the development of the role of the case manager. Such a role requires a number of skills. The role has been defined in several ways; however, it is clear that central to the responsibilities of such a position is the advocacy and care of specific individuals. The development of such a role follows from a concern that the individual child should not become lost in the system. In most instances the development of the role of the case manager should require not new personnel but rather the reorientation of the roles of individuals within the organization.

Let us review some of the other problems engendered by organizations in the development and utilization of interdisciplinary teams in agencies that deal with children and youth with special needs.

Lack of Understanding of the Team Process

The bureaucratic model, as we have seen, is based upon a hierarchical authority structure, whereas the team is based upon the attempt to bring appropriate knowledge and skills to bear upon a particular problem. In a team process, each profession represented in an agency, whether it be a school, hospital, residential facility, or some other organization, should have an appropriate role that is least restricted by a preexisting organizational structure.

An Organizational Structure Which Does Not Make Adequate Provision for the Team To Function

If an organization is committed to the utilization of the team concept, then it must adapt its processes, rules, procedures, and resource disposition to the needs of the team. Such adaptations should include the provision of adequate time, space, and personnel. The imposition of a team system upon an organization that is working at or near capacity will only lead to frustration and failure. The question that must be asked is what organizational changes must be made in order to integrate and take full advantage of the use of the team?

Lack of Organizational Involvement in Educating Persons for Teamwork

One of the ways in which the services to children by the team may be improved is through better education of the team members in what is expected of them within the organization. This is not say that the team members do not know their individual professions but rather to say that they need more help in coordinating their efforts on behalf of the client.

Looking again at the school as an example, we can see the importance of instituting a process which involves all in team-building activities. The individual teacher is still very much responsible for what happens in the classroom. Unless the individual teacher is involved and supportive of the educational plan for a student, there is little hope that the plan will be implemented in regard to that student or that the portions of the plan to be done by others will receive the full support of the teacher. It must be recognized that the teacher is often the central person in managing as well as implementing the educational plan for the student. Full realization of the potentialities of the team process for children with special needs must involve the teacher since the teacher is often the person most directly in touch with the student on a day-to-day basis and can materially affect the way in which the plans of the team are implemented.

It is apparent that schools, residential facilities, hospitals, and other human service organizations must change in relation to the new ways in which services are being delivered. The team approach, with its reliance upon the skills of many professionals, each dealing with a particular aspect of the child's problem but sharing and integrating information and care with others on the team, presents a unique opportunity to help the child. It is easy to see that the team system is difficult to implement especially in more traditional settings.

"Matrix organization" attempts to deal with the conflict between bureaucratic organizations and the team approach by setting up a dual organizational pattern or matrix. Each individual has a position in the matrix that permits communication on both a horizontal and vertical basis. N. Tichy (1977) provides an excellent case study of the development of a matrix organization in a primary care setting, the Dr. Martin Luther King Jr. Health Center, and points to the opportunities and difficulties of operating in a setting that contains a dual reporting and authority system. For such a system to work, all levels of the organization must be prepared to deal openly and creatively with conflict or with emphasis of one axis of the matrix over another.

It would seem that Drucker is right: we do not know enough about the human service institution. Neither do we know enough about teams and how they function within various types of organizations.

Chapter 5

Teamwork

If we look at how members of the interdisciplinary team spend their time and energy, we find a remarkable diversity of activities. The team approach does not mean that the team members must abandon those activities that define their professional identity. Although there may well be some shifts in the boundaries of professional roles and responsibilities, team members continue to perform many or most of their typical tasks; i.e., teachers continue to teach and psychologists continue to provide psychological services. What is noteworthy about the team concept is the coordination among members of the team, in contrast to the semi-independent stance of more traditional professional roles. Of course, even in nonteam professional interaction, there is necessarily *some* coordination of activities; what is unique about team functioning is the *degree* of such coordination. Team members will still spend considerable time in those activities regarded as their own "territory," but a significant proportion of their time will be used in coordination activities—sharing information about the child's progress and coordinating educational and treatment plans. This kind of coordination is crucial to effective team functioning.

In previous chapters we have examined in some detail the major components of an interdisciplinary team: the professionals who make up the team, the child to be served, and the school or organization milieu in which the team operates. Each component brings together a number of variables that may affect the team's behavior directly or indirectly. We are now ready to examine the processes that emerge from the interaction of these components. We will be looking at the next two elements of the Team System Diagram (see Figure 1–1, Chapter 1): team goals and activities. We will address such questions as What is teamwork? How do teams interact? What do team members *do?* and How do team members serve the exceptional child?

TEAM GOALS

One of the first tasks facing a newly established interdisciplinary team is to determine the purpose of the team and the goals that it is to address. Whether the team is operating in a school, a residential setting, a hospital, or a clinic, professionals have been brought together to provide certain services to a group of exceptional children and their families and must identify what those services are to be and how they are to be delivered.

Team goals may be regarded as the aims that give direction to the team's actions. Generally, goals are agreed on either formally or informally by the majority of team members. Team goals are usually stated in terms of what the team members wish of the team. For example, an interdisciplinary team in a developmental disabilities clinic may state that their primary goal is to provide effective diagnostic and treatment services to developmentally disabled children. General statements of this sort are often supplemented by a number of more specific objectives related to the diagnosis and treatment of children, work with families, and educational planning.

Teams vary greatly in the extent to which their goals are clearly spelled out and in the number of goals identified. Sometimes team goals are too general and ambiguous to give a clear indication of where the team is heading or what its tasks are. Goals should be stated specifically enough to give direction to the team's activities.

When a new team is formed, its principal goals may be spelled out either by the team members or by some external agent that initiates its formation, such as a principal or clinical director. In either case, considerable effort must be spent in identifying and clarifying these aims, since, if the team is to operate as a functioning unit, there must be some sense of shared goals. This does not mean that all members of the team will necessarily "buy into" all of the team goals or that some participants may not have other goals that have not been agreed upon or even discussed by the group. Such "hidden agenda," although often unarticulated, may be a powerful force serving either to facilitate or disrupt team functioning. Furthermore, a sense of congruence between personal goals and team goals may be an important determinant in the team member's enthusiasm and level of participation. A team whose members are unable to articulate and agree upon some minimum number of shared goals is not likely to function effectively for any length of time.

This may be illustrated by a case in which a principal initiates a team approach in the school with the stated purpose of providing better coordination of services by the regular classroom teacher, the special education teacher, the school psychologist, and the speech therapist. While all the participants may be able to agree readily that "better coordination of services" is an appropriate goal, this statement is too ambiguous to be meaningful. When the team members begin to discuss what "better coordination" means to each of them, they may find that they have quite different perceptions of the overall goal of the team. Fur-, thermore, they may have some personal goals that they may be reluctant to discuss openly. For example, the regular classroom teacher may be quite resistant to the team approach, seeing it as an encroachment on a teacher's autonomy in the classroom and fearing that children from special education may be placed in a mainstream classroom situation for which they are not yet ready. Thus this teacher's major goal may be to have as little involvement as possible in the team. At the same time, the special education teacher may also be reluctant to share responsibility with the team and may harbor some secret reservations about the regular classroom teacher's ability to provide appropriate instruction to the exceptional children who will be assigned to the regular classroom. The school psychologist's major goal may be to use the team as an opportunity to influence classroom management. The speech therapist may wish to receive more referrals from the special education teacher and may view the other team members as possible allies in this effort.

These goals of the professionals involved on the new team have little in common and may lead to serious disagreements among the team members. It is important that some common ground of agreement be identified early in the group's discussions, or the team approach may never be fully implemented. On the other hand, if the team members are able to discuss their feelings openly, they may be able to agree on some tentative goals. For example, seeing that each of the other three team members can serve as a consultant to the classroom teacher as children are mainstreamed, they might identify a goal of assisting the regular classroom teacher with specific problems arising as new children are moved from special education settings into the regular classroom. Such a mutually agreed on goal can serve as an initial focus for the team's efforts. As the team works together, other goals may be identified and articulated by the group.

Determinants of Team Goals

When we think of team goals, we tend to think in terms of the team's overall purpose of providing quality services to exceptional children and their families. Certainly these goals are a major portion of the team goals. However, as shown in the Team System Diagram (Figure 1–1) the three elements we have discussed—the child, the professionals, and the organizational milieu—all feed into goals that determine team activities.

Goals of the Child and the Family. Part of the task of the team is to help identify realistic and appropriate goals for the children it serves and for their families. The child's family is often involved in goal setting with the team. Child guidance clinics usually ask parents to help set treatment goals, and IEP teams are required to involve parents in determining educational goals for chil-

dren receiving special education services. However, parents are sometimes reluctant to indicate their goals, fearing the ridicule of the professionals if their
ideas are not feasible.

Professional Goals. Professionals on the team obviously play a crucial role
in determining team goals. Some of these goals may seem to be unrelated to the
welfare of the child. For example, team members may wish to pursue individual
professional goals—to clarify the role of the social worker in the school, to
educate other members of the team in the appropriate use of psychological
services, or to provide more consultation to the regular classroom teacher.
Whether these professional goals become team goals depends on the extent to
which they are understood and accepted by all team members. Unless these
goals are clearly articulated, they may remain part of the unverbalized hidden
agenda of the individual professional.

Organizational Goals. Finally, the organization itself contributes to the goals
of the team. For example, to provide quality educational programs for exceptional children may be a major goal of the school. Again, whether organizational
goals are ever adopted as team goals depends on how well they are communicated to members of the team and accepted by them.

Although the team may not accept all of the goals of the organization, the
professionals, or the family, each component will have some measure of influence. The team may express goals such as adopting a new record-keeping system
which will be used on a school-wide basis or utilizing case conferences as
teaching sessions to improve mainstreaming efforts. Although such goals do not
deal directly with a specific child, they may ultimately improve the quality of
care provided to *all* clients.

Short-Term and Long-Term Goals

Another distinction can be drawn between team goals that are *short-term* (to
be accomplished in a minimum period of time) and *long-range* (goals that may
take months or even years to reach). Whether the team focuses primarily on
short-term or long-term goals depends on the organization in which it functions
and how its role is defined. The primary goals for a crisis intervention team or
a surgical team are usually short-term; the major task of the team is to deal with
an immediate crisis. Long-term goals are also important to these teams, but
immediate priority is given to short-term problems.

In other teams the highest priority is given to long-range problems. For instance, a rehabilitation team working with spinal cord-injured patients or a team
working with mentally retarded children may focus on goals that are months or
even years away. Immediate problems will be handled as they arise, but in such
teams the emphasis is on Where will this child be in one year—or two years—
or even five years? Of course, the team needs to determine intermediate steps
in reaching such long-term goals.

For many teams short-term and long-term goals are equally important, and team members engage in a number of activities related to both. In fact, such a balance of goals can be important in the effective functioning of the team. The team that seldom looks at more long-range goals (either for children or for the team itself) may be avoiding certain issues that present potential conflicts or may have lost a sense of perspective concerning its overall direction. On the other hand, the team that tends to focus only on long-range issues and neglects to develop short-term goals may be avoiding recognition of certain immediate problems.

P. L. 94–142 requires that the IEP indicate both annual (long-term) goals and short-term objectives. Thus, the IEP team must not only identify the educational goals that the child can be expected to attain within the year but also set up some more immediate instructional objectives that can serve as intermediate steps as the child moves toward the annual goals. As Hayes (1977) has observed: "If the annual goal is to be accomplished, the teacher must have some sequence in mind when planning instruction. However, for the purposes of Public Law 94–142, it is not necessary to list each and every step the child will take along the way. Short term objectives are not intended to be lesson plans" (p. 18).

It may be easier for the team to agree on long-range goals than on the more immediate objectives. Team members may generally agree about the direction in which they wish to move with a particular child but have serious differences about how to get there.

Task and Maintenance Goals

Most of the goals we have mentioned have involved some task to be completed by the team. This is because teams are primarily task oriented. This is one of the ways in which interdisciplinary teams are different from other kinds of groups. However, in addition to these *task-related goals,* the team will also have goals related to the smooth functioning of the group, improving communication among team members, and reducing hostility among members of the team. Such goals are often not clearly recognized or discussed by the team, and at times the failure to deal openly with such goals can cause problems in team interaction.

Goals that focus on the group process itself, rather than on team tasks, can be referred to as group-maintenance or *team-maintenance goals.* Maintenance goals focus on factors that might interfere with the harmony and smooth functioning of the team. It is often recognized that the dynamics of the group is an important element in the group's success. However, teams often tend to ignore or overlook maintenance goals because team members feel they are too busy to discuss group processes. Consequently, it may be difficult for the team leader to get the team to address even obvious problems in team interaction. Team members often feel that, since they are all professionals, they do not need to like each other in order to work together. While this may be quite true, serious dissension among team members may bring the real work of the team to a halt and result in a serious crisis. Furthermore the poor morale that stems from disharmony within the team may lead to a frequent turnover in personnel, further disrupting the team's efforts. Thus it may be more effective in the long run to give some attention to team maintenance on a regular basis, rather than waiting until real problems threaten to erupt.

The relationships among these three dimensions of team goals—*determinant* (client, organization, and professional), *type* (task related and team maintenance), and *time* (short-term and long-term)—are illustrated in Figure 5–1. Since the activities of the team follow directly from its goals, the same three dimensions can also be applied to team activities.

Figure 5–1 Team Goals and Activities

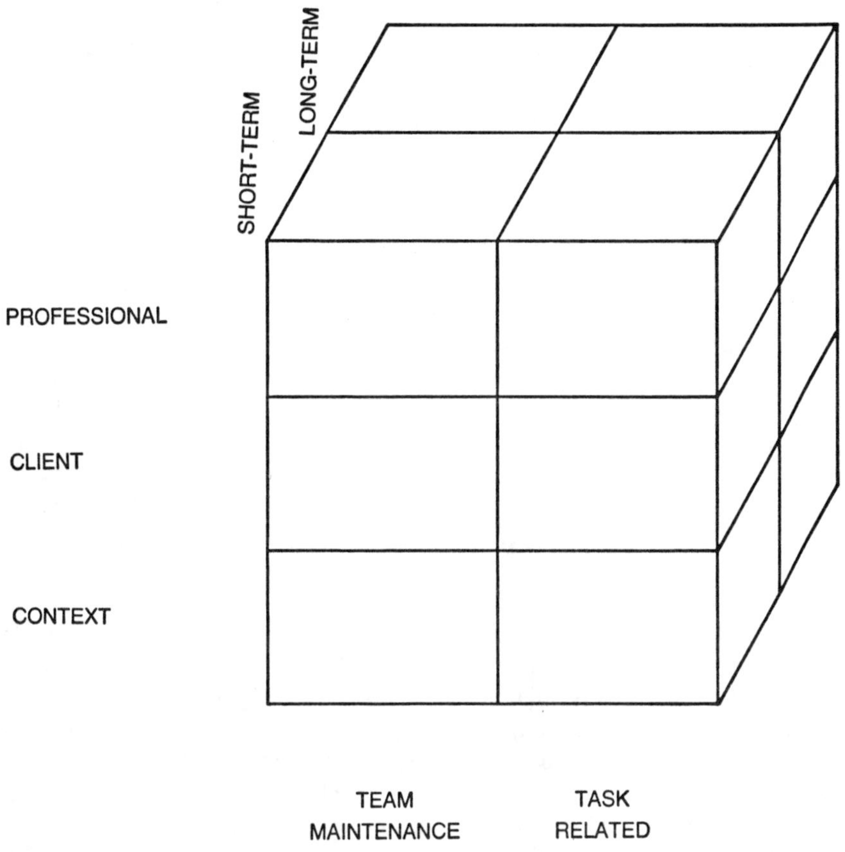

Goal Conflict

While teams are expected to spend some time initially trying to clarify goals, often little attention is given to goals once the team has begun to operate, because of time pressures and the demands of more immediate tasks. However, when difficulties arise in team functioning, they can often be traced to ambiguous or conflicting goals among team members. For example, the social worker in a children's psychiatric outpatient clinic may think that involving the family as participants in the decision-making process is an important team goal. However, if this goal is not shared by other team members, they may resent attempts to involve the family in team meetings.

In Chapter 2 we discussed some of the different theoretical approaches of the varied professionals on the team. For example, the special educator and the speech therapist may view the child's problems quite differently and thus lay out very different goals for the child. Such differences may divide the team into various subgroups or "camps," each advocating a particular set of goals for the child in question.

The importance of clear and explicit team goals was pointed out by Fenton, Yoshida, Maxwell, and Kaufman (1979), who investigated goal consensus among the members of special educational placement teams in the public schools in Connecticut. Questionnaires regarding team goals were returned by 1,428 elementary and secondary school personnel who were members of 230 placement teams. Respondents were asked to indicate which of 11 goals listed (taken from the state regulation regarding responsibilities of placement teams) were seen by them as team responsibilities. Included among the 11 goals were items such as:

- Determine the student's eligibility for special education.

- Determine student placement.

- Formulate appropriate year long educational goals and objectives for the student.

- Communicate with parents about changes in the student's educational program.

- Review the continued appropriateness of the student's educational progress. (Fenton, Yoshida, Maxwell, & Kaufman, 1979, p. 640)

Team members were asked to indicate for each goal whether the team should make suggestions, the team should make decisions, or the team was not responsible for the activity. Team recognition of goals was defined in terms of agreement among three-fourths of the team members regarding a specific goal.

Teams reaching that level of agreement ranged from 11 percent ("determine criteria for review") to 37 percent ("formulate long-term goals"). Greater agreement was reached on responsibility for goal setting, placement decisions, and program appropriateness, with less agreement about responsibility for eligibility, diagnosis, and communication with parents.

The authors summarize their findings:

> From the data obtained in this study, it is clear that (a) not all placement teams have an accurate idea about the scope of their responsibilities, and (b) placement team members recognize duties differently according to their roles; specifically, more administrators and support personnel recognize official placement team duties than do regular education teachers. (p. 641)

The disagreement regarding group goals found among the team members surveyed has important implications for team functioning. As the authors indicate, if team members have some consensus regarding the goals of the team, they may be able to work together toward those goals, even if some of the organizational goals are not recognized. "However, if members disagree among themselves as well as with the state guidelines or Public Law 94–142 regulations, group functioning will be impeded" (Fenton, Yoshida, Maxwell, & Kaufman, 1979, p. 643).

There are many sources of potential goal conflicts in the team approach. Conflicts may emerge between team members, between the team and the organization, or between team members and the child's family. Occasional assessment of the team members' perceptions of team goals may prevent some of these problems. Thus an important aspect of team maintenance is the periodic review of team goals, with an attempt to reach or maintain consensus among team members regarding those goals. In Chapter 8 we will explore more fully the concept of goal conflict and how such conflict may be resolved.

TEAM ACTIVITIES

Team goals reflect what it is the team wishes to accomplish. Team activities are the actions team members take to reach those goals. Thus team activities can be described along the same dimensions referred to in Figure 5–1. Activities can be task related or related to team maintenance, short-term or long-term, and focused on the child or the organization or the professional.

The overriding task of most teams is to attend to the problems presented by the children and their families. Solutions to the children's problems is sought through team rather than individual effort because the team can bring a greater number of resources (skills, knowledge, information) to bear on the task and thus presumably arrive at a better outcome than can one professional acting alone. The price for this improvement in outcome is a loss in efficiency due to the process of the group itself. This decrease in efficiency has been termed "process loss" (Steiner, 1972). For example, five professionals meeting for one hour usually cannot accomplish what one of them working alone could do in five hours. This is because only part of the team's time and effort is spent in actual problem-solving activities; the rest of the time may be devoted to team interaction and maintenance activities. The proportion of time devoted to team maintenance usually decreases the longer the team works together, but there will always be some degree of process loss when a team approach is used.

Most of the activities of the team focus on providing services to children. However, some time is spent dealing with organizational matters and in activities aimed at professional colleagues. Thus the team member may find it necessary to engage in curriculum planning, committee meetings, and similar activities. These meetings may be either task related (for example, making decisions about textbooks or schedules) or maintenance oriented (for example, clarifying roles or leadership within the department).

The task-related activities of a team can be further divided between those carried out by the individual team members and those performed by the team as a whole. Four major tasks related to the services provided by the team can be identified: (1) assessment, (2) decision making, (3) intervention, and (4) evaluation. These are shown in Figure 5–2, where some of the typical team and individual activities are indicated for each type of task. For example, during assessment, individual team members will report and interpret data they have collected about the child. The team will then integrate the information provided in the reports of various team members, identify the child's problem areas, and develop some tentative goals for the child.

As Figure 5–2 indicates, when the *assessment* has been completed, the team will usually meet to make *decisions* about the child, formulating some long-term goals, examining the treatment or educational options that are available, and planning specific intervention programs for the child in question. Responsibilities for carrying out these programs is divided among team members, who then implement the planned program and report on the child's progress to the team. The team coordinates and monitors the interventions by the individual team members. Finally, the team will *evaluate* the outcomes and provide feedback to team members regarding the outcomes of the programs. Although it is common for the team to meet in staffings or case conferences to make decisions and monitor the progress of the child, in some cases the decisions may actually be made by the team leader, based on the information supplied in the reports of the team members, and staffings may be used only for exceptional cases.

It should be noted that particular teams will not necessarily engage in all of the activities outlined in Figure 5–2. Some teams focus primarily on evaluation

Figure 5–2 Individual and Team Activities

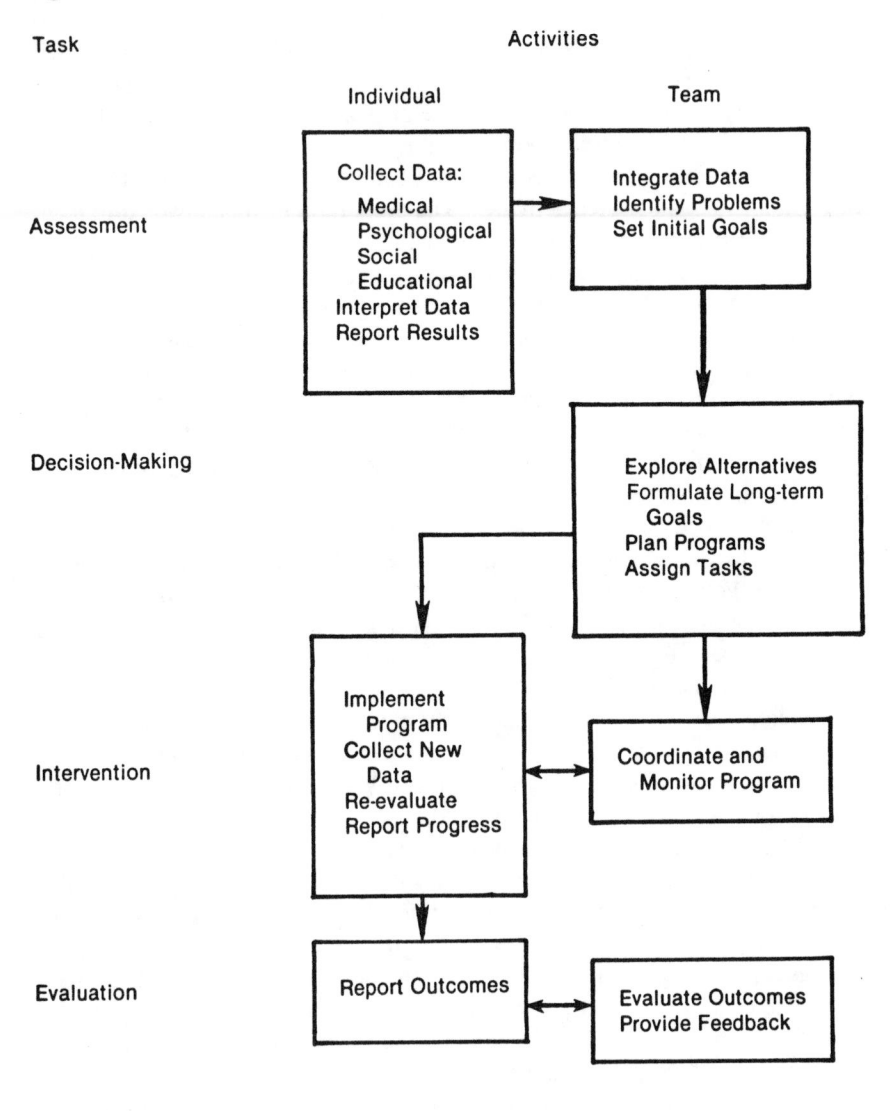

or assessment of the exceptional child, making recommendations for services that are provided by other teams or agencies. Some teams focus on intervention by providing educational and treatment programs to children and their families. We will look at some of these different kinds of teams as we examine each of the four tasks identified in Figure 5–2.

Assessment

One of the major tasks of the team is the evaluation or assessment of the children it serves. Generally, each team member is responsible for gathering, interpreting, and reporting specific information about the child. As a result of this division of labor in assessment, we often speak in terms of "educational data," "family history data," "medical results," and "personality measurement" as though the child could be divided into parts and each part measured separately. We sometimes lose sight of the "whole child" and forget that categories such as physical, mental, social, and educational have been created for our own convenience. Such categories are not inherent in the child, who functions as a whole being. It is part of the function of the team to reintegrate and reinterpret the *whole* of the educational, psychological, medical, and social assessment data gathered by the professionals.

Usually individual team members collect and interpret the information their profession regards as within its particular province. The information is shared with the team through a written report, a verbal presentation, or both. Sometimes, of course, there is overlap in the information sought, and two or more professionals may ask some of the same questions and collect similar data. This is a potential source of conflict if one professional feels that the information somehow "belongs" to her or his profession and that another professional is encroaching on that territory.

Assessment of exceptional children presents certain unique problems to the professionals who are involved in the process. Salvia and Ysseldyke (1978), in their analysis of assessment in special education, indicate that the major purpose of assessment in educational settings "is to provide children, parents, teachers, school psychologists, and other professionals with information to assist them in making decisions that will enhance students' educational development" (p. 14). They describe how tests may be used in screening, placement, special educational programs, program planning, program evaluation, and monitoring individual progress. Newland (1980) discusses in detail some of the assumptions inherent in psychological and educational assessment and some of the problems with these assumptions in the evaluation of exceptional children. For example, standardized psychological tests make the assumption that "*the subjects* being tested *have been exposed to comparable,* not necessarily identical, *acculturation*" (Newland, 1980, p. 76). Yet, as Newland points out, many exceptional children, particularly the severely physically handicapped, may have had very restricted experiences as a result of their physical impairments.

The major focus on nondiscriminatory testing reflected in P. L. 94–142 has emerged from the concerns of professionals about the appropriate assessment of handicapped, minority, and culturally disadvantaged children. Ysseldyke and Regan (1980) have proposed that "nondiscriminatory assessment can best be approximated by using data on intervention effectiveness, rather than data obtained from norm referenced tests, to make most psycho-educational decisions" (p. 465). Restricting the use of norm-referenced tests to classification, they would base decisions about individual children on intervention strategies that have or have not worked with that child in the past.

Sources of Error in Assessment

One of the assumptions underlying assessment described by Newland (1980) is that "*error will be present* in the measurement of human behavior" (p. 76). Information based on observations and measurements of the child by team members can never be perfectly accurate. Some error in measurement must always be assumed to be present.

This can be easily demonstrated with even a relatively simple measure such as body temperature. Ask several persons to take and record the body temperature of the same child and the results are likely to show variation due to error in measurement. Complex psychological and educational measurements are even more subject to error than are physical measurements.

Several sources of measurement error have been described, including observer error, error in the instrument, and error arising from variation in what is being measured (Noll, 1965; Walker & Lev, 1953). Observer error refers to individual differences between observers; that is, two observers will often "see" things quite differently. Observer error also includes variation within the same observer. "A single observer's own readings will commonly be found to vary from one observation to the next, even though the actual conditions are unchanged" (Noll, 1965, p. 9).

Instrument error results from the fact that no device, no matter how well calibrated, is perfectly accurate. There is sometimes variation between instruments and occasionally within the same instrument. Even reliable psychological and educational tests involve some error of measurement. This is particularly true with physically handicapped children, for whom certain items included on the test may be inappropriate and unreliable.

Finally, there is the error attributable to variation in the individual being measured (or in his environment). For example, measurement error is likely to result when a child's oral temperature is taken immediately after he has swallowed hot soup or when an intelligence test is given in a cold and uncomfortable room. In these cases, measurement errors stem from the variability of the subject's response. Often the team member is unaware of conditions that immediately preceded the testing or measuring period—conditions that might have a significant effect on the consistency of the child's responses. Team members who make observations under different conditions may find quite different results with the same child. This can lead to puzzling contradictions in the information reported at the case conference, and the team must either collect additional data or arrive at some explanation that resolves the inconsistencies. Furthermore, exceptional children may be more variable or erratic in their behavior than nonhandicapped children. Factors such as fatigue, emotional instability, pain, or hyperactivity can lead to increased measurement error when observing the behavior of exceptional children, or administering standardized tests to them.

Newland (1980) also calls attention to the important distinction between initial *observation* and the *interpretation* of the information that has been collected. The data collected includes only that which can be observed from the physical attributes of the child or from the child's behavior. Anything that is not directly observable is *inferred* from observable indicators. Such inferences usually involve hypotheses about the current status of the child or predictions about the child's future status. For example, a physician measures the height and weight of all patients coming into his office; those whose weight exceeds the norm for their height are advised to lose weight. In this case, the doctor has inferred that the patients will be "healthier" if their weight is closer to the norm for their height and age. This inference is based on the frequency of health problems associated with overweight in other persons. However, it should be pointed out that this is only a statement of probability and is not necessarily true for a particular client. Similarly, the doctor who finds an abnormally high white blood cell count could infer that there may be an infection but might be unable to predict where the infection is located. However, when this sign is coupled with pain and tenderness in the lower right abdomen, the doctor may well predict an infected appendix. In this case, the doctor is again using a predictive model based on probability statements.

It is equally important with educational, social, and psychological data, to keep in mind the distinction between observation and inference. Many of the concepts used by team members, such as *motivation, intelligence,* and *self-concept,* are unobservable attributes that reflect inferences based upon other, directly observable, behaviors. When we make inferences about the child's motivational level on the basis of observed performance, we are *interpreting* the child's behavior, not merely describing it. Unless this distinction is made, inferences may be reported as observations rather than interpretations, leading to confusion and additional error in the assessment process.

Weitz (1964), for example, has pointed out how selection and abstraction distort the information conveyed and the interpretations made in the interaction of a counselor and a client. His point is relevant to the collection and interpretation of information by other professionals as well. The six steps identified by Weitz are:

1. The client participates in some event.
2. Out of all the elements in the event, the client selects some; these he perceives and responds to.
3. Out of all the responses made by the client in the situation, he selects some; these he reports to the counselor.
4. The counselor listens to the client, and while he is listening, he symbolically projects some of his own similar experiences into the client's description.
5. Out of this total description—including the counselor's projections—the counselor selects some elements; these he perceives and responds to by drawing inferences and formulating structures.
6. Out of all of these inferences and structures, the counselor selects some; these he reports. This report by the counselor, involving high order abstractions in some cases far removed from the original event, is his tentative problem identification or diagnosis. (p. 81)

Thus the final report of the professional may contain a great many higher-order abstractions, "in some cases far removed from the original event" as Weitz indicates. In this way, perception of the child may be biased by the professional's own past experience and training. The teacher could be influenced by previous experiences with other children ("He reminds me so much of Johnny, who was also hyperactive") as well as by a particular professional approach or theoretical viewpoint. Differences in viewpoint *between* professions may be so great that they use very different "jargon" to describe the same event. However, even *within* a profession there may be very different perceptions based on divergent theoretical viewpoints, and this can lead the team member to focus on different events or to interpret them differently.

The extent to which different viewpoints may affect the assessment process is illustrated by Hobbs (1975).

Despite the progress described, diagnostic classification of emotional disturbance and cognate conditions in children remains a thicket of thorny problems. The terminology is strongly influenced by factors unrelated to the characteristics of the child. A particular child, for example, may be regarded as mentally ill by a psychiatrist, as emotionally disturbed by a psychologist, and as behavior disordered by a special educator. (p. 57)

It is the task of the team to integrate the different viewpoints presented in the individual reports of the professionals on the team. On the basis of all the information presented in the case conference or in the written reports of the team members, the team begins to identify the problems of the child and the family that need to be addressed. At this point the team may set some tentative initial goals that help to give some direction to the activities of the team in working with the child. One of the advantages of the team approach is that it offers an opportunity to identify and correct some of the misperceptions of individual team members. By pooling information, the team can minimize individual biases and errors in observation.

Ideally, the team assessment consists of collecting objective information with a minimum of inference, interpreting the data, and forming hypotheses regarding the child. As we have seen, however, the process is usually not so simple, and there will always be some degree of error in data collection and assessment procedures. It is important that the professional not make premature inferences and conclusions during the period of information gathering. When the team member feels sufficient data have been collected, the information is summarized, organized in a coherent way, and finally, interpreted.

It should be noted that data collection does not then cease—it continues so long as the child is being served by the team. The information gathering and assessment process is an iterative one, with new information giving new meaning to what has been previously learned. For example, a child presents certain problems, several hypotheses are suggested, and a tentative assessment is made. Various additional tests are then given, and this new information may either confirm or contradict the initial assessment. In the latter case, new hypotheses will suggest themselves and more tests may be given to confirm the new evaluation. The process of assessment is a continuing team activity.

The Team Approach in Assessment of Exceptional Children

One method of achieving nondiscriminatory assessment as mandated by P. L. 94–142 is the use of multidisciplinary teams in the assessment process. As Bailey and Harbin (1980) point out, there have been many attempts to reduce bias in evaluation through developing new testing procedures, establishing special group norms, and moving from norm-referenced to criterion-referenced tests. However, these efforts are not sufficient to eliminate bias, and other conditions must also be met. For example, the discrepancies between the skills needed in the classroom and the child's present skills must be evaluated so that the child can be placed in the appropriate setting. Furthermore, Bailey and Harbin (1980) recommend the use of an ecological perspective in evaluation in order to take into account settings such as the home, school, peer groups, and the community. They suggest that the evaluation process must be conducted by an interdisciplinary team of professionals who (a) can select and use data gathering techniques in a nondiscriminatory fashion, (b) can truly work together as a team in making educational decisions, and (c) understand how bias can enter into the decision-making process and thus make systematic attempts to identify and control sources of bias. (p. 595)

Flathouse (1979) has drawn attention to the need for multidisciplinary assessment of the multiply handicapped deaf individual.

No single discipline can provide the diverse experience and expertise necessary for the effective assessment of multiply handicapped deaf children. . . . Thus it should include information from a multitude of disciplines, representative examples of behavior in numerous situations and both subjective and objective data from parents, educators, psychologists, specialists from such disciplines as medicine, audiology, and speech pathology, and other providers of direct child care services for handicapped children. (p. 563)

In a study designed to examine the need for a multidisciplinary team approach in the identification and evaluation of learning disabled students, Alley, Deshler, and Mellard (1979) surveyed 420 professionals and 30 parents to determine their subjective judgments about identifying characteristics of learning disabled populations. They conclude:

The complexity of the condition of LD demands a multidisciplinary perspective for the purpose of identifying disabilities. While the LD teacher can contribute important information to identification decisions, our study suggests that other professionals can also make significant contributions to the identification process. (p. 103)

To implement the requirements of P. L. 94–142, the Bureau of Education for the Handicapped (BEH) of the Office of Education drew up and published regulations that provide a framework for carrying out various provisions of the law. According to the regulations pertaining to evaluation of students who may be in need of special educational programs, a team must be involved in the assessment process. The regulations state: "The evaluation is made by a multidisciplinary team or group of persons, including at least one teacher or other specialist with knowledge in the area of suspected disability." And further: "The child is assessed in all areas related to the suspected disability, including, where appropriate, health, vision, hearing, social and emotional status, general intelligence, academic performance, communicative status, and motor abilities.'' In addition to evaluation, placement procedures must also involve a group of persons, ''including persons knowledgeable about the child, the meaning of the evaluation data, and the placement options.'' In a BEH publication outlining criteria for evaluation procedures, Jones (1978) explains:

> Explicit in both evaluation and placement procedures, then, is the requirement that a team of individuals will be involved in deliberations about the child and his/her educational placement. While there will be variation in team composition as a function of the issues at hand, the team is expected to be multidisciplinary, to include regular and/or special education teachers, and to include specialists knowledgeable about the student's actual or perceived problem(s). Parents, parent surrogates, or advocates must be included as well. By whatever name (e.g., planning team, planning and placement teams, assessment team, placement committee, evaluation and placement committee, educational assessment service, school appraisal team, etc.) a multidisciplinary team is central to what is to be done, how it is to be done, and how the information gathered is to be used. (Jones, 1978, pp. 46, 48)

Jones presents criteria for evaluating the effectiveness of the planning and placement teams and indicates the desirability of considering the potential contribution of the following specialists in the assessment process: school administrator, school psychologist, special education administrator, physician, parents, school social workers, student teachers, educational diagnostician, speech pathologist, physical therapist, occupational therapist, audiologist, school nurse, counselor, curriculum specialist, methods and materials specialist, ophthamologist/optometrist, vocational rehabilitation counselor, and others. Input from such a broad spectrum of professionals would indeed ensure a comprehensive base of assessment information.

Within the same volume, Mercer (1978) points out that P. L. 94–142 requires that the sources of information used in making placement decisions include ''aptitude and achievement tests, teacher recommendations, physical condition, social or cultural background, and adaptive behavior'' (p. 93). In order to meet this mandate for multidimensional assessment, Mercer suggests that evaluators must make use of three different models: the medical model, the social adaptivity model, and the general intelligence model. ''Each of these assessment models answers a different set of questions about the child, is based on its own definition of normal/abnormal, its own set of assumptions, and its own set of values'' (p. 93). She points out that when all three models are used in assessment, the evaluation team must involve a number of disciplines. According to Mercer, an ''optimal configuration would include: an educational psychologist or school psychologist; special education personnel, resource teacher, or educational diagnostician; school nurse; school social worker, counselor, or visiting teacher; classroom teacher; other specialists (in audiometry, speech or vision, or a physician when needed); parents or advocate; and whenever feasible, the child.''

While P. L. 94–142 has been important in emphasizing the usefulness of an interdisciplinary team approach to assessment of children in need of special educational programs, there have been other pressures for multiple sources of assessment information. Insurance companies and other ''third party payers'' often require evaluation by an interdisciplinary team. The Joint Commission on Accreditation of Hospitals includes in the *Standards for Facilities for the Retarded* (1971) the statement that ''interdisciplinary teams for evaluating the resident's needs, planning an individualized rehabilitation program to meet identified needs, and periodically reviewing the resident's response to his program and revising the program accordingly, *shall* be constituted'' (p. 42).

Thus, a number of factors, including the complexity of the problems presented by the exceptional child, the need to guard against discriminatory testing, the desire to integrate information collected from a number of different sources, and the requirements of external mandates, lead to the use of interdisciplinary teams in the assessment of exceptional children.

Decision Making

When sufficient information has been collected, the team will begin to make decisions about the child. In some cases, decisions represent a consensus of the total membership of the team; in other cases, decision making is regarded as primarily the responsibility of one member of the team. Nevertheless, it is a *team* task, even if the team leader or some other member regularly makes the final decision.

Elements of Decision Making

There are two key concepts involved in the decision process: *choice* and *alternatives*. The option to choose among two or more alternatives is crucial to decision making. If either element is absent—that is, if the individual is not in a position to choose or if only one course of action is available—then there is no decision to be made. Teams often complain that although a considerable portion of the team meeting is devoted to an exploration of various alternatives, the team really does not have the authority to choose among them. The decision has already been made or will be made by someone else.

In any decision situation there must be an identification of the nature and range of options available. In many situations the decision maker must limit the range of alternatives to be examined in coming to a decision. This in itself constitutes a prior choice, since some very attractive or viable alternatives may be eliminated early in the decision-making process. The importance of this initial narrowing of choices is often not recognized, even though it may in fact represent the *most* important decision. Sometimes one may not be aware that such narrowing has occurred. For example, the acceptance of one theoretical framework is an effective way of limiting alternatives, but this may occur quite naturally, without extensive deliberation.

This idea is illustrated by the concept of the decision tree. A decision tree attempts to map the consequences of a decision. This is illustrated in Figure 5–3, which represents some of the decisions involved when a child experiences difficulties in the regular classroom situation. The classroom teacher, representatives of the local education agency (LEA), and members of the evaluation team may all participate in the decision-making process. Although this example is greatly simplified, it shows how, as one moves through the tree and reaches certain decisions, other possibilities are deleted, thereby truncating the tree. Theoretically, a decision tree might be constructed that would illustrate *all* of the possible decision consequences from an initial decision point. It has been pointed out, however, that the decision tree for evaluating a single opening chess move would consist of 10^{120} branches (Steen, 1975). It is clear that the professional's role is to prune the tree to the point where it is manageable, by eliminating as many of the unfruitful branches as possible, so that attention can be given to the most promising alternatives.

Another element of decision making that should be noted is that the impact of decisions and subsequent actions is sequential. Prior decisions alter the status of the person and thus alter the information upon which subsequent decisions are based. It is important to recognize this when dealing with a client over a long period of time or when evaluating previous decisions made by other professionals. Decision trees illustrate that decisions may lead down irreversible paths, thus making a seemingly unimportant decision crucial to the eventual outcome.

There are many factors that may affect the decision process. Ideally, a decision maker functions rationally, that is, on the basis of an evaluation of the data, using that data to reduce the chance of error. Unfortunately, humans do not always act rationally. Furthermore, the professional who is able to make relatively rational choices in one situation may become quite irrational in another area. Thus the decision maker may be influenced by irrelevant variables that are not really related to the decision at hand.

Despite the interest in decision processes, we still know very little about how people actually make decisions. This is partly because much of the empirical data about decisions comes from laboratory situations, where the risks are quite different from those inherent in *real* decision making. One fact is quite clear however: individuals react very differently to a decision task. We are all familiar with the decision maker who must have "more data" before a decision can be made, even when the available data seem abundant to the point of redundancy. There is also the individual who puts off a decision until events take over and

Figure 5-3 Example of a Decision Tree

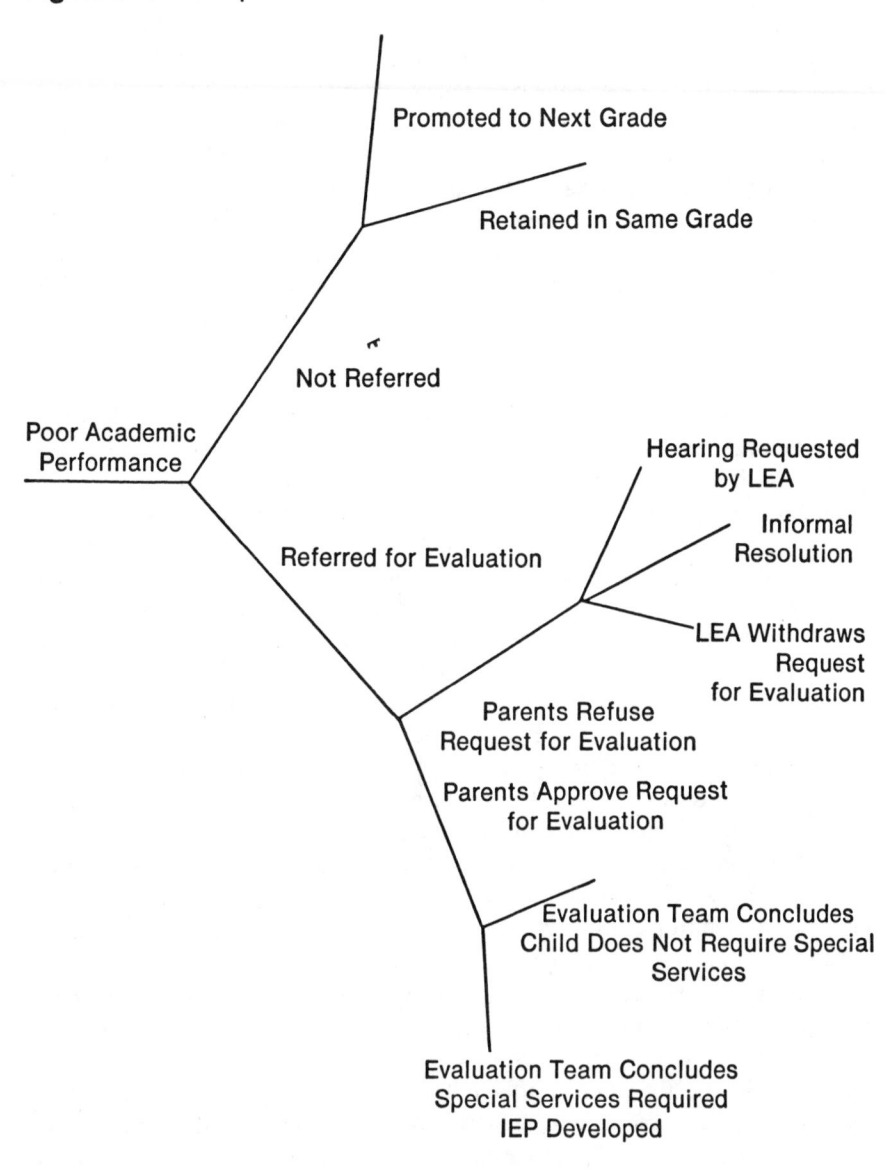

a decision is no longer possible. These reactions often occur because of an aversion to risk. Since most real decisions of any importance present an element of risk *for the decision maker,* delaying and avoiding a decision may be seen as an attempt to escape from risk. Collecting additional data may help reduce risk up to a point, but, when it becomes a ritualistic response to any decision, it is no more than a rather thinly disguised avoidance mechanism.

This behavior is often reflected in the case conference. For example, a social worker may indicate, "We don't have enough information right now to take any action. We should wait until I have spoken to the family." Or the teacher may indicate, "We should wait until next week when the psychologist will be here. Let's see what information he has before acting." While it is important to have sufficient information before making a final decision, to use this as a consistent way of avoiding *any* decisions is dysfunctional. This reluctance to make decisions may be seen by other team members as resistance or opposition to the team's decisions. Of course, if several team members take such a position, decision making may virtually cease.

Decision Error

Earlier in this chapter we discussed the concept of error in measurement. Let us now examine how error occurs in decision making and how to keep error at a minimum. Scheff (1963) has offered an interesting analysis of the role of error in medical diagnosis using the statistical concept of hypothesis testing. Two types of errors in statistical decision making have been identified, *Type 1 errors and Type 2 errors.* Simply stated, Type 1 errors are those in which a true hypothesis is rejected, while Type 2 errors are those in which a hypothesis that is really false is accepted as true.

This concept is well known to everyone familiar with the instruction to the jury that to be convicted of a crime, an individual must be found guilty "beyond a reasonable doubt." That is, it is more important to avoid convicting an innocent person (rejecting a true hypothesis of innocence) than to set free a guilty one (accepting a false hypothesis of innocence).

Scheff sees an analogous situation in medical decision making. It is often assumed that disease is progressive and to avoid or delay treatment will be harmful to the patient. Thus a Type 1 error (rejecting a hypothesis of illness when the patient is indeed sick) is to be avoided whenever possible. The consequences of Type 2 errors (accepting the hypothesis of illness when the patient is actually well) are seen as far less serious. The patient may be inconvenienced, may have unnecessary financial expenses, and in some cases may even suffer unnecessary pain and discomfort from diagnostic or operative procedures, but, nevertheless, conservative decision making is generally regarded as "good medicine." It is only when the frequency of Type 2 errors becomes unduly large (as when numerous complaints are filed about unnecessary surgery) that the values underlying such medical decisions are called into question. The alternative outcomes in medical decision making are identified by Scheff:

> A physician who dismisses a patient who subsequently dies of a disease that should have been detected [Type 1 error] is not only subject to legal action for negligence and possible loss of license for incompetence, but also to moral condemnation. . . . Nothing remotely resembling this amount of moral and legal suasion is brought to bear for committing a Type 2 error. Indeed this error is sometimes seen as sound clinical practice, indicating a healthy conservative approach to medicine. (Scheff, 1963, p. 99)

There are, of course, situations in which the medical expert will be particularly careful to guard against a Type 2 error. Where the medical treatment itself is extremely dangerous (as with some types of surgery), it is as important to avoid unnecessary treatment as to provide needed treatment. Treatment for rabies provides a good example of the dilemma of medical decision making. Suppose it is not certain whether the patient has actually been infected. Failure to treat when the patient has been infected (Type 1 error) means almost certain death. Yet rabies treatment itself carries a certain degree of risk as well as pain, so a Type 2 error may also be harmful to the patient.

There are several points to note. First, data used in medical decision making is not always clearcut, and in many instances decisions are made on the basis of mere probabilities. Second, it is important to weigh the relative impact of various errors in each situation, since the risks vary from one situation to the next. Third, we have focused on the impact of error on the *client,* but it should be noted that error poses risks to the *decision makers* as well. For example, in misdiagnosing an illness, the decision maker has made an error that could ruin his or her professional reputation and result in a suit for malpractice. On the other hand, an error that finds a person ill and a candidate for additional tests or consultations is not as risky since the decision is equivocal. The costs will probably not be catastrophic for any one patient and will not entail high risk to the decision maker. Thus, in high risk medical situations, physicians tend to seek a conservative alternative in order to minimize the risks to themselves and to the patient. While this may sound like optimum practice, there is some question as to its social utility in terms of the increased cost of treatment and cost to individuals in terms of increased pain and unnecessary reduction of the quality of life for periods of time.

Traditionally, such conservative decision making was also prevalent in psychiatric diagnosis and treatment, since it was thought that to allow a potential psychiatric patient to be untreated might well be dangerous to the patient or the community. More recently, court decisions and legislative actions have dramatically changed the atmosphere by applying legal rather than medical rules of decision making to the psychiatric patient. By recognizing that depriving a patient of his freedom through psychiatric commitment proceedings is in some ways analogous to putting the patient in jail, the risks of a Type 2 error become clearer. Scheff (1963) argued: "One might argue that the Type 2 error in psychiatry, of judging a well person sick, is at least as much to be avoided as the Type 1 error, of judging the sick person well. Yet the psychiatrist's moral orientation, since he is first and foremost a physician, is guided by the medical, rather than the legal, decision rule" (p. 101). Nevertheless, there have been significant changes in psychiatric diagnosis and treatment since Scheff's article appeared. The changes that have taken place with regard to the placement of exceptional children within the school system reflect a similar issue. Once the negative results of labeling and classification of exceptional children became clear (and the dangers of a Type 2 error were recognized), there was much greater resistance to the identification and placement of exceptional children. The due process regulations included in P. L. 94–142 are part of this change in attitude regarding the risks to children of labeling and segregation.

"Groupthink" versus Effective Decision Making

Another approach to the decision-making process has been suggested by Janis and Mann (1977). Following a review of the literature in effective decision making, they have identified seven criteria for evaluating the procedures used in selecting a course of action.

> The decision maker, to the best of his ability and within his information-processing capabilities
> 1. thoroughly canvasses a wide range of alternative courses of action;
> 2. surveys the full range of objectives to be fulfilled and the values implicated by the choice;
> 3. carefully weighs whatever he knows about the costs and risks of negative consequences, as well as the positive consequences, that could flow from each alternative;
> 4. intensively searches for new information relevant to further evaluation of the alternatives;
> 5. correctly assimilates and takes account of any new information or expert judgment to which he is exposed, even when the information or judgment does not support the course of action he initially prefers;

6. reexamines the positive and negative consequences of all known alternatives, including those originally regarded as unacceptable, before making a final choice;
7. makes detailed provisions for implementing or executing the chosen course of action, with special attention to contingency plans that might be required if various known risks were to materialize. (p. 11)

Failure to meet these criteria is regarded by Janis and Mann as defective decision making. Thus good decision making involves carefully examining the full range of alternatives, weighing the pluses and minuses of each, and collecting new information for use in evaluating the alternatives. They have examined some of the ways in which individuals and groups fail to engage in good decision-making procedures.

One of the patterns that often leads to poor decision making has been called "groupthink" (Janis, 1972). Groupthink occurs in groups of high cohesiveness, which are insulated from outside influence, under conditions of a directive leadership, high stress, and little hope of finding a better solution. Symptoms of groupthink include the illusion of invulnerability, rationalization, and the suppression of dissent within the group. Groupthink leads to defective decision making and less than optimal solutions to problems. Janis has suggested several ways that the conditions that lead to groupthink can be avoided, such as encouraging the group to air objections and doubts, assigning the role of devil's advocate to one or more group members, and bringing in outsiders to challenge the views of group members and to question group decisions.

These findings seem to have direct applicability to team decision making. It is important that the team leader create an atmosphere in which a wide range of alternative courses of action can be considered, that the possible costs and benefits of each are carefully taken into account and that new information is diligently sought and considered. Furthermore, the team that works closely together with much cohesiveness may need continually to guard against becoming too insulated from the larger organization and against other conditions that may lead to groupthink.

It is not clear at the present time the extent to which decisions reached through team discussion and a sharing of information actually differ in some systematic way from decisions reached by individual professionals acting alone. For example, it is possible that since group norms generally tend to be rather conservative, conformity within the team may serve to stifle originality and creative contributions by team members, resulting in more conservative decisions by teams than by individuals, even when groupthink is not a factor.

In contrast to this view is the interesting paradox of what has been termed the "risky shift" in group decision making. Some research results suggest that in certain situations, decisions reached by groups may in fact reflect a greater willingness to take risks than those reached by individuals.

Risky Shift in Decision Making

The risky-shift phenomenon was first demonstrated by Stoner (1961), who studied male graduate students in industrial management. Each subject was first asked to indicate (independently and privately) the level of risk he would be willing to accept for a series of life dilemma problems. For example, an individual is offered a job with a new company. The job has an uncertain future but offers higher pay and the possibility of a partnership if the company survives. The present job offers lifetime security and a good pension but a modest salary. The subject is required to indicate the lowest probability of the company's succeeding that would make a move worthwhile (e.g., 1 in 10, 5 in 10, etc.). The group then discussed each problem until a decision was made regarding the degree of risk acceptable to the group. Instead of showing a decrease in risk taking, as might be expected from studies in group conformity, the group decisions were *riskier* than the average of the individual decisions.

The original experiment has been replicated frequently in order to verify these findings and attempt to explain them. The risky-shift phenomenon has been demonstrated with a variety of subjects and tasks, and several hypotheses have been suggested to account for it.

Most of the studies in this area have made use of a *choice-dilemma questionnaire* (Kogan & Wallach, 1964) that contained 12 real-life dilemmas similar to the example above. In each case, an individual is faced with a safe alternative with a lower payoff or a riskier choice with the potential of greater gain, and the subject must select the degree of risk that he or she views as acceptable. Other studies have used problem-solving tasks (with subjects choosing the level of difficulty of items they wish to attempt as a measure of risk taking) and gambling situations.

What are the significant factors in the group that cause individuals to shift their decision? This question has stimulated a great deal of research. Most of the studies have involved group discussion until consensus was reached. Although it was earlier thought that establishing consensus might be the critical factor, Wallach and Kogan (1965) demonstrated that the shift could occur with discussion alone but not with consensus alone. On the other hand, "information exchange" without discussion has also led to a risky shift (Blank, 1968; Teger & Pruitt, 1967).

In an extensive review of the literature on the risky-shift phenomenon (Dion, Baron, & Miller, 1970), four major explanations were identified: diffusion of responsibility, persuasion, familiarization, and the cultural value hypothesis. We will briefly examine these explanations, since they have some bearing on how teams reach decisions about their client.

1. Diffusion of Responsibility

Stated in its simplest terms, this hypothesis suggests that a risk-taking situation may induce anxiety or fear of failure in subjects and that the sharing of responsibility with the group reduces these fears and allows for a greater degree of risk. Although some research (Wallach, Kogan, & Bem, 1964) provided support for such an explanation, other studies (Marquis, 1962; Pruitt & Teger, 1969) have raised some questions. In further modification and elaboration of the responsibility-diffusion notion, it has been suggested that the diffusion may be based on affective bonds developed between group members during group discussion. In a study (Dion, Miller, & Magnon, 1970) as reported by Dion, Baron, and Miller (1970), conducted in response to certain methodological problems encountered in previous attempts to examine the affective bond idea, group cohesiveness was experimentally manipulated to produce a group high in cohesiveness. However, the researchers offer an interesting interpretation of the results, in that "as group members become more attracted to one another they also become more loath to minimize *personal* responsibility or displace responsibility for failure onto their fellow group members" (Dion, Baron, & Miller, 1970, p. 320). Such a possibility would have real implications for the operation of a shift toward greater risk in ongoing teams in which cohesiveness had developed. In view of the contradictory evidence around the responsibility-diffusion hypothesis, some researchers have turned to other possible explanations.

2. Persuasion

What Dion, Baron, and Miller (1970) have called the "persuasion" hypothesis holds that high-risk takers are more influential and persuasive in the group, and thus the shift of the group toward greater risk is in reaction to this leadership. In support of this theory, several studies have found a relationship between the initial risk allowed by individuals and the influence on group discussion attributed to them by group members in postsession ratings (Wallach, Kogan, & Burt, 1965). However, it has been pointed out (Kelley & Thibaut, 1969; Shaw, 1976) that the parallel between the shift in the group and the opinion of the high-risk takers may be an artifact of the situation. If the group shifts toward greater risk, it will *appear* as though they are shifting toward the opinion of those who initially held this position. Even when it is demonstrated that the group members *perceive* high-risk takers to be more influential, this may only reflect an assumption on their part that since the group has shifted toward higher risk, the high-risk takers *must* have been influential. There have been attempts to pursue this further by examining personality differences of initially high- and low-risk takers. But, as Dion, Baron, and Miller suggest, there is a need for more direct evidence, based on observation of the group process with independent evaluation of the relative influence of various group members. There also seems to be a need for additional research on the role of persuasion by team leaders and other influential team members on the decision-making process.

3. Familiarization

Most researchers who have dealt with the risky-shift phenomenon have seen it as a group effect and have looked for explanations in terms of, What does the group do to change the risk taking of individuals? However, a few (Bateson, 1966; Flanders & Thistlethwaite, 1967) have sought an explanation in terms of individual rather than group processes. The familiarization hypothesis suggests that what is important in the risk-taking experimental paradigm is the greater familiarity with the problems presented. This presumably leads to a concomitant reduction in uncertainty and an increased willingness to take risks. In the usual risky-shift experiment, group discussion serves to increase familiarity with the pros and cons of each specific alternative, and it is the additional experience or understanding of the item rather than the group process per se that leads to a shift in risk. Although initial studies by Bateson (1966) and by Flanders and Thistlethwaite (1967) demonstrated a shift to greater risk following familiarization alone (without group discussion), later studies have failed to replicate these findings (Ferguson & Vidmar, 1970; Myers, 1967; Pruitt & Teger, 1967). Thus familiarization does not seem to offer a clear and sufficient explanation for the risky-shift phenomenon (Dion, Baron, & Miller, 1970), but it may be an element in team decision making that should be examined further.

4. Cultural Value

As reviewed and summarized by Dion, Baron, and Miller (1970), R. Brown's (1965) theory of risk taking assumes that cultural values encourage risk-taking under some conditions and caution under others and that a risky shift would occur in those situations in which risk is supported by cultural values. Under such conditions the risk value would serve to direct the group discussion so that individuals could gain relevant information about the decision and about the position of other group members. The discussion would not only give the individual additional support for risk taking but also reveal the degree of risk others are willing to take, thereby encouraging the individual to move in a more risky direction. Experimental results seem generally supportive of this explanation, but contradictory findings have also been reported.

In summarizing research on the risky shift, Dion, Baron, and Miller (1970) conclude that, although at the present time the cultural value hypothesis offers the strongest single explanation, "when we reach a complete understanding of group decision-making and risk-taking, it should not surprise us if propositions from several competing theoretical positions turn out to be true" (p. 370). The authors further point out that up to now very little attention has been given to such phenomena in "real" groups. "Real" groups may differ in several ways from those used for experimental purposes, including differences in status and in the consequences of the decision. For example, group members brought together in a research study have not had the previous experience with each other that team members have had, they do not have the status differences that exist in teams, and they are usually dealing with hypothetical problems rather than with decisions that will have real impact on the group or other individuals.

The data concerning the riskiness of group decisions does have implications for group decision making in other contexts, however. It suggests, for example, that while groups may sometimes come to more conservative decisions, this is not *necessarily* the case. More recent research (Myers & Lamm, 1976) has suggested that "risky shift" may have been a misnomer, since the shift may be toward either greater or lesser risk. Thus the term "group polarization" has been used to refer to changes in group responses as a result of group discussion (in jury decisions, ethical decisions, and other choice situations) in addition to risk taking. As Dion, Baron, and Miller (1970) indicate, research on the shift to risk has also shown that the decisions of the group may at times be less rational and less responsible than individual decisions (Bem, Wallach & Kogan, 1965). Such findings are important in examining the effectiveness of group decision making in the human service professions.

Team Decision Making

A study reported by Winter (1976) applied findings from the risky-shift literature to the team approach. Using college students as subjects, Winter found that willingness to provide rehabilitation services to hypothetical clients who could be regarded as "high risk" was greater among groups than among individuals, and that persuasion may have been a factor in the shift to risk. Winter concluded that "a team approach used in making decisions about acceptance or rejection of applicants for rehabilitation services may provide the impetus for more acceptant and liberal views about clients and may thus provide for more extensive delivery of rehabilitation services to individuals with severe conditions" (p. 580).

Wagner (1977) described an earlier study in which he compared service plans made by teams and by individual practitioners. A major conclusion was that "team service plans are more holistic and that team practitioners, when compared with nominal groups of independent practitioners, expressed more of a need to become involved in the totality of the client's life" (Wagner, 1977, p. 213). In addition, he found teams considered "significant others" more frequently, while individual practitioners developed more specific recommendations and more unique service plans. These findings suggest that team decision making may indeed lead to outcomes different from those following decisions made by professionals acting alone.

Some authors express concern about the results of team decision making. While more decision-making responsibilities are being delegated to interdisciplinary teams, in some cases team members may be unclear as to what those responsibilities are. Fenton, Yoshida, Maxwell, and Kaufman (1979), in the study described earlier, found that many members of interdisciplinary placement teams responsible for decisions concerning the delivery of special education services did not recognize the teams' decision-making responsibilities. Rae-Grant and Marcuse (1968) warned that one of the hazards of teamwork is the idea of "shared responsibility": "The myth that the total team is effectively discharging responsibility for a given patient may mask the fact that no one fully accepts responsibility or feels himself to be ultimately accountable for what happens" (p. 4). They also point out that some members may see the anonymity of team decision making as an excuse for less responsible behavior. Weiner and Raths (1959) found that team diagnostic and prognostic decisions are not more accurate as a result of the team meeting. They suggest that some of the team's time may be wasted and that other team activities might be more useful.

Nagi (1975) indicates that two major aspects of team decision making are structure and substance. By *structure* he is referring to the "hierarchical" and "egalitarian" models of decision making in teams and to the constraints imposed on the team by the parent organization. *Substance* refers to "what agreements and disagreements take place among team members in regard to the substance of the decision" (p. 191). Differences in professional background and other characteristics of individual team members can be expected to lead to certain disagreements. Rubin and Beckhard (1972) stress that such differences can make it difficult to reach consensus on the team's decisions, with the result that team members feel less commitment to those decisions. A recognition that all members may be involved in implementing a decision is one of the major arguments for shared decision making.

An important vehicle for team decision making is the case conference, team meeting, or staffing. At this meeting, team members are able to share assessment information, discuss alternative courses of action that are available to the team, and arrive at decisions which often represent the consensus of the group. The opportunity to discuss the pros and cons of various options openly may lead to better solutions. However, in view of the professional time and costs involved, the question arises as to whether the benefits stemming from the team meeting are sufficient to justify such an approach. Nadolsky and Brewer (1977) investigated decisions and recommendations made as a result of staff conferences in a rehabilitation agency. Looking at the consensus expressed by staff following staff conferences, the authors conclude that the conferences did not bring the opinions of staff closer together on ratings of the client's readiness to work, although there did seem to be relatively consistent opinions among staff concerning the type of living accommodations needed by clients. They conclude "that the intrinsic value of the staff conference is questionable since it is a costly procedure and probably provides a minimal contribution to the group decision-making process" (Nadolsky & Brewer, 1977, p. 248).

One complaint frequently heard about team meetings is that decisions are already made before the meeting and the conference is merely used as an opportunity to share the results of prior decision making. Some support for this is found in a study (Goldstein, Strickland, Turnbull, & Curry, 1980) that examined 14 IEP conferences. The authors report that "of the 14 conferences observed, in only one instance was the meeting actually devoted to specifying goals and objectives jointly between the parent and educators" (p. 282). Rather, in most cases, the conference was devoted to the resource teacher reviewing an already developed IEP with the parent. While parents were given an opportunity to contribute new information that might lead to changes in the educational plans, the observed conferences do not seem to have been decision-making groups.

To date, the most extensive investigation of the team approach in special education placement and planning decisions has been a series of studies by Yoshida, Fenton, Maxwell, and Kaufman (1978a, 1978b) of the 230 placement and planning teams in Connecticut schools. Earlier in this chapter we discussed their study of team goals that revealed that many team members apparently do not fully recognize the responsibilities of the placement teams (Fenton et al., 1979). In that study, they found that the responsibilities that were least recognized by team members were "those that were prescriptive in nature: establishing long-term goals for the student, developing short-term instructional objectives, and determining criteria for review of the student's progress" (p. 641). Interestingly, activities recognized by administrators were more likely to be recognized by other team members also, while those which were less frequently recognized by administrators were also less likely to be recognized by other professionals on the team.

A related study (Yoshida et al., 1978a) examined the extent to which placement team (PT) members perceived that they participated in team conferences and their degree of satisfaction with team meetings. Two factors related to participation in team decision making were identified: Factor I, labeled "Specific PT Tasks," was based upon items concerned with contributing and interpreting information, proposing and evaluating alternatives, and finalizing decisions. Factor II, labeled by the authors "Decision-Making Climate," included items about the participants' freedom to disagree with other team members and sense of participation in the decision making about a student.

> The results of this study clearly show that PT members of different professions differ in the magnitude of self-perceived participation during the PT meeting, especially in five activities concerning Specific PT Task participation. . . . Appraisal personnel (school psychologist, school social worker, and school counselor) and administrators generally have higher participation scores than do medical personnel or special and regular education teachers." (p. 242)

School psychologists and special education teachers were most satisfied with team meetings, and regular education teachers were least satisfied. The authors expressed concern that expectations of the team approach leading to better decision making for exceptional children may not be fulfilled, and that the instructional personnel who are ultimately responsible for implementation of the decisions may not be active participants in the decision-making process and therefore may not be fully committed to their implementation.

This question is explored more fully in another report by the same authors (Yoshida et al., 1978b). In this study, oral and written communication with program implementers (special education teachers, regular education teachers, and support personnel) who were absent from the team meetings were examined. Results indicated that while special education teachers received most of their information in both oral and written form, regular education teachers and support personnel more often received information only in an oral form. Furthermore, an average of three members of the team communicated with the absent program implementer. The authors point out that the use of oral communication by several school staff members may lead to considerable distortion and/or inconsistency in the information given to the individual who is to carry out the program that has been decided upon. While it is possible that each member gives the same version of the team decision to the program implementer, it is likely that, particularly where only oral communication is used, each professional may give an individual and quite different interpretation of the decision of the team. The authors suggest that the use of written communication, since written documentation of team decisions is required by P. L. 94–142, might reduce distortion in the transmission of decisions to those responsible for implementation. Another method to ensure accurate communication with program implementers suggested by Yoshida et al. is to assign one team member the responsibility for all such communication. They conclude that "regardless of the methods used, PTs must develop procedures for verifying that the PT decisions and the student's program are transmitted without distortion in order to insure that the decisions arrived at are the ones implemented" (Yoshida et al., 1978b, p. 182).

Intervention

Once decisions regarding placement or treatment of the exceptional child have been made by the team, the plans that have been agreed to must be carried out by members of the team or by other teams or agencies. Many of the efforts of the team are devoted to these intervention activities designed to resolve the problems presented by the child and the family.

The kinds of medical, psychological, social, and/or educational intervention strategies employed by the team depend upon the goals of the team; the kinds of problems presented by the child; the school, agency, or institution in which the team functions; and the theoretical approaches adopted by members of the team. Interventions may be carried out by individual team members or by the team working together, but generally there is a division of labor, with tasks assigned according to professional roles and competencies. Thus, medical personnel are responsible for medical treatment, educational personnel for education programs, etc. However, there are usually a number of areas of overlap, where the responsibilities are open to negotiation or to sharing among team members. Furthermore, there must be coordination of services offered to the child and the family by the individual professionals, and this is a major function of the team approach.

An example of the way in which an interdisciplinary team can be used to provide services to exceptional children is found in the Experimental Education Unit at the University of Washington (Haring, 1977). In a description of the interdisciplinary educational team used at the unit, Blackhard, Hazel, Livingston, Ryan, Soltman, and Stade (1977) indicate that the team includes the classroom teacher, a communication disorders specialist, a family liaison specialist, an occupational therapist, a pediatrician, and an administrator. In addition to assessment activities and developing long- and short-term objectives for the severely/profoundly handicapped children served, the team is also involved in planning programs, providing direct services for the children at the unit, and suggesting intervention strategies. The agreed upon program may be managed by the classroom teacher or by the appropriate specialist. In some cases, the specialist may model the appropriate intervention for the teacher and provide support or inservice training during the program. The team regularly reviews the progress of the child and modifies the program if necessary. Each professional team member involved with the child is responsible for the provision of certain services that he or she is the most qualified to administer. The administrator of the team does not provide direct services but is a catalyst that keeps the educational team functioning.

Thomas and Marshall (1977) have described an ecological model for the clinical evaluation and coordination of services. The model, which is based on the Child Study Center at Oklahoma Children's Memorial Hospital Program, includes four phases: data collection (phase I); pooling data in a multidisciplinary staffing and making initial program recommendations (phase II); initial programming (phase III); and periodic reassessment and program modification (phase IV). Medical, developmental, and family information is gathered and integrated during the staffing, and the delivery of services is coordinated so that the family sees each part of the total habilitation plan for the child. Included in the team of specialists are physicians or pediatricians, audiologists, child development specialists, clinical psychologists, teachers, social workers, and others as needed by the child. The authors emphasize the importance of the agency's flexibility in adapting a child's program to meet specific needs rather than forcing the child to function in a stereotyped program.

Intervention approaches used by an interdisciplinary team working with developmentally delayed or impaired children is described in a book edited by

Allen, Holm, and Schiefelbusch (1978). Baer (1978), in an early chapter in the book, points out that even a team approach does not necessarily lead to integration of treatment procedures, since different team members often operate from different bodies of knowledge and different assumptions. The interventions also differ among disciplines. "Thus, psychologists practiced catharsis while educators appealed to dominant sensory modalities, physical therapists worked on motor skills while physicians prescribed drugs, and nutritionists prescribed diets and calories while speech teachers modeled phonemes and sentence structure. One team member's efforts often seemed incomprehensible to other team members" (p. 58). Baer proposes a behavioral analysis model that can provide the basis of integrated intervention efforts on the team and describes a behavior management program that can be used in educational interventions with children. In other chapters, the roles of the pediatrician, the nurse, the psychologist, the communications specialist, the social worker, the physical and occupational therapist, the nutritionist, and the early childhood education specialist are discussed in terms of their contributions to the interdisciplinary team. The specific competencies of each professional are explored, and the kinds of interventions they may use in working with developmentally disabled children are described. Holm (1978) makes the distinction between child development teams that focus on assessment and evaluation and those that also become involved in management and treatment of the child. She points out that, to avoid chaos on the team, one individual needs to be responsible for each case and that this "case manager" role can be rotated among team members, although it may be best to try to match the competencies of the professional in charge with the particular problems presented by the child.

Holm distinguishes between *multidisciplinary* teams in which members work "side by side" as they carry out their own evaluations, *interdisciplinary* teams which encourage professionals to substitute for each other, and *"transdisciplinary"* teams in which members incorporate knowledge and skills from other disciplines into their own practice. This distinction is also made by McCormick and Goldman (1979), who say the difference between multidisciplinary and interdisciplinary approaches is "that the interdisciplinary model advocates establishing formal communication channels and assigning a case manager in an effort to avoid compartmentalization and fragmentation of services" (p. 153). While the interdisciplinary model implies a commitment to group decision making and coordination of services, they feel that responsibility is often diffused. The transdisciplinary approach differs primarily in terms of program implementation. "There, rather than being apportioned among the disciplines according to their specialty, responsibility for child behavior change becomes the responsibility of one (or possibly two) team member(s). The other team members are available on a continuing basis for consultation and direct assistance" (p. 154). For example, they indicate, a group of children in need of intensive language programming might be served by a teacher and a speech-language pathologist, who implement the program with consultation from other members of the team. Hutchinson (1974) emphasizes the learning opportunities in a transdisciplinary approach, since team members are expected to share their knowledge and skills with others on the team. Interventions are carried out by the team member or members assigned to that task by the team or by the parents, who are trained appropriately. Thus the number of professionals actually providing direct services to the child is reduced, and there is less possibility of fragmentation. As Hart (1977) indicates, the composition of team members in a transdisciplinary team does not differ markedly from that of multidisciplinary or interdisciplinary approaches; however, the implementation and responsibility are apportioned differently, with each member taking on some of the responsibilities of other professionals on the team. Holm (1978) expresses some concern about the possibility that a professional might adopt some of the skills from a number of disciplines and "obliterate the distinction between solo practice and a team approach" (p. 103). She suggests that, while this may be appropriate at times, a single practitioner cannot really replace the interaction of disciplines implied by an "interdisciplinary" team.

Renne and Moore (1977) draw a distinction between multidisciplinary assessment and transdisciplinary approaches to assessment. They view multidisciplinary assessment as a serial process in which team members make individual assessments and reports. "The transdisciplinary process, on the other hand, is one in which representatives of the various disciplines contribute their individual expertise in addressing *a specific set of concerns*" (p. 11). Thus, several professionals might make observations about the child's communication skills. The focus is on synthesis of information, not merely adding it together.

Sirvis (1978) applies the transdisciplinary viewpoint to the development of IEPs for physically handicapped students. She views the IEP as a way in which the various professionals who are involved in the delivery of services to physically handicapped students share information and planning. "The formal IEP meeting should result in delineation of priorities for education programming, persons who will provide the necessary interventions, and how the program will be evaluated for possible reconsideration. The IEP also identifies those related services that are to be provided by other members of the transdisciplinary team" (p. 82).

Many examples of intervention procedures with exceptional children that make use of the team approach for coordination of services can be found in schools, hospitals, and other settings. The requirement of P. L. 94–142 regarding evaluation teams and IEP conferences has accelerated a move toward the team approach that was already in progress in special education and related disciplines. The effectiveness of the interdisciplinary team in reducing the fragmentation of services that has been criticized so frequently is still being demonstrated. However, it appears that often a team can fill a monitoring and coordinating function in the provision of programs for exceptional children, thereby improving the services provided to the child and the family.

Evaluation

The interventions of the interdisciplinary team must be periodically evaluated so that the child's program can be redesigned if the goals and objectives that were originally suggested are not being met. The kinds of evaluations that are conducted are based upon the type of intervention strategies employed, the kinds of data available, and the needs of the organization. Some behavior modification programs may contain an evaluation component as part of the treatment procedure. Other programs may demand a reassessment of the child and the family on a regular basis, with appropriate modifications in the intervention or treatment if adequate progress has not been made.

Evaluation of the outcomes of the team's efforts is an ongoing process that is a part of each of the activities described above. Has enough data been collected? What other information is needed? How can we account for this finding? Which alternative would lead to a better outcome for the child and the family? Is the new program having the expected results? Team members constantly receive feedback and evaluate the effects of their actions on the client. A more formal evaluation of the effectiveness of the team's intervention efforts usually comes at the end of the child's program or during follow-up procedures. The evaluation process will be discussed further in Chapter 8.

Chapter 6
Dynamics of the Interdisciplinary Team

In the last chapter we examined the *work* of the team—the assessment, decision making, intervention, and evaluation activities carried out by the members of an interdisciplinary team. In this chapter we will look at how the team organizes itself and the factors that influence the operation of the team. While there has been little research dealing specifically with the maintenance activities of interdisciplinary teams, there is a considerable body of information regarding the dynamics of small groups that has implications for the functioning of human service teams.

Interest and research in small group dynamics have accelerated rapidly in the last half century (Hare, 1976; Shaw, 1976). Social psychologists and others have conducted extensive research on the variables affecting group interaction and productivity, investigating a variety of groups including work, problem-solving, and decision-making groups. Some of this research has involved observations of existing groups in their natural settings; more often it has involved the creation of short-term experimental groups in laboratory situations. Although many questions regarding the operation of small groups remain unanswered, research with a variety of subjects and types of groups has led to the identification of a number of common factors. Five major characteristics that distinguish a "group" from a "collection of individuals" have been identified. "The members of the group are in interaction with one another. They share a common goal and set of norms, which give direction and limits to their activity. They also develop a set of roles and a network of interpersonal attraction, which serve to differentiate them from other groups" (Hare, 1976, p. 5). In looking at the team and how it functions, we will examine these characteristics and certain related concepts of group dynamics, such as power, status, conformity, coalition formation, and size and composition of the team.

THE TEAM AS A SMALL GROUP

The interdisciplinary teams that provide services to exceptional children and their families consist of small groups of professionals who meet in face-to-face interaction with a common purpose. Such teams vary along a number of dimensions, including size and composition, characteristics of members, physical setting, tasks to be performed, and type of interaction. However, as we look at some of these characteristics that are shared with groups in general, we should also note that interdisciplinary teams have certain unique attributes that differentiate them from other small groups. For example, as we have seen, teams are usually part of a larger institutional setting, such as a school, hospital, clinic, or similar organization, and it is more likely that roles will be assigned on the basis of professional expertise or job title than by group consensus. Furthermore, teams do not usually emerge spontaneously, as other small groups often do. Rather, membership in the team is usually a specific job responsibility. Thus team membership may be imposed from without, and this involuntary aspect of participation is likely to affect the individual's interaction within the team. Also, the rewards for participation may come from outside the team rather than from within it. Raises and promotions may be seen as rewards for being a "good" team member or a frequent participant. On the other hand, outside factors may sometimes interfere with team performance if staffings or team meetings are seen as unrewarded and a "waste of time" so far as professional aspirations are concerned. The effect of outside pressures on the performance of individual team members and on the performance of the team is one of the factors that deserves more study.

Generally, the interdisciplinary team operates within certain other constraints imposed by the work setting and by the task itself. Frequency of meetings, stability of membership, and size of the team may be influenced by organizational or administrative factors. Unlike groups in which the leadership is selected by the group members, teams will often have formal leaders assigned by virtue of their position or professional status, although other informal leaders may emerge from the team itself. Related to this is the issue of autonomy—that is, the extent to which team decisions are put into action rather than being vetoed at another level. Such outcomes have impact not only on the decision-making process but also on the continued involvement and motivation of team members.

Team Norms and Conformity

One of the characteristics of small groups noted by Hare (1976) is the development of norms concerning the expected behaviors of group members. Norms provide guidelines for the individual and also serve to indicate the behaviors that can be expected of others (Shaw, 1976). Such standards produce a uniformity of behavior that further serves to identify and maintain the group. Team norms may call for sociable and cooperative behavior on the part of members, for regular attendance at team meetings, for contributing to the work of the team, and for not monopolizing the team discussion with irrelevant material. Norms may cover such diverse matters as dress codes, appropriate language or jargon, and even the seating arrangements in team meetings. Some norms will be discussed and agreed on by the team as a whole. However, often norms are unspoken, and the insensitive or new team member may be unaware of certain subtle cues used by other team members to control behavior.

Those who deviate from the norms established by the team may face sanctions ranging from being ignored to dismissal. Thus the group uses various forms of pressure to ensure conformity on the part of its members. Within the organizational structure, teams, of course, develop additional sanctions (reprimands, firings) that may be employed against nonconforming members. When norms are well established, the team may work quickly and harmoniously, but overconformity may tend to stifle new ideas and solutions and reduce team effectiveness.

Hollander (1958) noted the variation in the severity of sanctions imposed on a group deviant. He pointed out that deviation is more easily tolerated in participants who have "earned" the right to deviate (which he calls "idiosyncrasy credits") through previous contributions to the group. Thus high-status members are less likely to be punished for deviation from group norms than are low-status members. Furthermore, some norms demand rigid adherence, while others are more easily bypassed; some norms are accepted by all group members, while others may be opposed by a significant majority (Shaw, 1976).

Conformity is particularly important in decision-making groups, where the final outcome is hindered by the failure to examine various alternatives adequately. If team members fail to give full consideration to certain possible solutions because of fear of ridicule or disapproval, then team decisions may not be as good as if all alternatives were considered. Several authors (Argyris, 1969; Hackman, 1975; Hackman & Morris, 1975) have noted that "conservative" norms regarding group behavior tend to dominate the group so that interpersonal risks are minimized and deviant behaviors are quickly punished. Such conformity may be dysfunctional for team effectiveness. On the other hand, the risky-shift results discussed earlier suggest that group decision making is not always more conservative than individual decisions.

Fry, Lech, and Rubin (1974) emphasize that the norms of the team are particularly important because they influence other aspects of team functioning. They discovered that inflexible team norms—such as "doctors are more important than other team members," "conflict is dangerous," and "silence means consent"—may be dysfunctional. They conclude that "the cost of failing to develop norms of flexibility, support and openness of communication is high indeed" (p. 38) since the team is then unable to become self-correcting.

Role, Status, and Power

Another important characteristic of groups is noted by Hare (1976): the development of a set of roles or role expectations regarding each member of the group. Some of the roles that may be assumed by group members include "energizer," "information-seeker," "opinion-giver," "evaluator-critic," and "harmonizer," as identified by Benne and Sheats (1948). As the names suggest, the energizer is one who "prods the team to action or decision, attempts to stimulate or arouse the group to 'greater' or 'higher quality' activity," while the harmonizer "mediates the differences between other members, attempts to reconcile disagreements, and relieves tension in conflict situations through jesting or pouring oil on troubled waters" (Benne & Sheats, 1948, p. 44).

Once established, roles are likely to be self-perpetuating, so that deviations from the expected roles may disturb other members. However, role expectations in interdisciplinary teams are also based on other factors, such as professional affiliation and position in the organization. Thus, a physical therapist will be looked to by the team for relevant information regarding the patient's range of motion, and a social worker will be expected to have knowledge regarding the family situation. It is important to distinguish role expectations based on team membership and on behavior in team meetings from those based on professional identification.

Hayden and Gotts (1977) have described some of the roles of team members involved in a program for the early education of exceptional children and suggested a process for role definition that may be useful in implementing such a program. They propose first developing a description of the program, including intake, diagnostic, program planning, direct services, and follow-up activities that are necessary to achieve the goals of the program. Secondly, the areas of work should be assigned to staff members and behavioral description of the staff who carry out the activities developed. Then the work that is being done should be compared with the original model to identify gaps, and descriptions of these areas should also be developed. Finally, role descriptions should be formulated from the final behavioral descriptions. While Hayden and Gotts give examples of roles that might result from such a process, they warn that it is not possible to establish role descriptions that will work in all settings, because of the differences in programs. They also stress the importance of differentiated and defined roles.

The concept of "team" in no way implies that everyone has the same role or that all must be able to do everyone else's work. The team concept works so well because in fact the individuals who make up a staff have many different interests, talents, skills, and capabilities, and these are drawn upon and utilized. Team work does imply that each individual has a clearly defined role to play and that the roles are related to each other in such a way as to ensure the accomplishment of the common goals. (Hayden & Gotts, 1977, p. 248)

Goldstein, Strickland, Turnbull, and Curry (1980) suggest that the roles and responsibilities of some of the members of the IEP committee are not clearly defined and that further specification of training in those roles might be important. "Unless each participant understands what his or her contribution is to be and actively assumes that role, the multidimensional purpose of the IEP conference will be defeated" (p. 285).

Some role ambiguity and overlapping of roles on the interdisciplinary team are probably to be expected. Whenever different professionals are working together on a single set of problems, there is bound to be some confusion about who is to do what. Thus, total role differentiation may not be possible or even desirable. If role definition is too rigid it may reduce the flexibility of the team unduly. Similarly, some degree of overlap between positions may actually help to bridge the gap between the disciplines and to prevent fragmentation in the delivery of services. However, excessive ambiguity in team roles may reduce team effectiveness.

Fenton, Yoshida, Maxwell, and Kaufman (no date) examined the expectations of special education placement team members of their own roles and the roles of others on the team. Principals, school psychologists, special education teachers, and regular teachers rated the appropriateness of 25 activities for four target roles, including their own. Results indicated that team members had a restricted view of their own roles and of the roles of other professionals on the team. Since the largest number of activities was seen as appropriate for principals and the least number for regular teachers, the authors conclude that

one possible explanation of the findings in this study is that the expectations which members have for their own roles and for the roles of others reflect the relative influence, or lack thereof, of member's hierarchical position within the school organization. The regular teachers may perceive themselves and be perceived by others as having less status within the school hierarchy and therefore their potential participation in the placement team may be restricted accordingly. (p. 12)

Even more important in this study is the finding of significant differences between team members' expectations about their own roles and the expectations of other team members about those roles. Such ambiguity may be dysfunctional to teamwork by reducing members' commitment to team activities. Fenton et al. suggest that inservice training might be helpful in clarifying the roles of various team members.

These results support the relationship that has been observed between the prestige or status of an individual and the role of that person on the team. Although members may "earn" status by playing a significant role (such as "harmonizer") in the interaction process, to a certain extent status in the team is likely to reflect the prestige of the individual's profession. Status variables have been shown to have important effects on a number of group processes. For example, studies have indicated that higher-status individuals receive more communication, are better liked, and give less irrelevant communication to other members than persons of lower status in the group (Thibaut and Kelley, 1959).

Both role and status also relate to social power, or the ability to influence other members of the group. External prestige often influences other team members even as concerns problems that are unrelated to the expertise of the high-status individual. Thus the nurse may take the advice of the physician very seriously in choosing a new car, even though the doctor's expertise may not extend to that subject. In a study of role relations in mental health teams, Zander, Cohen, and Stotland (1959) found a consistent power structure with psychiatrists at the top and psychologists and social workers subordinate. That such external power relationships might be expected to carry over to decisions within the team is implied by the findings of Leff, Raven, and Gunn (1964) that psychiatrists tend to be more influenced by other psychiatrists than by psychologists, whereas psychologists appeared to be equally influenced by both.

In a study of the effects of power in groups of mental hygiene workers (Hurwitz, Zander, and Hymovitch, 1968), it was found that high-power members communicated more often than low-power members, were better liked, and received more communication from both high- and lower-power members. The authors suggest that low-power members experience uneasiness in their interaction with high-power members and react in an ego defensive manner in the group situation. Such reactions are likely to affect not only team dynamics but also the actual decisions reached by the team. This is because the opinions of high-power individuals are likely to be given greater weight regardless of the accuracy of their judgments.

The power of the team member may be based on one or more of several possible sources: French and Raven (1959) have identified five bases of power in small groups. Reward power and coercive power are related to the subject's perception that the individual has the ability to mediate rewards or punishments. These rewards and punishments might be verbal (such as praise or criticism) or more tangible (such as a promotion or a salary increase). Legitimate power is based on internalized cultural values, acceptance of the social structure, and/or designation by a legitimizing agent. Thus a physician has a legitimate right to prescribe medicine, and the principal of a school has a legitimate right to enforce certain regulations. Referent power is based on the subject's identification with a power holder, as when the boss's secretary attains power through association with a powerful figure. Finally, expert power refers to the subject's perception that the power holder has special knowledge or expertise. R. Martin (1978) has analyzed the consulting role of school psychologists and mental health professionals in terms of referent and expert power and suggests ways of maximizing their influence as consultants. Team leaders may have several sources of power both within and outside the team.

THE TEAM LEADER

One of the major roles on the team is that of the team leader. Leadership has long been thought of as a personal trait, a collection of skills possessed by individuals to a greater or lesser degree, a continuum along which individuals might be ordered according to how much of the trait they possessed. However, more recent studies (Gibb, 1969; Steiner, 1972) have tended to focus on leadership *behavior* rather than leadership *traits*. In reviewing previous attempts at definition of the group leader, researchers have noted several approaches (Carter, 1953; Gibb, 1969). The leader has been variously defined as the individual who holds a particular office (''chairman'' or ''president''), helps the group move toward its goals, is identified as leader by other group members, has influence over others, is the focus of group behaviors, or engages in leadership behaviors.

Although the leader may emerge spontaneously from the interaction of a team, in most cases team leadership is awarded by the parent organization. Thus a teacher may be asked to coordinate an educational team or a psychiatrist to head up a mental health team. However, unless the team members accept the legitimacy of the appointment, the designated leader may not be able to fulfill the functions of team leader. Since frequently the individual so designated does in fact already wield considerable influence over group members, that individual is usually accepted to some extent as a team leader.

Regardless of whether a leader has previously been assigned by the organization, it is possible for one or more leaders to emerge during the interactions of the team. Leadership functions may be concentrated primarily in one team member or may be distributed across a number of members. In some teams, leadership roles may shift as the task progresses, so that individuals with differing skills may exert more influence during various phases of the team's activities.

In an analysis of the primary health care team, Parker (1972) identified five aspects of ''team leadership'': patient coordination and management, team management, charismatic or spiritual leadership, primary patient relationship, and medical decision making. These roles need not all be filled by the same individual and some may shift from one team member to another. While some, such as medical decision making, are directly related to the responsibilities and competencies of the physician, other leadership roles can be filled by any team member. Similar leadership roles might be identified in the educational team.

Since the leadership functions that have been identified cover a broad range of activities and behaviors, it is unlikely that they could all be carried out by only one member of the team. Krech and Crutchfield (1948), for example, have indicated 14 functions that might be performed by a group leader: the leader may be seen as executive, planner, policymaker, expert, external group representative, controller of internal relationships, purveyor of rewards and punishments, arbitrator, exemplar, group symbol, surrogate for individual responsibility, ideologist, father figure, or scapegoat. As Cartwright and Zander (1968) have pointed out, "It becomes evident that one person could seldom be effectively responsible for them all" (p. 305). Thus various members of the team may share these functions, assuming those that are ascribed to them by other team members or for which their behavior is most suited.

A distinction is frequently made between a "task leader" and a "social-emotional leader" (Bales and Slater, 1955). The task leader assumes those functions of coordination and planning necessary for task performance, while the social-emotional leader is responsible for team maintenance activities, often serving as a mediator and calming force for the group. Cartwright and Zander (1968) discuss the two major categories of group functions, "goal achievement" and "group maintenance," pointing out that while one leader may perform both types of functions, in some situations task-oriented or social-emotional "specialists" may be required for effective group performance. For example, although the principal may have been assigned responsibility for coordination of task-directed activities, the counselor may maintain team interaction by mediating disputes, encouraging and motivating the other team members, and relieving team tensions. The social-emotional leader is often better liked by the group than the task leader, but the latter may be more respected. The overall effectiveness of the team will be determined in part by the interaction of these leaders. Competition between them can be quite disruptive to the team, while agreement on significant goals and cooperation in methods of approach can facilitate both goal achievement and team maintenance.

When only one team leader emerges, that leader must demonstrate skills in dealing with both task-oriented and social-emotional functions. Which functions are most essential is likely to vary with the nature of the task, the characteristics of the team, and other variables. Fiedler (1968), for example, has demonstrated that a leader primarily concerned with task completion is likely to be most effective when the situation is one defined as either very easy or very hard, while the more interpersonally oriented leader is more successful when the situation is of intermediate difficulty.

Interestingly, Fiedler concludes that, since the effectiveness of the group depends on how the leader's style fits the specific situation at hand and since most people will be effective leaders in certain situations and not in others, more effort should be given to changing the group situation to fit the leader rather than attempting to change the leader's personality and leadership style to match the situation. Fiedler offers several specific suggestions for changing the group situation. For example, the leader's power can be changed (by increasing or decreasing his authority), or changes can be made in the structure of the task or in the composition of the group.

On the other hand, Shaw (1976) suggests that the leader may be able to vary his or her style with the favorableness of the situation, becoming more responsive to social-emotional factors in moderately difficult group situations and more directive as the situation becomes extremely favorable or unfavorable. He notes that "the group leader often errs in this respect especially when the group/task situation becomes highly unfavorable. Empirical evidence suggests that he should become more directive, whereas all too often he becomes less directive in his interactions with other members of the group" (p. 395).

The applicability of these concepts to the interdisciplinary team has yet to be empirically demonstrated, and the area is in need of further investigation.

TEAM INTERACTION

Among the group characteristics noted by Hare (1976) were the development of a network of interpersonal attraction and the interaction of group members. Positive and negative feelings for each other often become the focus of attention in therapeutic groups. However, in interdisciplinary teams such feelings may be ignored in the face of more immediate task demands. Yet affective reactions to other members can exert a powerful force in almost any kind of group, and, although team membership may offer more tangible rewards (such as promotions, salary increases, and professional status), the approval of other team members may be the strongest and most immediate payoff for teamwork.

Initially team members enter a new group clothed in the professional "position" they hold in the organizational setting. Each position is associated with certain role expectations, status values, and "rights and privileges"—all this quite apart from the individual who occupies that position. Similarly, there are certain built-in relationships between professions that will affect interactions. For example, the role expectations of a principal and a teacher, a psychiatrist and a social worker, or a teacher and a psychologist will to a considerable extent structure these relationships regardless of how the individuals regard one another. Yet, while professional positions will affect the amount and type of interaction between those individuals who fill them, attractions and antagonisms are often reactions to people rather than to job titles. It may be that personal characteristics most strongly affect the team members' interactions with others in the group.

Interpersonal attraction has been related to physical attractiveness, similarity of attitudes and beliefs, and compatibility of needs (Shaw, 1976), and it is likely that such factors also affect patterns of attraction and antagonism within the team. Even professionals are more likely to like those who have beliefs, attitudes, and ideas similar to their own. Sociometric techniques can be used to measure these patterns by asking participants to rank all the members along some dimension or to identify members of the group with whom they would or would not like to work, or whom they like best.

The network of interpersonal attraction within a team may represent a unique configuration that is an important aspect of the group's identity. In addition, these patterns of interpersonal relations (along with the interprofessional perceptions explored earlier) play a major role in determining the productivity of the team.

The extent and type of interaction among educational team members has been examined by Armer and Thomas (1978), who were interested in collaboration in pupil personnel services teams. They developed and revised an Interdisciplinary Collaboration Scale which was used along with a judge's rating of team interaction and frequency of team meetings with school personnel. Results of the study indicated that "high collaboration teams were often reported as meeting regularly with faculty and administrators and were more often perceived as working as a team" (p. 175). In some schools, the teams that were highly collaborative were also seen as more cooperative and independent and were viewed more positively on the evaluative dimension of a semantic differential measure of attitudes.

An investigation of the type of interaction in interdisciplinary health care teams was reported by Feiger and Schmitt (1979). Several meetings of four interdisciplinary teams were videotaped and coded for interaction initiated and received by team members and also for the kind of interaction ("asks for information," "gives opinion," etc.). The results suggested that none of the teams fit the model of collegial interaction developed by the authors and that the four teams differed in their interaction. Since the personnel on the teams were identical except for the physician, this seemed to reflect differences in the physicians on the teams. They also found that the degree of collegiality in the interdisciplinary team was positively related to patient outcome measures.

COMPOSITION OF THE TEAM

The effectiveness of any team is to a great extent a function of the individuals who compose its membership. As Shaw (1976) has suggested, age, sex, and other personal attributes of group participants are important because they affect the behavior of the individual, the reaction of other members to that individual, and the overall composition of the group. An important element in the group's composition and ultimate effectiveness is the homogeneity of the group with regard to these individual characteristics.

In discussing the difficulties in assessing the effects of group composition on productivity, Steiner (1972) has observed:

> Heterogeneity with respect to a given attribute may augment potential productivity but greatly increase the complexity of the process which must occur in order for the group to realize its full potential. Thus, for example, a group whose members each possess unique information concerning a topic may have the potential to produce a high quality judgment because their total available information is very great. Such a group is likely to experience greater difficulty in evaluating and pooling information than a group with more homogeneous members. (p. 197)

Since an interdisciplinary team is by definition a heterogeneous group, we may expect, according to Steiner, some difficulty in integrating information. This may be offset by more effective outcomes because of the diversity of the information available to the group.

The composition of teams may vary in a number of ways. Let us briefly examine some of those factors and note how they may affect team functioning.

Professions

In most cases, the team will be professionally heterogeneous, with a number of disciplines and specialties represented. However, teams may be composed primarily of closely related professions, such as special education teachers and regular classroom teachers, or of a diverse group of professionals, such as physician, teacher, psychologist, and social worker. As indicated above, teams composed of professionals of varied skills and expertise will have more total information available in their deliberations than will a group with more limited, overlapping, and perhaps even redundant information, but the heterogeneous group may experience greater difficulty in assimilating and integrating such diverse data. Although the potential quality of judgment may be much higher in a heterogeneous grouping, the complexity introduced by those differences may prove counterproductive.

Additionally, Steiner notes, "Probably heterogeneity is also more likely than homogeneity to promote antagonisms among members" (Steiner, 1972, p. 107). Since professionals of varied disciplines, experience, and training will view the client in terms of frames of reference or theoretical models drawn from that training, the more heterogeneous the team members, the more varied their ways of approaching the client's problems. In Chapter 2 we examined some of the ways in which medical, psychological, social, and educational approaches might differ. Even the language or professional jargon of the various disciplines may lead to confusion and misunderstandings. Such antagonisms may divert attention from the task of decision making, introducing considerable static in the process and reducing the effectiveness of the team.

Sex

The effect that the sexual composition of the team has upon the group processes is somewhat uncertain. Most teams are mixed groups with a fair proportion of male and female members; however, occasionally all-male or all-female groups are found in professional settings. The most striking effect may be found in teams where the great majority is of one sex and only one or two representatives of the opposite sex are present. This situation seems to make all participants more aware of sex roles and may tend to give greater or lesser weight to the input of the minority participants. Thus, the opinions of a sole male participant may have greater influence on the team's deliberations than would his contribution if he were merely one of several male participants. In the same way, a sole female member may be reluctant to appear too "aggressive" in an otherwise all-male team.

Just as heterogeneity along other dimensions, such as professional background, introduces greater complexity into team dynamics, a mixture of male and female team members also seems to complicate interactions and opens up new sources of influence. Results of research on small groups have been somewhat conflicting. For example, mixed-sex groups have been found to perform more efficiently than all-male groups (Hoffman & Maier, 1961) and less efficiently than either all-male or all-female groups (Clement & Schiereck, 1973). Mixed-sex groups have also been found to be more conforming than same-sex groups (Reitan & Shaw, 1964). Shaw (1976) suggests that mixed-sex groups may be more concerned about socio-emotional factors, while same-sex groups may concentrate on task orientation. Another finding suggests that culturally stereotyped sexual roles may result in greater conformity among female participants and greater competitiveness among male participants.

The effects of sexual composition in interdisciplinary teams is also complicated by the relationship between sex and profession. There tends to be a preponderance of female team members in middle-status professions, such as teaching or nursing, and more males in higher-status professions, such as administration or medicine. It is often difficult to separate the effects of profession and sex in the operation of teams in human service settings.

Age

Predictably, the age of the team members will have some effect on the processes and outcomes of the group interaction. As with stereotyped sexual roles, cultural expectations related to age can affect the perceptions of team members and increase or decrease the weight given to an individual's opinion. A young principal may be treated differently than an older one. Since age is also likely to be confounded with professional experience and status, it may be difficult to isolate the effects of age alone. It should be noted, however, that, since the groups under consideration here are composed primarily of professionals, the age span is somewhat reduced. Most of the research dealing with age and group effectiveness has involved children and is not applicable to teams. It may well be that, compared to factors such as ability and experience, age is a relatively less important variable in interdisciplinary teams.

Other Factors

Other personal attributes, such as intelligence, dominance, authoritarianism, social sensitivity, and special skills or abilities, are also likely to affect the individual's contribution to the team activities. The unique constellation of attributes, abilities, and experience found in each team will determine to a great extent how the team operates and its effectiveness in carrying out its tasks. Results of several studies have suggested that differences in abilities and personality profiles within the group are more conducive to effective problem solving than is group homogeneity (Goldman, 1965; Hoffman, 1959; Hoffman & Maier, 1961; Laughlin, Branch & Johnson, 1969).

In summarizing a review of research on the effects of group composition, Shaw (1976) concludes:

> We have just begun the analysis of group composition effects. It is already clear that such efforts are far more complex than they appeared to be initially. We may hazard a guess that interpersonal compatibility is the basic variable in group composition; the large task facing group dynamics is the theoretical analysis of interpersonal relations so that the compatibility-incompatibility of individual characteristics can be identified. (p. 236)

COMMUNICATION NETWORKS

Communication between team members—that is, who talks to whom—is a central variable in team interaction. A good deal of research has focused on the determinants and consequences of communication networks in small group functioning. A communication network has been defined as "the arrangement (or pattern) of communication channels among the members of a group" (Shaw, 1976, p. 445). In an attempt to determine the effects of different communication networks on group performance, Bavelas (1948) developed a technique that has been used by a number of other investigators. In this design, subjects are placed alone in cubicles with connecting slots through which messages may be passed. By varying the available slots participants can use, the experimenter can control the channels of communication. If all slots are open, each participant can communicate with every other participant (termed a completely connected or comcon network). Other network designs, such as wheels, chains, and circles, can be formed by closing designated channels. Experiments in varying communication networks, along with variations in the task involved, the number of participants, and other significant factors, have been performed to study a number of relationships involving communication patterns.

One of the significant notions emerging from these studies is that of centrality of position in the network. Centrality has been defined and measured in a number of ways; however, the concept can best be illustrated by an example (Cartwright & Zander, 1968). In a five-person group arranged in a row (A–B–C–D–E), C holds the most central position (with the shortest total communication distance to every other member), while A and E are in the most peripheral locations. In a circle network, where all members are equidistant, all positions are equally central. The importance of the idea lies in the relationship that has been found between centrality and leadership: the individual holding the central position is most likely to emerge as the identified group leader (Shaw, 1976). Furthermore, centrality of position is also related to satisfaction; those members who have more channels of communication available indicate greater satisfaction than those with limited communication outlets. This finding has implications for team morale, since networks that provide only limited communication for a large number of members may suffer morale problems. One way to explain the relationship between satisfaction and centrality is that greater centrality leads to greater feelings of independence, autonomy, and power, thus producing a sense of satisfaction with one's position in the group (Cartwright & Zander, 1968).

Within the limitations of the network, various informal communication structures arise for purposes of exchanging information necessary to complete the task. Two basic organization patterns have been identified: the each-to-all pattern and the centralized organization (Shaw, 1976). In the centralized pattern, all of the data are channeled to one individual, who solves the problem and communicates this solution to the other members. This approach is used by some educational and human service teams. The each-to-all pattern involves sharing all information with all participants, who then solve the problem independently.

The particular communication network used by the group usually determines the type of organizational structure that emerges. Centralized networks usually lead to centralized organizations, while networks that do not place any member in a centralized position are likely to develop as each-to-all organizations (Shaw, 1976). Shaw also points out that centralized communication networks appear to be more effective with simple problems, while complex problems are more efficiently handled in decentralized networks.

It is difficult to generalize from these laboratory studies to the interdisciplinary team, but some parallels do come to mind. Some teams appear to have clearcut, almost rigid, communication channels, with a leader who controls and directs the discussion to an unusual degree. In such cases, the leader may direct questions to other team members and receive answers from them in turn, but there may be little or no communication between team members themselves. Such an extreme situation would clearly represent the centralized network and centralized organization. In contrast, in the decentralized pattern all members communicate freely with all other members, and each participant has access to the total available information.

Many authors who are concerned with the effectiveness of the interdisciplinary team emphasize the importance of open communication channels between team members (Haselkorn, 1958; Lacks, Landsbaum, & Stern, 1970; Nagi, 1975; Rubin & Beckhard, 1972). Wagner (1977) points out that Shaw's (1964) findings (that groups with more communication channels perform best on complex tasks, while groups with fewer channels are better with simple tasks) suggest that "all-channel" networks may be most effective for the "complex human relations problems" dealt with by the team, as compared with the "wheel" network used by the individual practitioner.

Rubin and Beckhard (1972) indicate that, since each team member is a resource, there must be open channels of communication to all other members. Haselkorn (1958) considers communication a crucial element in interprofessional collaboration and examines some of the problems that may interfere with communication. Lacks, Landsbaum, and Stern (1970) developed a training laboratory experience to increase communication in a children's psychiatric team as a way of improving team performance.

We will examine some other aspects of team communication in Chapter 8. The interested reader can find a further discussion of communication among team members in Horwitz (1970) and Brill (1976). The two literature reviews by Tichy—one covering literature on teams (1974), the other dealing with relevant behavioral science research (1975)—are also pertinent to this topic.

TEAM COHESIVENESS

Another important element in team interaction is the cohesiveness of the team. Although cohesiveness has been defined in a number of ways, most would agree with Cartwright's statement (1968) that it "refers to the degree to which the members of the group desire to remain in the group" (p. 91). Interpersonal attraction among group members has often been used as a measure of group cohesiveness, since attraction to other members appears to be an important component of an individual's attraction to and desire to remain in the group. Cohesiveness is regarded in some ways as the "glue" that holds the group together. The more cohesive the team, the higher the likelihood it will maintain itself over a period of time and exert influence over its members. Thus cohesiveness is an important factor in determining the willingness of team members to contribute to the work of the team and thus to its outcomes.

Earlier, we indicated that several factors found to be related to interpersonal attraction may also be important in determining group cohesiveness. Certainly, groups whose members are attracted to one another by common interests and attitudes, compatible needs, and other shared characteristics seem more likely. to "stick together." However, other factors may also affect the cohesiveness of teams. Thibaut and Kelley (1959) have pointed out that a participant's attraction to the group depends on the relative costs and rewards that group membership will bring. Most people have had many group experiences in the past, and these experiences form a standard against which present or future groups can be compared. According to Thibaut and Kelley, the more one's expectations of the outcomes of membership exceed that comparison level, the more one will be attracted to that group. An individual may be drawn to a team because of its goals, its activities, the kind of leadership demonstrated, or other incentives. Cartwright's article (1968) indicates that the motives of the potential group member are also important. These include the need for affiliation, prestige, recognition, or other rewards the group may offer.

Thus, according to Cartwright, cohesiveness depends on four sets of interacting variables: the needs of the participants, the incentives offered, the expectations of the members about the outcomes, and the comparison levels held by group members. Even in situations where team membership is a mandatory "part of the job" rather than elective, these factors are likely to be important in determining whether members feel they are an integral part of a team or simply going through the motions.

While some optimal level of cohesiveness seems to be important in the effective functioning of the interdisciplinary team, high cohesiveness was one of the factors that Janis (1972) identified as an antecedent condition to "groupthink." As Janis and Mann (1977) point out, "when the cohesiveness of a group increases from a low to a moderate or high level, each member becomes more psychologically dependent on the group and displays greater readiness to adhere to the group's norms" (p. 131). Thus the highly cohesive team may become more conforming and less likely to question group norms or team decisions. Furthermore, as the team becomes more cohesive, it may be more difficult for new members to participate fully in team activities and for the team to accept opinions and information coming from sources outside the team.

COALITIONS

Along with the factors that tend to bring team members together into cohesive units are a number of factors that lead to divisions and conflicts. Ideally, teams are cooperative ventures in which members pool their individual resources in order to arrive at a better outcome. Thus members of a mental health team will pool their talents, professional training, and experience, and the information they have gathered about a child and the family, in order to make a diagnosis, predict the child's future behavior, establish a treatment plan, or carry out the treatment. Such an endeavor is assumed to produce an outcome beneficial to the child and to team members as well.

However, as we have seen in our discussion of team cohesiveness, individual prestige, recognition from other members, a promotion, or a salary increase may also be considered incentives for some team members. As in most group situations, competitiveness can also affect the actions of team members, and most teams are likely to contain elements of both cooperation and competition. In the parlance of game theory, such teams are said to be engaged in mixed-motive games.

The sociometric techniques used to study interpersonal attraction within groups often reveal a number of subgroups within the larger unit. These smaller groups, held together by friendship or mutual liking, are generally referred to as *cliques*. Although cliques may affect communication patterns within a team, they will not necessarily affect the outcome or decisions made by the team as a whole. When a subgroup is drawn together to affect outcomes, the term *coalition* is used. For example, a clique may decide to work together against an individual or another subgroup within the larger group, and in this case a coalition would emerge.

Most of the work on coalition formation has taken place in laboratory settings with individuals who are initially strangers. These studies generally do not operate long enough or in such a way as to reveal the role of interpersonal attraction in coalition formation (Carlins & Raven, 1969). Research on coalitions often makes use of triads, in which two members join together in opposition to a third person in order to control the outcomes of the group.

Several theories of coalition formation have been suggested, and these have tended to focus on how coalitions form in relation to the resources available to each potential participant. For example, the minimum resource theory (Gamson, 1961) contends that coalitions are likely to form between persons who control the minimum resources necessary to control the outcome. Thus if A has five points, with B and C each having three points, a coalition would most likely occur between B and C. Although some attention has been given to the role of additional factors, such as interpersonal relations, most research in this area has attempted to control for such variables rather than to investigate them.

The complexities of coalition formation in natural group settings remain generally unexplained. Since the participants may be seeking any number of possible rewards in addition to the expressed purpose and expected outcomes of the team conference, we might expect that coalition formation would be highly unpredictable. Gamson (1961) refers to this lack of predictability as the "utter confusion theory," reflecting the lack of understanding of the variables determining coalitions.

Despite our frequent inability to understand or predict the specific coalitions that may emerge in teams, they can be a significant factor in determining outcomes. Using a children's mental health team working with exceptional children as an example, we can visualize a number of ways in which coalitions might operate. Sometimes coalitions seem to form around professional identification—with psychiatrists, psychologists, social workers, or other professional groups uniting along professional lines to oppose recommendations made by other group members or other coalitions. Often two or more professional groups join against a third, as when the psychiatrists and the social workers in the team unite to oppose the opinions of the psychologists. Ideological or theoretical values can also lead to the formation of coalitions. For instance, team members with a psychoanalytic bent may join together in opposing a treatment plan based on techniques of behavior modification, or two or three therapists whose primary interest and expertise is in individual treatment may object to a recommendation of group counseling for a child.

Coalitions may be seen as both indicative of and contributing to the potential conflict and divisiveness within a team. Coalitions may be subtle and more or less "under the table" or may be clearly recognized by the group. They may be relatively permanent (with members of the coalition consistently supporting the position of other coalition partners, with an implicit understanding that they will in turn be supported) or unstable and changing (with considerable switching of coalition membership as issues change). It would appear that the more stable the team, the more likely the formation of clearcut coalition subgroups. It should be noted, however, that sometimes when a particular coalition exerts excessive power over group decisions, there is a corresponding loss of morale among the other members, who may feel that their input is not valued. Thus the rewards offered them by group membership are considerably diminished, and cohesiveness may be reduced to the point where team effectiveness is seriously threatened and/or the group may disintegrate. In other cases where a powerful coalition threatens the functioning of the team, new coalitions may be formed to counteract this threat. Individuals who may oppose each other on ideological or other grounds may unite against a common threat, at least on significant issues. This continual realignment of team participants in various subgroups makes it difficult to predict the direction of coalition formation in natural groupings outside the laboratory situation.

OTHER FACTORS

There are a number of other factors that may set limits or in some way structure the interaction of team members. They include the size of the team, the physical environment in which it meets, its degree of formality, and the length and frequency of its meetings.

Size of the Team

Much attention has been given to the question of an optimal size for decision-making groups, but results are not clearcut since size interacts with a number of other variables. A task that is divisible and can be shared by individual team members working alone or in smaller units will require enough participants to complete each task component. In these cases, often the optimal size relates directly to the number of task components. In the interdisciplinary team, optimal size may be dependent on the number of specialists required to provide services to a particular child or by the requirements of the school and institution. Public Law 94–142 specifies the composition of the evaluation team and the participants in the IEP conferences.

As a team increases in size, the number of possible relationships between members increases rapidly. For example, in a three-member group there are 3 possible paired relationships, but in a six-member group there are 15. It has been pointed out that while a larger group has more resources available for meeting task demands, the individual contribution of each member is reduced as group size increases and only the more forceful members can make their opinions known (Hare, 1976).

Physical Environment

The physical setting in which the team interacts may affect its operation in several ways. A light, airy room with comfortable seating arrangements and good temperature control will allow team participants to concentrate on the tasks at hand rather than be preoccupied with their own feelings of discomfort. A room that is too hot or too cold or has uncomfortable chairs may serve to unduly prolong (or shorten) the meeting.

The seating arrangement both shapes and is molded by the interaction of the members. As a particular team develops a mode of interaction, it will spontaneously modify the arrangement of chairs to fit its style of operation. A formal arrangement generally denotes a more constrained interaction. In any case, no matter what arrangement is adopted, often one or two individuals will place their chairs in an idiosyncratic position not in keeping with the total arrangement.

The physical setting may affect the performance of the team in more specific ways. Research has indicated that seating arrangements may affect the flow of communication and the quality of the group interaction and that "when members of a group are seated at a round table, there is a strong tendency for members to communicate with persons across the table and facing them rather than with persons adjacent to them" (Shaw, 1976, pp. 133–134).

Although the relationship between status and seating is not clearcut, evidence suggests that seating arrangements play a role in leadership selection when leaders have not already been assigned. Positions at the head of the table or in the most central location are generally regarded as having higher status than more peripheral positions. Students, particularly in medical settings, often comment on the relationship between professional status and seat location in team meetings. Frequently physicians sit together at the center of the group, with psychologists and social workers adjacent, and nurses, physical and occupational therapists, and other professionals seated at varying distances from the center.

Territoriality with regard to seating has also been noted. In cases where seats are not formally assigned, participants will frequently establish territorial rights to a particular chair in a certain location and return to that seat each meeting. New members are expected to take seats that do not "belong" to anyone else and may be resented if they unknowingly usurp another member's chair.

Formality or Informality of the Team

One of the dimensions along which teams may vary markedly is the formality or informality of their procedures. Medical team conferences often employ much more formal procedures than IEP conferences, for example. The degree of formality in a team meeting is apparent in the physical arrangement of the seating. Seats lined up in neat rows reminiscent of a formal classroom suggest a communication network and style of interaction quite different from that suggested by a casual, even somewhat sloppy, circle of chairs. Seating is only one rather obvious aspect of formality. More crucial to the eventual outcomes of the team is the formality of the group interaction itself. A casual and relaxed atmosphere may lead to more spontaneous and more frequent comments by the participants, while in a more formal context the interaction may be somewhat stilted and reserved. On the other hand, greater informality may encourage more irrelevant information and lead to a less effective use of the time and energy of the team members.

Length and Frequency of Team Meetings

The professionals who make up teams are faced with heavy demands on their time. Often they are members of several teams, committees, and other groups. Team sessions may last anywhere from a half-hour to a half-day, or in some rare instances even a full day. The effects of duration on the group process is mixed. In therapy groups or self-awareness groups the purpose of the session may be to move from cognitive to more affective expression, and here increased duration even to the point of marathon sessions may be quite conducive to meeting group goals. However, in teams that make decisions critical to the future, shorter sessions appear to be more effective.

It seems likely that the relationship between duration and effectiveness may be represented by an inverted U-shaped function, with both very short and very long sessions proving less effective than sessions of moderate length. Short sessions do not give the group an opportunity to share the information that needs to be shared and to integrate it in a meaningful way. Long sessions tend to be tiring, and participants sometimes become less involved and more careless in their judgments as the session progresses. Team members who become anxious to leave may agree to courses of action that they might otherwise oppose. Individuals have different levels of tolerance for long sessions, and those who have the stamina to sustain their position may find that their input gains weight as the conference continues and other members begin to tire.

Team meetings may be held once a day, once a week, once a month, or even less frequently. Sessions may be scheduled regularly or called when a decision is pending or a problem arises. The frequency with which the team meets is related to the interaction between team members. Teams that meet infrequently may not develop a high degree of cohesiveness. On the other hand, too frequent meetings can be resented by busy professionals who may lose interest in the team, decrease their involvement, and thus reduce their input. With frequent sessions, potential antagonisms between members are more likely to surface, and this too may reduce productivity.

Stability

Some teams are highly stable, with a fixed group of participants meeting frequently over a long period of time. Unstable teams are those whose membership frequently shifts, with different members attending each session. There is little continuity or cohesiveness in an unstable group and much less opportunity to develop shared perceptions and a shared language. The rules by which decisions are made may change markedly from session to session, depending on who is in attendance. If the group is too unstable, it may not meet the criteria for a team spelled out in Chapter 1.

At the other extreme are those teams that have interacted so closely and for so long that the individual team members have come to perceive and respond to events in a very similar manner. Certain situations seem to demand this kind of consensus, so a great deal of effort is sometimes devoted to developing a common framework. For example, when a behavior modification procedure or token economy system is introduced in an agency or school, there must be agreement among the staff as to the behavior that will be rewarded. This agreement is difficult to achieve if there is rapid turnover in the team or if members attend irregularly.

It can be seen that each interdisciplinary team reflects a unique constellation of variables that affect its functioning. Because of the complexity of team interaction, it is often difficult to predict in advance (and even to explain on an ex post facto basis) why certain teams work effectively and others do not. Yet some specific suggestions for improving team performance can be made. Chapter 8 will address this question further.

Chapter 7

The Family of the Exceptional Child

The family is the first and most important representative of the social environment for the exceptional child. The infant or small child is limited primarily to contact with the immediate family and perceives the outside world only through interaction with the family. If these early contacts are positive ones, the child will tend to view the world in an optimistic light. If the interaction with the family is unhappy, the small child is likely to see the world as a rather frightening place.

As the infant grows, the family continues to play a major role in the emotional and cognitive development of the child. If the child is exceptional, the role of the parents is likely to be even more crucial to the child's adjustment. As the child enters school and gradually moves into a "wider social radius," as described by Erikson (1963), the parents continue to play a significant role in guiding the child toward positive interactions with outside social institutions. One of the primary social institutions with which the parents must negotiate is the school system. Particularly for the handicapped child, how well the parents are able to interact with the professionals in the schools and other community agencies may determine, to a large extent, the child's ultimate success or failure. In this chapter we will examine the dynamics of a family with an exceptional child and the relations between parents and professionals.

PARENTAL REACTIONS TO THE EXCEPTIONAL CHILD

A number of authors (Farber, 1972; Ross, 1964; Seligman, 1979) have described some of the reactions of parents to the birth of a handicapped child. Ross points out that attitudes toward a child are being formed even before the child's birth. Typically, the parents will share the more general social attitudes of what is beautiful and attractive, and they will have strong feelings about how children should look and act long before the child actually appears on the scene.

The parent may develop certain expectations of the child's height, weight, sex, hair color, and other characteristics. The child's failure to meet these expectations may lead to a sense of failure on the part of the parent, with accompanying guilt, anxiety, and feelings of inadequacy.

Furthermore, young couples often find themselves under a number of conflicting pressures from friends and family who are free with advice ranging from "don't tie yourselves down too soon" to "have your children while you are young enough to enjoy them." Many people besides the parents-to-be have an opinion about the coming child. If the baby who finally appears is deficient in some way, the new parents may experience a deep sense of loss and disappointment.

In this regard, an analogy with the "mourning" process has often been made. Briefly, the parents who discover that the expected child is severely handicapped may experience an initial period of shock and numbness, followed by a gradual awareness of what has happened and, finally, a period of grief, which the parent eventually works through (Solnit & Stark, 1971).

Along with this process, the parent may experience not only grief but also anxiety and guilt over the failure to produce a perfect child. Ross (1964) points out that the mother may in some ways perceive the child as a "product." While a perfect child may be seen as evidence of her cleverness and maturity, a defective child may be seen as evidence of incompetence. The baby may also be regarded as a gift to her husband. Giving an imperfect gift points up her failure and induces a sense of guilt. In extreme cases, the child may even be seen as punishment for previously committed sins.

Gath (1979) has summarized the reactions of a group of parents to the birth of a child with Down's Syndrome.

> Without exception, the parents regarded having a child with Down's Syndrome as a bitter blow and all experienced grief. The duration of intense grief varied but 90% of the parents were still talking about their grief at the end of the two years. The grief reaction appeared to go through stages as described in other studies. . . . After the initial feeling of numbness and unreality a period of denial sometimes, but not invariably followed. Then came many tears which were often accompanied by aggression. Anger was expressed against the doctor who had told them, or the obstetrician who had not done a termination, sometimes against the spouse or other relatives or more vaguely toward God or "Fate." Gradually weeping and recrimination became less frequent and constructive efforts were made to get over practical difficulties. (p. 14)

To defend against the anxiety associated with the perception of the child's defect, the parents may make use of one or more defense mechanisms. In general, parents may be expected to respond to the birth of a handicapped child in the same way that they react to most stress situations and to adopt those mechanisms that they use to deal with other sources of anxiety. Ross (1964) and Seligman (1979) have identified several defense mechanisms that may be used by parents of handicapped children to help them deal with what might otherwise be an overwhelming sense of anxiety.

Defense Mechanisms

Denial is a common defense and one of the most primitive. Children often use denial as a protection against facing unpleasantness and quickly convince themselves that they "didn't do it," even in the face of considerable evidence to the contrary. In like manner, the parent may be unable to face the reality of the child's handicap and may continue to deny the child's impairment even in the face of what would appear to be quite obvious symptoms. As Ross points out, as long as the parent can avoid situations in which comparisons with other children are inevitable, they may continue to deny that the child is significantly different from other children of the same age. Parents may tend to overprotect handicapped children, thus keeping them away from situations in which the handicap is apparent, or may push too hard because the children "just won't try." Denial may be supported by family, friends, and even by professionals who are also made anxious and uncomfortable by the child's condition. These individuals may hold out unrealistic hopes to the parents or provide false reassurances that "it's only a stage" and the child will "soon grow out of it." On the other hand, if others (including professionals) *do* attempt to help them face reality and accept the child's deficit, the parents may reject the information and advice. Instead they may seek opinions from others and search for a doctor or other professional who will tell them what they want to hear.

If denial does not adequately protect against anxiety and guilt, the parent may employ additional defenses. One of these is blaming others—projection of one's own impulses or feelings onto others. "It's *his* fault." The unspoken part of that is "it's not *my* fault." According to Ross (1964):

> The object of the projection is often a physician who did "something" wrong. Not only the blame, but also all the anger resulting from the frustration involved in having a defective child may then be turned against this professional person or, for that matter, against the entire profession he comes to represent. The slightest inadvertent (and unrelated) error is lit upon and becomes enlarged out of all proportion because it serves to support the defensive economy. (p. 64)

At times parents may resent the exceptional child and unconsciously blame the child for being born. Because such feelings are unacceptable to the parent's self-concept, they must be denied. However, if denial is not sufficient to stem the guilt, the mechanism of reaction formation may be used. "I am not angry at my child—I love him." Thus, the parent covers up the anger and resentment by stressing the opposite, positive, feelings. The use of reaction formation can easily lead to overprotection of the child by parents who are trying to cover up their own angry feelings.

The defense of undoing is related to reaction formation and the guilt associated with having failed to produce a perfect child. Unconsciously accepting the blame for the child's condition, the parent attempts to "undo" this damage by taking extra care for the child and giving into the child's demands, even when they are unreasonable or inappropriate.

Ross (1964) describes how the parents can protect themselves from anxiety by ritualization, focusing on medical and technical factors associated with the child's handicap. The parents may become so preoccupied with caring for the prosthesis, giving medicine, supervising exercises, and attending to other rituals associated with caring for the child that they are not sensitive to the child's emotional needs. Ross indicates that this "mechanization of parent-child relations" enables the parent "to shift the focus from feelings attached to the child's condition and thus to isolate his own emotional reactions" (p. 67).

Other defenses exist. In some cases the parent's behavior may go beyond ritualization and take the form of acting out hostility toward the child by punitive exercises, rigidly followed diets, or other unpleasant treatments. Guilt is avoided because the actions are good for the child and because hostility is expressed in a more socially acceptable manner. Other defenses that may be used by the parents include sublimation, intellectualization, and rationalization (Ross, 1964; Seligman, 1979). These are often more constructive than the previously mentioned defenses, and the results are usually less destructive to the child. For example, in sublimation the parent may use the energy stemming from the anxiety around the child's disability in working for agencies or parent organizations devoted to advocacy and other activities that promote the welfare of exceptional children. Intellectualization allows the parents to control the feelings associated with the handicapping condition by *thinking* about the disorder instead of experiencing the emotions. Such parents may engage in research or other professional activities focused on the disability itself. The parents may use rationalization to reduce anxiety by looking at the "silver lining" in the situation— "she really has such a sweet disposition—she is the joy of my life."

Mechanisms such as the ones we have described help the individual retain some personality integrity in the face of what might otherwise be an overwhelming stress. As the parent works through the mourning process and comes gradually to accept the reality of the child's handicap, such defenses may become less and less important. In some cases, where the defenses are quite strong, they may prove dysfunctional in that they disturb the parent's relations with family, friends, and professionals, and even interfere with the child's care. For example, if the parent continues to deny the child's handicap at a time when professional intervention is required, real harm may be done to the child by the parent's inability to cope with anxiety.

PATTERNS OF PARENT-CHILD INTERACTION

Once the parent has made an initial adjustment to the exceptional child in the family, certain patterns of parent-child interaction begin to emerge. Such interactions, once established, tend to become circular. Accepted without undue pressure to perform and without undue parental guilt, which may lead to over-possessiveness, the child is likely to be easier to get along with and not as fussy or cranky. The child's presence in the family is more gratifying and less stressful, and the parent is more likely to continue to behave in a warm and accepting manner. On the other hand, the rejected child will feel neglected, insecure, and unhappy and will tend to place greater demands on the parent. Such a child may be whiney, have frequent temper tantrums, and generally behave like a "difficult" child. The parents are likely to get relatively little gratification from their interaction with the child, may feel burdened by the demands placed on them, and may find the interaction increasingly stressful. In these circumstances the parents may begin to devote a large part of their time with the child to simply minimizing stress, either through rigid overcontrol and discipline or through bribery in order to keep the child quiet.

The interactions between parent and child are also affected by other family circumstances. The overworked and harrassed homemaker with three preschool children will respond differently to the new baby than the first-time parent. While parents with several children might welcome a placid quiet baby who causes little disruption in the home, the new parents of a first baby might find such an infant "too quiet" and prefer a more lively and alert baby who may be more interesting and fun to play with. Thus the needs of the parents and the temperament of the infant combine to produce a unique configuration of parent-child interactions.

While parent-child interactions can take many forms, there has probably been more written about parental *overprotection* than any other interaction pattern in the families of exceptional children. Robinson and Robinson (1976) identify several sources of overprotective behaviors among the parents of retarded children. First, they point out, with the slow-learning child it may be easier and quicker for the parent to continue to feed, dress, and bathe the child than to teach the child these skills. The busy parents may have neither the time nor the patience to teach the child to tie shoelaces when they can do it themselves in a few seconds. Secondly, "the prolonged period of infancy and heightened

dependency'' of the retarded child may lead to overlearning of dependent relationships by both parent and child. Finally, they note that overprotection may
be a defense against hostility and guilt associated with the exceptional child.

This notion that overprotection may reflect rejection of the child is also suggested by Wright (1960), who indicates that, while overprotection may be based
on genuine love and concern for the child, it may also reflect guilt over the
parent's feelings of rejection of the child, impatience with the child, or the need
to keep the child dependent on the parent.

Another source of overprotection may be found in the ambiguity of the situation for the parents. Because of their limited experience with handicapping
conditions such as their child's, it is sometimes very difficult for parents to
know *what* demands they can realistically place on the child, and *when* it is time
to place them. Indeed, as Wright points out, the use of the term "overprotection" involves a matter of judgment, and the parent may not agree that the
behavior is overprotective. "Instead he is usually convinced that the child is not
in fact fully capable of self-help in the particular instance. As he sees it, it is
the realities of the situation that require his help and protection" (Wright, 1960,
p. 306).

Since the parent may have few guidelines as to what can reasonably be expected of the handicapped child, where to draw the line between loving protection and overprotection is a debatable point. The whole question of depend-
ence-independence is a difficult one for exceptional children and their parents,
and it is a more complex issue than it at first appears. In fact, the rejecting
parents may put such unrealistic demands on the child for greater independence
that they actually produce a more dependent child.

It is particularly in this area of determining what the child can realistically be
asked to accomplish that the parent may be in need of help and professional
advice. It is important to keep in mind that not all parental reactions are emotionally determined. Some reactions are due to lack of information and the
ambiguity of the situation. It is here that the parent is likely to turn to professional workers for assistance.

EFFECTS ON SIBLINGS

It should be recognized that the birth of an exceptional child affects not only
the parents but other members of the family as well. Other children may suffer
a lack of attention and affection because of the parent's preoccupation with the
disabled child. Sibling rivalry may be exaggerated, and the nondisabled child
may be severely punished for even relatively mild actions against the handicapped sibling.

Research seems to indicate that children are likely to reflect the attitudes of
their parents toward handicapped children in the family (Grossman, 1972; Klein,

1972). If the parents perceive the child as a shame or a burden, other children in the family will react the same way. If the parents accept the child as a full member of the family, the siblings will do likewise. However, resentment may develop if the nonhandicapped children are given too much responsibility for the supervision and care of the disabled sibling (Telford & Sawrey, 1977).

In an extensive study of the family adjustment to a severely retarded child, Farber (1959, 1972) found that the effects were greater upon the normal sister than upon the normal brother. Girls who interacted more frequently with the retarded sibling were more adversely affected than sisters who were less involved, and siblings (both male and female) were more adversely affected when the retarded child was highly dependent. Fowle (1968) also found that oldest sisters seemed to be more adversely affected by the retarded sibling than oldest brothers. Grossman (1972) found that the effects of exceptional children on siblings was related to age of the siblings and the socioeconomic condition of the family but that about half of the 83 college-age siblings studied had actually profited from the presence of a retarded sibling in the family, in that they seemed more tolerant and compassionate, and more focused in terms of personal and vocational goals than a matched control sample. However, the sample also included siblings who were adversely affected by the presence of a retarded brother or sister and who experienced negative reactions, such as guilt and anger.

The dynamics of a family with an exceptional child were further explored by Farber (1959, 1972), who found that the factors related to the family adjustment included the socioeconomic status and religion of the family, the sex of the retarded child, the amount of support from relatives, the extent of community participation, and the size of the family. Thus the birth of a handicapped child appears to have far-reaching effects upon the family. The complexity of the variables involved suggests a need for a great deal of additional research before the dynamics of the family are fully understood. However, it is clear that parents often need professional help as they try to work through their feelings about their child's disability and strive to provide a loving and supportive atmosphere for their children. How the professionals respond to that need may determine how successfully the parents are able to cope with the responsibility of caring for an exceptional child.

PARENTS AND PROFESSIONALS

During the course of treatment and education of their exceptional child, the parent comes into contact with a variety of professionals.

They range from the physician who makes the original diagnosis to the speech, occupational or physical therapist who engages in habilitative work with the child, and the teacher who may have him in his classroom. Psychologists, social workers, nurses, psychiatrists, and school administrators may enter the case at one time or other. With all these professions involved, one might think that the parents are well served, yet the very proliferation of specialists may complicate rather than clarify the issue. (Ross, 1964, p. 74)

How the parent interacts with these individual professionals and with the team itself has important implications for the care of the child. Yet often the relationships are less helpful than might be expected, and both the professional and the parent emerge from the interaction frustrated and disillusioned. It may be useful to examine some of the elements in parent-professional interaction that can lead to difficulties and to discuss how such problems might be avoided or alleviated.

Barriers to Interaction

As Wright (1960) has pointed out, both parents and professionals come together with certain attitudes that interfere with the development of good parent-professional relationships. Some of the attitudes that inhibit communication between parents and professionals may need to be changed if they are to work cooperatively in the child's treatment. More and more, the parent is expected to assume a major responsibility in the child's program and to be an active participant in the planning and decision-making process. P. L. 94–142 calls for the formal involvement of the parents in the educational planning for exceptional children. Yet there are still many barriers to effective communication between parents of exceptional children and the professionals who are caring for their children.

Parental Barriers

Among the barriers to parent-professional interaction presented by parents are the defenses against anxiety that were described earlier in this chapter. The parent who is continuing to *deny* the child's handicap or the extent of the limitations imposed by the disability will be threatened by the attempts of the teacher or physician to deal realistically with the child's condition. *Projection* may involve blaming the professional for the child's condition or for failing to provide what the parents regard as appropriate treatment. *Reaction formation* or *undoing* may lead the parent to reject the help of the professional and to attempt to carry out the child's program singlehandedly.

In addition, the parent may have some strong feelings about the role of the professional with the child that interfere with a cooperative relationship. For example, the parent may be *afraid* of the professionals who are working with the child or feel that the professional will *blame* them for the child's condition. There are often socioeconomic and status differences between the parent and the professional that add to the parent's sense of inferiority and inadequacy in interactions with the physician or teacher. Their own lingering *guilt* about the child's condition may contribute to the parents' discomfort in communicating with professionals. In some cases, the parent may show a hostility that seems to be based in *jealousy* of the professional's relationship with the child. If the child has become particularly attached to a favorite teacher and constantly chatters about this paragon to the parents, they may begin to feel that the teacher is usurping their role and their relationship with the child.

Some parents are cooperative and eager to help but develop an excessive dependence on the professional that leads to unrealistic demands for time and attention. In such cases the parent may constantly call or write the teacher or pediatrician for advice about each new development. Such demands may eventually "turn-off" the professional so that the parent no longer receives even an average degree of attention. The parent may also approach the professional with unrealistic expectations about the child's prognosis and what the professional is going to accomplish. Failure of the teacher to produce the results the parent had counted on then leads to disappointment and resentment. In contrast, the overprotective parent may feel the professional is pushing the child too hard and expecting more of the child than is reasonable.

At times the parents' difficulty in relating to the professionals involved with the child may reflect the parents' attitudes to the child himself. The rejecting parent who neglects or abuses the child, psychologically or physically, may be defensive and hostile in interactions with professionals, fearing that the abuse will be uncovered and lead to punishment.

Professional Barriers

It is important for professionals to keep in mind that they, too, may have interfering attitudes that prevent good communication with the families of the children they are serving. While some of the barriers between parents and professionals have been breaking down in recent years, there are still many ways that professionals can improve their interactions with family members.

According to Wright (1960), one of the attitudes of professionals which may interfere with a constructive relationship with parents is the idea that *"the trouble with children is their parents."* She explains:

> This attitude in professional circles is more common and more resistant to change than we like to think, for it rests upon many supporting experiences of an emotional as well as rational nature. To begin with, there is the resentment against one's own parents which the rehabilitation worker, like other adults, may feel. The rehabilitation worker

has added proof in his own practice of the lack of wisdom of some, if not many, parents when they fail to carry through the recommended plan or openly defy it. Moreover, he has the edict of the theorists who have laid on the parental doorstep the tremendous responsibility for maladjustments in children. (p. 290)

For some professionals, this attitude is related to an identification with the child and the child's needs and a consequent rejection of the parents and their importance in the child's life. Thus the teacher may complain, "Johnny would make good progress if his parents would stop interfering and leave him alone." The teacher may proclaim that the parents are too overprotective or, conversely, that they fail to follow through with the program that has been established. In either case, the implication is that the child is the teacher's responsibility and the parents are "outsiders" to the treatment process.

Related to this attitude are the problems arising from the professional identity of the teacher or physician or psychologist. The perception of oneself as an "expert" on the problems presented by the child may lead to the idea that one has the answers to those problems. While the professional may recognize the contributions of other professionals on the team to the improvements in the child's condition, the parents may not be viewed as full participants in the team approach. They may be regarded primarily as sources of information in the assessment process, not as equals in the decision-making process. In a study of activities that educational-planning-team members thought parents should participate in during team meetings, Yoshida, Fenton, Kaufman, and Maxwell (1978) conclude, "in short, parents are expected to provide information to the planning team, but they are not expected to participate actively in making decisions about their child's program" (p. 532).

Professional jargon is another indication of the failure to involve the parent in the child's program and to include them in the planning process. Dembinski and Mauser (1977) found that one of the major recommendations that parents of learning disabled children have for educators, psychologists, and physicians is to "use terminology we can understand" (p. 582). The authors conclude that training programs for these professionals must include specific skills on interacting with parents of learning disabled children" (p. 584). Bitter (1976) has emphasized that professionals working with deaf children should use language that parents understand and should help them to interpret the terminology and reports of professionals. Gorham (1975) makes a similar point in her advice to professionals working with exceptional children.

Write your reports in clear and understandable language. Professional terminology is a useful shortcut for your own notes, and you can always use it to communicate with others of your discipline. But in situations involving the parent, it becomes an obstacle to understanding . . . . Information that he does not understand is not useful to him. The goal is a parent who understands his child well enough to help him handle his problems. (p. 523)

PARENTS OF EXCEPTIONAL CHILDREN AND THE TEAM

According to P. L. 94–142 and earlier legislation and court decisions, parents have the right to due process in the evaluation and placement of their exceptional children and in the planning of an appropriate educational program for them. Yet the actual role of the parents in these activities is somewhat vague and ambiguous, and the extent of their involvement in the development of an appropriate program for their child varies from state to state and in some cases from school to school. Yoshida, Fenton, Kaufman, and Maxwell (1978) found that of 24 activities of the school planning team only 2 activities were seen as appropriate for parental participation by more than 50 percent of the planning team members. The 2 activities were "present information relevant to the case" and "gather information relevant to the case." These findings suggest that parents may not be encouraged by team members to participate actively in the decision-making activities of the team, even though such seems to be the intent of legislative and court guidelines. Furthermore, a study by Hoff, Fenton, Yoshida, and Kaufman (1978) suggests that even when parents are present at the planning team meeting, they may not actively participate in the decision making or even understand the decisions made. Only 50 percent of the parents studied were able to describe accurately the placement decision reached; their reports of the other components of the decision made (eligibility, goals, and review date) were even more inaccurate. The authors suggest that parental participation in the planning team meetings alone may not be sufficient to ensure that parents understand the special education planning and placement decisions and that they are really giving *informed* consent to those decisions.

Losen and Diament (1978) suggest that parents will need to become active in their child's planning team's meetings *before* the placement decision is reached. They also recommend that the number of staff members in the meeting be limited so as not to overwhelm the parents and that during the conference discussion be limited to specific objectives identified in advance. Swick, Flake-Hobson, and Raymond (1980) and Seligman (1979) give other specific suggestions for conducting conferences between teachers and parents of exceptional children.

Teams working with exceptional children sometimes have difficulty in adjusting to team meetings in which parents are expected to be active participants in decision-making activities and not merely sources of information. The discomfort of the professionals in these circumstances may lead to "mini-meetings'' before the team meeting or to team meetings in which members are so inhibited by the presence of the parents that they cannot openly discuss the problems of the child. Yet honesty and openness from the professionals with whom they come in contact are often what parents ask for and need. The barriers to communication between professionals and parents that we described earlier do not disappear when the professionals band together in an interdisciplinary team. Indeed, the team may simply become a more formidable and impersonal ''professional'' with whom the parent must interact. It may take a concerted effort on the part of the team members, individually and together, to help the parent become an active participant in the team and a partner in the treatment and educational process.

Chapter 8

Improving Team Performance

Throughout this book we have been concerned with those factors that affect the performance of an interdisciplinary team and the services it provides. In previous chapters we have also examined some of the processes in which teams engage and how these may affect outcomes of the team. In this chapter we will review several aspects of the team system that have impact upon team performance and suggest some methods that might be used for improving the way in which teams function. In addition, we will examine team evaluation research as a means of improving our understanding of teams.

Two major functions of the team, task-related activities and team-maintenance activities, have been identified and explored. These two functions are obviously related, since time and energy devoted to one is then not available for the other. To the extent that the team must spend time and energy in organizing itself to complete the task and in dealing with interpersonal relationships, there will be a loss in efficiency, referred to as *process loss* (Steiner, 1972). According to Steiner, this loss is the difference between the *potential productivity* of the group (given the demands of the task and the resources of the group) and its *actual* productivity. Thus, in some ways interaction may hinder the performance of the task.

On the other hand, according to Hackman and Morris (1975), there are also some potential *process gains* as a result of group interaction. Although these gains sometimes go unrecognized, they make it possible for the group to achieve a more effective outcome than might have been anticipated from knowledge about individual members. For example, group interaction may increase the amount of effort members are willing to expend, increase the total pool of knowledge available, and help the group develop strategies for carrying out the task. Thus, by working cooperatively, group members may arrive at solutions that are better than the sum of the members' independent efforts. This, of course, is one reason for using the team approach.

The extent of both process loss and process gains (i.e., the actual effectiveness of the group) will be determined by a number of factors. As Steiner (1972) indicates, the productivity of the group depends on the demands of the task, the resources available to the group, and the process of the group. We have discussed how increasing the size and the heterogeneity of a team may increase the resources available. But, at the same time, by increasing the complexity of the interpersonal interactions, process loss may also be increased. Let us examine some other factors that may affect team effectiveness.

PROFESSIONS

Professionalization can present a number of barriers to the development of the team. The professional has been educated to act as an autonomous individual, and the team as a system takes from the professional some degree of autonomy. This can be a barrier to team effectiveness. Linked to *autonomy* is the notion of *specialization,* which in effect supports the impetus to act alone without reference to others.

In order to deal with the questions of professional autonomy and specialization, it is necessary first to discover how both factors are perceived by team members. The boundaries of professional responsibility are not clearcut, and perhaps some team time should be spent on the question: Where does my ability to decide autonomously what treatment will be accorded to a child start and end? For example, if a teacher continually ignored the school administrator's suggestions concerning actions, there would certainly be a need for these two professionals to address their differences.

Often this type of question can be confronted at a team meeting designed to deal with the question of professional responsibilities and prerogatives. Such an agenda may do much to clear the air concerning who does what and who decides who does what. However, care must be taken in structuring such meetings so that they do not become just another battleground for interprofessional conflict. At times it is helpful to develop subgroups within the team to tackle the question of how two or more professions can work together in everyone's best interests. This process may be mediated by a third person, one who understands the professions involved and has no personal axe to grind. Such mini-consultations can focus on various groupings of individuals and professionals without involving all the team at once. Often such an approach seems less threatening to those involved if the need for such meetings is first discussed in a general way with the total team.

Topics that might be discussed include but are not limited to professional autonomy, specialization, division of labor, delegation of authority and responsibility, the knowledge base of the various professions, and professional stereotypes. If such a discussion is treated as a *routine exercise* in improving team function, with the assumption that no one of the professions adequately understands the skills and competencies of another, much will be done to dispel the common concern among professionals that they really should know what another profession can contribute but would be embarrassed to ask, or the common misconception that they really do know the abilities and skills of the other profession when in point of fact they do not.

Let us consider at this point some specific techniques for teams to use in improving their team performance.

One useful exercise concerning professional roles and stereotypes can be developed using the Interprofessional Perception Scale (IPS), described in Appendix A. Since the instrument is essentially based on "how I see you, how I think you see yourself, and how I think that you think I see you," it can be an excellent takeoff point for discussing a number of areas of interprofessional interaction. Subjects such as ethics, competence, status, autonomy, and interprofessional understanding are addressed. Of course, care should be taken to explain the purpose of using the IPS and also the differences in perception that are uncovered. Sometimes it is best to have individuals complete the IPS anonymously and tabulate the results in the same way, using group data to stimulate discussion. At other times it is best to use data from more general populations, thus depersonalizing the responses and thereby reducing to some extent the threat to those present.

Another aspect of professionalization that sometimes creates a barrier to effective team operation is the question of *ethical standards*. The various human services professions differ considerably in the content of their professional codes of ethics. To a large extent the differences may be the result of professional territoriality. Such differences make it difficult to generalize from one code to another. Some codes of ethics ignore the team as an approach to patient care. This is especially true on the subject of sharing information. If observed to the letter, some professional codes of ethics in effect preclude some professionals from participating in teams. Some codes also fail to provide clearcut standards governing the activities of nonprofessionals on the team (Golin & Ducanis, 1977).

It would seem appropriate that the various professional organizations that promulgate codes of ethics convene to discuss the effects of those codes on the interdisciplinary approach. Until that happens, however, it will be necessary for individual team members to interpret their codes to other team members so that there will be mutual understanding of the constraints such standards impose. Since some professions have more highly developed codes of ethics than others, it would seem appropriate that the former use their knowledge to help the latter refine and develop their own codes.

A related problem is that of differential *legal responsibility* for the client. Briefly, it is necessary for the various professionals on a team to ascertain their individual and joint legal responsibilities. It should be remembered that the team approach does not necessarily abrogate individual responsibility. Such clarification may do much to improve relationships between team members when decisions must be made and responsibility for performance fixed.

A highly sensitive area of interprofessional relationships is *status*. An individual's status is often determined to a large extent by her or his profession. Status influences communications, decision making, and the overall operation of the team. It is generally best to recognize professional hierarchies openly and to discuss their possible impact on team functioning; this does much to mitigate their negative influences over a period of time.

One negative influence is often found in the area of communication: those more junior on the status scale tend to defer to others of higher status even when they have better and more accurate information concerning the problem at hand. One way to alleviate this problem is to establish clear protocols of operation that reward participation in information giving and decision making.

Interprofessional differences are sometimes amplified by the use of professional *jargon*. If team members are speaking different languages, communication will certainly be hindered. Once the problem is recognized, team members can take pains to explain the technical terms they use, checking with other team members to be sure meaning is communicated clearly. Unfortunately, professional jargon is sometimes used as a symbol of status and expertise, and some professionals hesitate to explain their jargon, as though sharing it implied a loss of their unique skills and knowledge. This attitude is often seen in the interaction of professionals and nonprofessionals on the team. Too often the professional conveys a sense of "You really can't understand what I am saying because you don't have sufficient training to comprehend these professional concepts." This does little to encourage effective sharing of information.

There are, of course, other factors that can enhance or hinder communication within the team, and several of these were discussed in Chapter 6. A team that is interested in improving its communication patterns may want to address these questions:

- What are the formal and informal channels of communication in this team? Is the communication network one that adequately serves the needs of the team?

- Is sufficient time available to team members for adequate communication? Do physical arrangements enhance communication?

- Do the present record-keeping systems enhance communication?

As long as the interdisciplinary team is composed of persons rather than machines or computers, there will be conflicts among team members. An appropriate team goal, then, is not to eliminate conflict but to minimize its negative effects.

Conflict Management

A number of the conflict management techniques described in the literature (Blake, Shepard & Morton, 1964; Burke, 1969; Robbins, 1974; Vogt & Ducanis, 1977) are applicable to team conflict situations.

The initial reaction to interpersonal conflict is often to *smooth over* differences and avoid any overt disagreements. This is seldom an adequate solution to the problem. While there may be some temporary relief, it is likely that the conflict will emerge again, perhaps in a more virulent form.

Another approach often employed in dealing with team conflict is *compromise and bargaining*. Unfortunately, this may result in outcomes that satisfy neither party, so resentments continue. An *authoritarian* approach, whereby the team leader enforces a resolution to the conflict, may also do nothing to quell resentments. A more promising approach is to use *problem solving* to reach a rational solution that is satisfactory to all parties. The particular problem-solving techniques used will vary with the nature and extent of the conflict but generally will involve: (a) identifying the conflict (problem identification), (b) exploring solutions, (c) trying out one of the solutions, and (d) evaluating the solution.

Reducing Role Conflict

A common source of conflict among team members involves ambiguous and overlapping roles. This issue has been addressed at several points in this book because it is such a pervasive problem for interdisciplinary teams.

In part, role ambiguity and role confusion arise because team members are filling several different *kinds* of roles simultaneously. These include:

- *personal roles*—based on individual attributes, such as personality factors
- *professional roles*—based on professional competencies
- *team roles*—based on team interaction and including such roles as leader, follower, mediator, etc.

Team members may respond to any of these multiple roles, and, while there may be some correlation between roles (for example, personal roles are often related to team roles), sometimes this is not the case.

The greatest problems for the interdiscplinary team seem to come from the conflicts around professional roles resulting from overlapping responsibilities and competencies. The following steps provide a framework for addressing issues of role conflict.

1. *Clarify role perceptions and expectations.* This can be done through open discussion or by writing statements anonymously on 3'' x 5'' cards which are later read to the group. In either case, each team member should indicate his or her perceptions of the role of each other member.

2. *Identify professional competencies.* Now members have an opportunity to indicate their competencies and explain more fully what their professional responsibilities entail. Often it is difficult for team members to ask each other about their skills or knowledge. This step provides a mechanism for eliciting such information without acknowledging ignorance.

3. *Examine overlapping roles.* Base the discussion on information provided in Step 1 and Step 2.

4. *Renegotiate role assignments.* Negotiation is much easier once there is a better understanding of other members' expectations and competencies.

GOAL DEFINITION AND GOAL CONFLICTS

In Chapter 5, we indicated the need to define team goals clearly and to identify goal conflicts that may potentially disrupt the team. Team members need to ask:

- Are team goals and objectives adequately defined?

- Is there a consensus among team members regarding priorities for the team?

These questions are relevant not only for new teams in their early stages of development but also for teams that have been in existence for some time.

The newly formed team may experience the greatest difficulty with defining goals, since initial goal statements are often rather vague and fuzzy. A goal definition exercise of some kind can help sort out the perceptions of various team members regarding goals and indicate the directions in which the team sees itself moving.

The team that is already functioning may experience some difficulty in the area of goal conflict. Team members may unknowingly hold quite different notions of some of the team goals, and this may lead to repeated disagreements regarding appropriate courses of action to be taken by the team. Again, a goal definition exercise can help identify hidden conflicts in team goals and provide a basis for negotiating and redefining those goals.

Goal Definition Exercise

The following exercise is one the authors have found useful with both newly formed and existing teams. By comparing the goal perceptions of various members, the team can identify and discuss areas of consensus and disagreement and determine priorities. The exercise has two phases and involves the following steps:

Phase One

1. Each team member is asked to write out briefly *three* major goals of the team. Each goal statement is written on a separate 3'' × 5'' card. Participants do not sign their names to the goal cards.
2. The goal cards are collected by the team leader or a designated person (who need not be a team member), shuffled to ensure a random order, and numbered. Then, *each card is read to the group*.
3. In this first ''run-through'' of the goal cards, the participants are asked to sort each statement into one of four categories: long-term task, long-term maintenance, short-term task, and short-term maintenance. This 2 × 2 matrix is shown in Figure 8-1.

At this step of the exercise, discussion is directed only at clarifying the goal statements and reaching consensus on whether the goal is primarily long- or short-term and task or maintenance related. Team members should not evaluate the goals at this point or worry about goal priorities or goal conflicts. The first phase of the exercise has revealed the pattern of goals as viewed by the team.

Figure 8-1 Goal Definition Matrix

	TASK	MAINTENANCE
LONG-TERM		
SHORT-TERM		

Whether or not the pattern that emerged is what the team expected is a question that should be discussed.

Phase Two

4. Team members are given a list of all the goal statements in each of the four categories. The team now has an opportunity to correct any errors in the initial sorting.
5. Taking one category at a time, the team is asked to review each statement in the category and eliminate any redundant statements or incorporate them into similar statements. Since there are likely to be a number of duplicate statements, this step should yield four considerably shorter lists.
6. The team is now ready to establish priorities by arranging the remaining goal statements in order of importance. Although this can be done numerically (by combining the rank order given to each goal by each participant), it is preferable to arrive at a team consensus through discussion.

This goal-setting exercise provides a structured way for the team to share perceptions about goals and priorities. Goal conflicts quickly come out into the open and can at least be discussed, if not resolved. The specific steps of the role negotiation and goal exercises are less important than their use as mechanisms for the process of team interaction and consensus. Other techniques that might be used include:

• Information sharing in groups and between individuals

• Mediated small group information sessions

• General information sessions

Each of these techniques should be used in a planned, orderly fashion that precludes the notion that "something is wrong." Indeed, there should be openly stated that, to improve the performance of any team, it is necessary to address a number of operational factors on a regular basis. If this attitude is accepted by team members, team development becomes a normal and effective *process* rather than a crisis or confrontational *event*.

In summary, to enhance its operations the team should attend to several areas related to professionalization:

• autonomy

• specialization

• division of tasks

- ethics

- delegation of authority

- knowledge base and overlaps

- roles and stereotypes

- legal responsibilities

- status

The more general problem of how to educate the professional for interdisciplinary team work is the subject of the following section.

EDUCATING THE PROFESSIONAL

If interdisciplinary teams are to function at an optimal level, professionals need to be trained or educated to function as part of a team. Of course, in order to function effectively as a team member, each professional must first be competent in his or her particular area of expertise. Training and practice in the field of specialization are necessary before an individual can make a major contribution to any team effort.

Once individuals are competent in their own professions, they must then develop competence in teamwork. For example, as Senator Edward Kennedy said, in pointing out the need for professionals to work with a team under the provisions of P.L. 94–142:

> The handicapped child receives a comprehensive assessment that includes information from teachers, parents, and other specialists such as physicians, psychologists, speech therapists, arts educators, occupational therapists, and social workers. Their cooperation is mandated, but even more important, it is a potential catalyst for creativity. (Kennedy, 1978, p. 7)

Other authors (Brown & Reece, 1978; Elmer et al., 1978; Martin, 1978; Reynolds, 1978; Stainback, Stainback, & Maurer, 1976) have pointed to the need to prepare teachers and other professionals for roles as team members.

This quotation demonstrates that the concept of educating for the team delivery of services is needed. Recognition of the concept has not always led to the development of such educational programs, however.

In recent years professionals in many of the human service professions have shown increased interest in developing the means to improve the interdisciplinary team through education. A variety of specialties, including mental health, alcohol and drug abuse, rehabilitation, and special education, have espoused the concept of interdisciplinary education for teams. However, before exploring this concept further, let us examine briefly the need for understanding the competencies of other professions and some of the goals of team education.

Goals of Team Education

The unique professional contribution of each team member is a major strength of the team approach. On the other hand, professionalization may at times be dysfunctional to the team effort in so far as it can lead to interprofessional conflict and misunderstanding.

Since most professionals are educated in a professionally segregated setting, there is usually little opportunity to understand the competencies of others. For adequate team functioning, team members should be familiar with other professions in order to best utilize coworkers' skills.

While most professional education is aimed at developing an individual who can function autonomously and independently within an area of competence, team education seeks to develop one's ability to function interdependently with other professionals, using one's own skills and those of others in an optimum way. Education for teamwork is part of what has been termed interdisciplinary education. Szasz (1970) lists some objectives for the interdisciplinary team, including an increased awareness of the need for a comprehensive approach; an understanding of the "attitudes, values and methods" of other professionals, as well as their skills; and the ability to use group dynamics in organizational relations.

Heilman (1977) reviewed the literature and conducted a number of interviews with experts in the field in order to identify the competencies needed by health care personnel to function as a health care team. This list of competencies was refined and reduced to 51 statements with relatively little overlap. These competencies were then rated by 20 experts from "of highest importance" to "of little importance or significance" for teamwork. Heilman concludes:

> First priority among the 51 competencies was given to the need for a recognized leader for the team; the leader was not to be predetermined, but was to be selected by the group according to the task at hand. The ability of team members to handle conflicting personalities and divergent ideas was also given high importance. The health professional's perception of his own role, his security and self-confidence, were listed in the upper third [in importance]. Likewise, each one's understanding of the roles of other team members, of the differences in each one's perception of his role, and of the expertise possessed by each

discipline on the team must be present if the team is to proceed harmoniously. (p. 81)

Heilman discusses the need to develop training programs "to assure the acquisition and use of the teaming competencies, with systematic plans for developing the [highest rated] competencies," the importance of orienting faculty to a team approach to health care, and the "demand on administrators and organizations to plan for the initiation of the team approach" (Heilman, 1977, p. 82).

Models of Team Education

Now that we have examined the need for interdisciplinary team education and some of its goals, let us look at some of the ways an education program dealing with teamwork might be provided. A variety of approaches can be envisioned, most of them variations of the same three models: preprofessional training, continuing education, and team development. *Preprofessional training* includes courses and programs in interdisciplinary teams designed for students as part of their professional training program. *Continuing education* programs include workshops and seminars in addition to formal coursework offered to professionals on an individual or group basis. *Team development* usually involves the use of consultants (either from within or from outside the agency) who work with an organization in order to initiate a new team or improve the operation of an existing team. Team development focuses on a specific team and helps the group analyze its functioning and make appropriate modifications in its operations.

Preprofessional Team Education

According to a survey conducted by the authors, a large proportion of the administrators of professional schools believe that educational preparation for teamwork is important, but most professional schools are not presently offering such coursework. Many advocates of team education believe the appropriate time for such training is during the period of basic professional preparation. This is a traditional approach that has often been used when innovations in professional practice suggest that an important content area or particular skill that is needed by the professional in the field is not being provided in the curriculum.

There are three elements of interdisciplinary team education at the preprofessional level:

1. cognitive (primarily didactic) information—including organizational theory, small group dynamics, and the sociology of the professions

2. affective (and experiential) learning—by participating in a team, the students learn through experiences how a team operates, how roles are established, how leadership emerges, etc.
3. clinical training—by participating as part of a team in assessment, and similar activities with the client, the student not only learns necessary clinical skills but also learns how to use those skills in conjunction with other professionals. These skills may vary not only with profession (e.g., special education, nursing, counseling) but also with the type of situation in which the student is placed (a special classroom, a neighborhood clinic, a hospital, etc.).

For several years the authors have conducted a course in The Division of Interdisciplinary Programs of the School of the Health Related Professions, University of Pittsburgh, for special educators and health professionals. The course considers the variables that influence the team, such as professional roles, organizational settings, group dynamics, communication, and legal, social, and financial factors. Students are expected to:

- demonstrate the ability to identify competencies and use other professionals in an interdisciplinary team.

- describe the impact of various organizational settings on team functioning.

- analyze and evaluate the influence of team dynamics and of various subcultural factors (such as professional roles and status) on the functions of an interdisciplinary team.

- evaluate various models for educating team members in the function of teams and team development.

- analyze and evaluate models of team decision making.

- demonstrate the ability to communicate effectively with other team members (including patients, professionals, and paraprofessionals) and to function in appropriate roles within the team.

The course includes didactic work (principally lecture/discussion of pertinent research) and an experiential component in which each student is assigned to a team within the class. The student teams are then required to develop unified reports on an operational team located in a facility within the region. This seems to be an economical means of having the students experience some of the opportunities and frustrations of teamwork. The teams are asked to develop reports on the basis of direct observations of the team they have chosen, along with interviews of various team members. Teams that have been studied have ranged from a residential school for the visually handicapped to an emergency medical rescue unit. Students in the course have come from 15 different professions.

Evaluation of the course has indicated that the participants feel the project is rewarding but frustrating in that they must work together to achieve the goals of the course (50 percent of the grade is based on the project). The instructors unobtrusively but systematically observe the teams and intervene only when a high-conflict situation arises. The final examination covers the didactic work and includes an item asking the participants to analyze the development of their team. Answers to this item have indicated that almost all of the participants were able to use the principles taught in the course to better perceive the dynamics of their particular team (Golin & Ducanis, in press).

There are a number of barriers that have to be overcome before effective preprofessional interdisciplinary education programs can be designed. The *institutional barriers* may be administrative, academic, logistic (time, cost), and attitudinal. *Individual barriers* include those associated with the acculturation of the individual to the profession, one professional's perception of another, and the trainee's background (socioeconomic status, level of training, and goals).

There may be a number of administrative problems in negotiating and managing an interdisciplinary program involving several professional schools. Not only may the schools have different ideas of what should be taught, but they may even teach at different times. Often professional schools are on schedules of varying lengths, so it is difficult to accommodate students from several different schools.

The question of *what* to teach and *how* to teach it are equally important. The faculty must decide whether the team education component will focus on cognitive aspects (through didactic material), affective aspects (with an experiential component), or both. Will the program take place in an academic or clinical setting? Faculty may be divided on how the program should be implemented, and the schools involved may have conflicting values on this issue. Although a program may ideally provide all components simultaneously, it may be difficult for the students to benefit from this approach. It may be that learning the theoretical basis for teamwork, in addition to learning how to interact with clients and with other professional team members, is so overwhelming that the student actually retains very little. Furthermore, most students are engaged in other coursework at the same time and may feel overloaded and not able to commit sufficient energy to the program.

Team education is often introduced as part of an existing course or as a new course. If the coursework is felt to be sufficiently significant, the new area becomes part of the required "core" of professional training in that discipline. This means either expanding the requirements of the professional program or eliminating another area that was previously required. Since programs cannot continually add requirements, eventually the addition of new areas means the elimination of old requirements.

The new area may also be competing with other innovative areas in the field as well as with existing curricular requirements. Thus attempts to modify the curricula of professional schools often lead to a serious examination of priorities within the program. "We just can't teach them everything they need to know" is a frequent lament heard in curriculum committees.

What *is* taught may at times be based primarily on political considerations within the school or be included because of pressures exerted by professional organizations or clinicians in the field. Particularly in periods of rapid change there is likely to be some confusion regarding which innovations are "fads" and which are likely to become a permanent part of the repertoire of professional behaviors. For example, when behavior modification was first introduced into professional practice, many psychologists, counselors, and teachers saw it as just another fad. At the present time, however, some knowledge of behavior modification is generally required in professional preparation programs. More and more professional schools seem to be taking the position that the interdisciplinary team approach is a genuine innovation and not just another professional fad.

The faculty involved in planning and implementing an interdisciplinary team program may experience many of the same problems in working together as do the members of a direct service team. They, too, must work together as a team, negotiate, and learn to understand each other's roles and capabilities. At the same time, the primary responsibilities of these faculty members rest in their own professional school. Thus, despite a striking commitment often found in those involved in team education, the realities of their position and limited time and energy may severely restrict what can actually be done.

Finally, a serious problem we have noted with preprofessional team training is that new professionals are still unsure of their own developing professional skills and their roles vis-à-vis other professionals. While a number of authors have noted the problems for interdisciplinary teamwork created by early socialization in the profession during preprofessional training (Frank, 1961; Lewis & Resnick, 1966), the other side of this coin is that lack of confidence in one's own professional skills may make it more difficult to interact with other professionals early in the training experience. In our classes, we have found that students who are not yet sure "who they are" professionally sometimes have difficulty interacting with other, more advanced, students in other professions. Erikson contends in his theory of human development (1963) that true intimacy comes only after the individual has developed a secure sense of identity and can "let go" of that identity sufficiently to merge with another. While interdisciplinary team relationships are considerably less intense than the kinds of relationships Erikson had in mind, it may well be that students are not ready to profit fully from an interdisciplinary team experience until they have developed sufficient clinical or professional skills to have some degree of confidence in their identities and abilities. Only then can they truly represent their profession to other members of the team so that all can learn from each other.

At the present time, most team educators seem to support the idea of early interdisciplinary training. The need for interdisciplinary experiences early in professional training was identified by Lewis and Resnick (1966) on the basis of the results of an interdisciplinary clinical elective for medical and nursing students. They found that, contrary to expectations, the objectives of the two groups did not become more similar as a result of the interdisciplinary experience, and the authors attributed this finding to professional socialization early in the student's training.

Educational institutions must decide what priority will be placed on interdisciplinary teamwork in the professional curriculum. Once the decision is made, the institutional and individual barriers to the development of adequate approaches may be addressed. Thus far, although a number of professionals support the concept, there have been significantly few who have been able to initiate and maintain programs.

Continuing Education

Continuing education and inservice programs are a means of upgrading professional skills and imparting knowledge of current research and innovative techniques to practicing professionals in a wide variety of fields. It reaches those who did not receive training in teamwork during their preprofessional education and gives further training to those who did. A major advantage of continuing education programs is that the practicing professional who sees the need for additional skills in a particular area is highly motivated to learn.

While many educators fear that the established professional may lack sufficient role flexibility for effective teamwork, it is also possible that the professional's knowledge of and confidence in his or her own role (as well as the roles of other professionals) may prove to be an advantage in a team education program.

It seems apparent, however, that if professionals are to be adequately educated for effective team interaction, both preprofessional and continuing educational programs are needed.

One example of a continuing education program is the one-day workshops designed by the authors to address the team-related problems of the participants. Specifically, workshop goals invite the participants to:

- examine the rationale, concepts, and basic principles of the interdisciplinary team

- explore barriers to satisfactory team performance

- develop methods for improving team effectiveness.

In addition to lecture/discussion of the team system, the participants are asked to provide a set of critical incidents they have observed that illustrate ineffective team performance. These incidents are then discussed and categorized. For example, at one workshop the critical incidents yielded the following distribution of common barriers to team effectiveness.

Organizational structure	23.4%
Goal conflict	14.8%
Interpersonal and interprofessional conflict	26.3%
Communication	35.5%

Further discussion then points up the need for role negotiation and better attention to communication patterns. The impingement of organizational structure on team operations and some approaches to conflict management are also discussed.

Evaluation of the workshops indicated that the participants thought the workshops were for the most part useful in helping them understand their teams and making them aware of the ways to improve team performance.

The continuing education approach holds a great deal of promise in that it can reach those practitioners who are most concerned with improving the effectiveness of team operation. It may also be less expensive than alternative approaches.

One problem is the question of impact or effectiveness in the actual improvement of team performance. Most continuing education programs tend to be of short duration—one to three days. They bring together persons from a number of agencies or schools, deal with a specific topic, and send the participants back to work. The assumption, of course, is that the individual will be able to apply what has been learned to the work situation. Unfortunately, there is little followup on this point.

Team Development

According to Woodman and Sherwood (1980): "Although there is general support for the finding that team building elicits positive affective responses from participants, the linkage between team building and improved work group performance remains largely unsubstantiated" (p. 166).

Team development focuses on the group processes of the team, helping members look at the goals, norms, tasks, decision making, etc., of the team, with periodic "checkups" to ensure that the team is functioning effectively. Although some of the training (in leadership skills, for example) can be conducted during individual professional preparation, Rubin and Beckhard (1972) say that "some training needs to be done with the team as a unit" (p. 333). Furthermore, since older teams may be less flexible, they also suggest that perhaps team development should take place as early as possible after the formation of a team.

There is much to be said about the advantages and disadvantages of the team development approach. Among the principle advantages is that the work can be directed to the specific problems of a team, giving little or no emphasis to areas of team operation that are working smoothly. Secondly, the persons who participate in team development are able to increase their awareness of how their own team and teams in general function.

One disadvantage is that this approach may be costly in time and money without yielding much apparent improvement in the way team tasks are addressed and completed. If outside consultants are asked to aid in team development, it is imperative that sufficient time be taken to evaluate what the team actually needs and that those needs be addressed in a nondestructive manner. For instance, one workshop participant told the story of a team that was functioning fairly well until a consultant was called in to improve their operation. "He came in and in just one day took us apart. We never did get together again in the two years I was at the agency." Talented consultants should at the very least do no harm, but inept consultants may create or exacerbate problems that will remain long after they are gone.

One of the most striking aspects of professional education is that we are presently training people for roles they will continue to fill 20 or 30 years from now. Not only must we make educated guesses about the skills and competencies that will be needed by professionals in the future, but we must also develop in our students a flexibility that will allow them to shift roles and responsibilities as conditions in their fields change.

Since it seems that the interdisciplinary team will continue to be an important aspect of educating exceptional children in the coming years, it is likely that preprofessional preparation for teamwork will become more common and that there will also be a growing need for expanded programs of continuing education and team development.

In addition, improving team performance requires that the organization in which the team functions be examined and, if necessary, reformulated. In the following section are some of the questions that should be asked.

ORGANIZATIONS

Organizations differ in detail but are similar in general characteristics. As has been pointed out, the pervasive organizational pattern in the Western world is bureaucratic. Given this type of structure, the impact of the organization upon team functions begins to take on more meaning and greater clarity. The interface between the organization and the team makes it necessary to attend to those aspects of the interaction that may be dysfunctional. Goals and objectives, power and authority, process and procedures, and rewards and sanctions are among those aspects that have influence upon team operations. As discussed in Chapter

4, the individual organization setting has much to do with the way the team is organized and functions.

The major question to be faced by any organization that espouses team principles for the delivery of human services is *commitment*. Is the organization willing to alter itself in such a way as to nurture and enhance the team function? If not, then the parent organization, if it is typically bureaucratic, will constantly be at odds with the team or teams within it. This is because the organization is built up along the same divisions of labor as the professions. It tends to emphasize and reinforce the divisions between disciplines and to restrict communication along hierarchical lines. Rewards and sanctions tend to be delivered through the same channels and for the same reasons. Teams, on the other hand, tend to be structured so as to emphasize the sharing of knowledge and communication across disciplines. Suffice it to say that any organization that seriously contemplates the development of effective teams must answer the following questions:

- Are the goals and objectives of the organization as a whole adequately communicated to the team structure? Are they understood?

- Are the goals and objectives of the team and the organization shared?

If the team does not share the goals of the parent organization, some accommodation must be reached. Either the goals are not appropriate or the team has not been integrated into the organizational structure.

- How is team membership defined?

- How appropriate are the roles assigned by the organization?

- How ambiguous are the roles? How is this ambiguity resolved within the organizational structure?

One of the main purposes of organization is to control and direct human behavior. The assignment of tasks and roles and the definition of what constitutes membership are important activities of any organization. The relationship between role definition and activity in a team system is crucial to the functions of the team.

- How is the authority structure of the organization reflected in the team? (Who decides? Who decides who decides?)

It is imperative for adequate team functioning that the authority structure reinforce the activities of the team. Crucial here is the position of the team leader in relation to the organization as a whole. What kinds of decisions can a team leader make? How are they enforced? May they be overruled? Does the team fit the formal authority structure or does the authority of the team evolve from other sources (such as from the individual personal or professional attributes of its members)? For example, if a particular team member is considered to be "the" expert in a particular field, it is likely that a team decision in that area would not be overlooked or overruled by persons who hold normative authority within the organization.

- How is the team integrated into the pattern of communication within the organization?

- How consonant with team organization are the systems of record keeping, storage, and retrieval of information?

- What are the organizational barriers to effective communication from and to teams?

When teams are made up of a number of professionals, each from a separate unit of an organization, it may be that organization-team communication is assumed to occur because of the dual membership. This is not necessarily true. Therefore, an analysis of communication patterns is an important and useful step in improving team and organizational performance.

- How do processes, rules, and procedures fit team operation?

Each organization has some fundamental processes by which it works to fulfill its goals. Such processes may not facilitate team functioning, since they originated when teams did not exist. A careful look at the way organization processes, rules, and procedures enhance or deter team functioning is in order.

- How do the reward/sanction systems relate to the team?

- What are the norms and values of the organization in relation to the team?

Perhaps no other area of organizational function is as important to team success as the system of rewards and sanctions imposed by the organization. If teamwork and team effort are not rewarded in some way, the team system will not function. The expected normative behavior of the individual in the organization and the informal value system also influence the way in which the team functions. These aspects should be critically appraised when attempting team improvement.

- Does the arrangement of space (e.g., offices, conference rooms) enhance or detract from team efficiency?

While it is often overlooked, the spatial arrangement of an organization can do much to either enhance or detract from the effective team operation. Territoriality and space can have a significant bearing on human interaction: proximity generally enhances communication.

- What evaluation procedures are used? How do they relate to the team?

In any organization, evaluation of activities closely reflects what is perceived as being valued and rewarded within the institution. The evaluation procedures must take into account the team system, or the system will of consequence suffer.

While this list of questions is by no means exhaustive, it does provide a starting place for examining how the team interacts with the organization. A careful examination, based on these parameters, may be helpful in uncovering areas where work must be done.

EVALUATION AND RESEARCH

In this section we are concerned with two aspects of the study of teams: evaluation and research. It can be argued that one term subsumes the other. In this instance the division is made on the basis that evaluative studies are concerned with the more short-term goal of direct practical intervention with specific functioning teams, whereas research studies are more concerned with long-term goals of theory building and theory testing. There is indeed some overlap, which in the long run will prove to be a positive influence: as theory is tested in operational settings, both theory and practice are improved.

The Need for Evaluation

A number of parties are concerned with the evaluation of the team approach: the child, the parent, the professional who is a member of a team, the organization in which the team operates, and those who pay for services, whether they are taxpayers or individuals. While we might assume that what is best for the client is best for all concerned, this is not necessarily true, and what may seem to be an unqualified "good" or benefit for one interested group may not be a benefit for others.

For example, saying the goal is the "best" in services is socially acceptable but just not accurate unless qualified by some statement concerning the acceptable *costs* of services. Therefore, it seems reasonable to evaluate those costs in relation to benefit received by the child.

To look at the need for evaluation from the individual *child's* point of view, we probably must make several assumptions. First among these is that the overriding interest is in the benefits that come to the child as a result of the work of the team. We must be careful to separate individual benefits from other social benefits of which the child and parents may approve but which do not reflect directly on the client. For example, since the cost of service is borne only in part by the family, if the team is a more cost effective means of delivering service but delivers that service at less than maximum quality, then the team approach is of dubious benefit. It is also assumed that the value is maintaining or enhancing the quality of life of the child. Another assumption is that there are alternative systems for the delivery of service and that each holds the possibility of greater benefit to the child.

We can also look at the need for evaluation from the point of view of the *professional*. The needs of the professional and the client coincide in some instances and not in others. For example, the professional certainly shares the client's interest in successful treatment (although what constitutes "success" may differ quite a bit for professional and client). However, the "efficient" use of time may be a crucial issue for the professional but much less important to an individual child, even though it benefits all the children served if time is used efficiently. Similarly, if the team functions well in educating its members, there are indirect benefits to all the children, even if the direct benefits to any particular child are not so apparent. The professional's main interest in the evaluation of team effectiveness may be in whether the team operation enhances the professional's ability to provide better service.

From the perspective of the *organization*, evaluation reflects the desire to assess how well the team is meeting broad organizational goals. While it would seem that such interests mesh both with the children's and the families' interests and with professional needs, this may not be the case. The organization may place its main emphasis on how smoothly the team accommodates itself to or fits in with the organizational structure, and its evaluation may take this thrust. The institution may also share with taxpayers and others a common interest in keeping costs down.

What To Evaluate?

There are many aspects of teamwork that can be evaluated: the improvement of the quality of life for the child, the cost effectiveness of the team, or the effectiveness of the team process as an educational medium for team members.

We can return to our general model of the team system shown in Figure 1-1 (Chapter 1) and use this to derive a paradigm for the evaluation of the team approach. Each part of the model is important to the evaluation process. If we can determine the goals of the team and relate these goals to activities and outcomes relative to the needs of the child, the professionals, and the organization, then we will have taken the first step in team evaluation. Thus the initial component becomes the identification of team goals (both task and maintenance goals) and the collection of data related to the achievement of those goals.

Clear statements of goals are vital to the evaluation process. Sometimes even when goal statements *are* available and an attempt is made to measure performance against these published goals, the evaluator is told, "But those goals do not really reflect what we are trying to do." There is a real need for teams to formulate in the most explicit terms possible both task and maintenance goals, and all members of the team should be fully aware of the goals that will be used in the evaluation process.

Once goals have been clearly identified and stated, it is necessary to decide what indicators of goal achievement are to be used. It is important that the indicators be closely related to the real goals, since the evaluation process tends to make people focus on those aspects of their performance for which they will be held accountable. Care must be taken in the selection of output indicators in order that they not become substitutes for the goals themselves.

For example, some years ago the State University of New York based the annual budget for its various academic departments on the number of students enrolled. Data were collected for the fall term of each year and extrapolated for the remainder of the year. Thus departmental budgets were in large part determined by the number of students shown to be attending classes during the fall term. Over time it was noticed that in some cases departments were showing fall term enrollments that were much larger than anticipated. Closer examination showed that the departments in question had moved a higher proportion of their required courses and large lecture sessions to the fall term, thereby maximizing upon the indicator used but not enhancing the real outcome since the total output did not change. Similar instances may be found where an "average daily attendance" or "beds occupied" figure is used as an indicator of productivity for funding purposes.

Questions about Team Evaluation

According to Deming (1975), one of the requirements of an effective evaluation system is a "meaningful operational measure of success or of failure . . . of some proposed treatment applied to specified material, under specified conditions" (p. 56). By "materials" Deming is referring to persons, patients, accounts, products, or "anything else." Of course, the treatment we are interested in evaluating is the use of a team. Keeping Deming's requirement in mind, let us look at some specific questions about team evaluation.

How is team "effectiveness" or "success" to be measured? The criteria of success or effectiveness may encompass a number of elements. For example, team effectiveness might be measured on the basis of improvement in the condition of children, more efficient use of professional time, or expressed satisfaction of team members, administrators, or children. Such measurement may involve the development of objective instruments to measure whatever outcomes are to be examined. It is possible then, that we might develop several different criteria of effectiveness and that these criteria may produce contradictory results. For example, an evaluation of the effectiveness of a particular team may show that services are less expensive, that the professionals on the team find their work more rewarding, and that school administrators feel there is a better allocation of resources when a team approach is initiated. On the other hand, there may be no difference in the child's progress. Whether such findings constitute "success" is a matter to be decided by those who request or initiate the evaluation. The use of appropriate evaluation procedures does not eliminate subjective judgment; it merely ensures that the data upon which judgments are based are as accurate as possible.

Which elements of the team approach lead to more effective outcomes? If the team approach itself is what we are to evaluate, what variables increase or decrease its effectiveness? Undoubtedly, some kinds of teams are more effective than others. What factors make for significant differences in team functioning? What is it about that specific team that is likely to be more successful? Is it the use of case conferences, the record-keeping system, the informal means of communication, the diversity of professional representation, or some other aspect of team functioning? When a team approach is newly implemented, it is often found that some aspects work and others do not. Generally those elements that work are retained, and those that are less successful are dropped (either by design, or through gradual disuse). The task of evaluation is to determine more accurately which elements of the team approach are effective in a particular setting and which should be modified or eliminated. Unfortunately, it is often quite difficult to separate out the effect of various aspects, and the whole team approach may be evaluated negatively simply because of problems with *one* aspect.

With which children is the team approach most effective? This question suggests a need to identify particular problems that are most amenable to a team approach. Often the client's problems extend over a number of areas and must of necessity involve input from a variety of professions. Insofar as the needs of the child define the team's task, we would expect that the team approach will prove more effective with certain populations.

Under what conditions does the team operate most effectively? We have already seen that the context in which the team operates may be an important factor in the team's effectiveness. What administrative support is needed if the team is to be successful? Are teams more successful in certain types of institutional settings or agencies than in others? Do teams function most effectively under particular administrative structures? These types of questions must be addressed in any evaluation project.

Types of Evaluation

The basic purpose of team evaluation is to improve decision making about the program and to provide information for choosing between various courses of action. Should a particular team be continued in its present form, discontinued, or modified? This kind of decision is based on the results of evaluation research. As Weiss (1975) has described it:

> Evaluation research is a rational enterprise. It examines the effects of policies and programs on their targets (individuals, groups, institutions, communities) in terms of the goals they are meant to achieve. By objective and systematic methods, evaluation research assesses the extent to which goals are realized and looks at the factors associated with successful or unsuccessful outcomes. The assumption is that by providing the "facts," evaluation assists decision-makers to make wise choices among future courses of action. Careful and unbiased data on the consequences of the programs should improve decision-making. (p. 13)

How to ensure the collection of such unbiased data is one of the major problems facing the evaluator. It should be noted that successful evaluation often requires the collection of a greal deal of information. As Weinstein (1975) indicates, "while data about individuals served and the services they receive are the heart of the information system, other data must also be available" (p. 398). Among the "other data" Weinstein includes information about facility staff, facility buildings, other resources used by the agency, finances and costs, and the geographic area served.

What procedures are available to help in the collection of data and the evaluation of a particular team operation? Although the methodological aspects of evaluation are not within the scope of this book, we will briefly examine two major approaches to evaluation and also look at some of the roles that seem to be appropriate in the evaluation of team effectiveness. More detailed information on evaluation procedures can be found in Anderson and Ball (1978), and Guttentag and Struening (1975).

Formative and Summative Evaluation

A useful distinction between two types of evaluation, formative and summative, has been made by Scriven (1967). Briefly, formative evaluation is used to help in the formation of a program by providing feedback on various components as the program develops, while summative evaluation assesses the overall effectiveness of a program after it is in operation. Formative evaluation research may include studies designed to pretest materials or measuring instruments, to collect data regarding characteristics of the target population, or to further define the goal of the program (Anderson, Ball, & Murphy, 1975). Formative evaluation is usually an *internal* operation or at least must be carried out in close cooperation with those designing and implementing the new program. Feedback is immediate and is used to modify the program *as it develops*. Results of a summative evaluation may be used to make decisions about modifying or eliminating a program *after the program has been developed and implemented*. Summative evaluation will often indicate intended and unintended positive and negative outcomes (Anderson et al., 1975).

Both types of evaluation are appropriate forms of team research; which type should be used depends on the purpose of the evaluation and whether the team approach has already been implemented or is still in a planning or developmental stage. Formative evaluation may be thought of as a tracking device that provides feedback during the process. It operates like a radar-controlled rocket, which makes midcourse adjustments on the basis of a constant flow of information concerning its direction and speed. Summative evaluation, on the other hand, operates like an artillery spotter, who reports whether or not the shell hit the target and then advises corrections for the next shot.

The decision to use either formative or summative evaluation should be based upon the needs of the particular project or program to be evaluated. The advantage of formative evaluation consists of the possibility of intervention at an early stage, so that later stages of the operation will work better. Thus, the evaluation itself becomes part of the process. This aspect can also function as a disadvantage because it makes it almost impossible to say what would have occurred had the evaluation not been taking place. In the specific instance we are examining in this book, formative evaluation seems most suited to the evaluation of the team approach.

Summative evaluation looks at the end result. Since it is concerned only with end products, it has the advantage of not intervening in the process, thereby changing it and confounding the results. This is not to say that data cannot be collected during a project that is being evaluated—only that the evaluator does not intervene in the process.

Role of the Evaluator

In any project, program, or process that deals with the achievement of particular goals, there is a need to define the evaluator's role. This role may be filled by one or more persons. Those who accept this role must critically appraise the achievement of goals by means of a formative or summative evaluation. The evaluation must be designed and implemented in a manner that is consistent with the project and that will aid in the improvement of performance.

Techniques for data gathering and analysis should be consistent with good research practice. The role of evaluator demands not only technical expertise in the collection and analysis of data but also interpersonal skill in conveying the results of evaluation. Evaluation is often looked upon with some trepidation by those being evaluated. Therefore, the evaluator must be skilled in handling what may be a very sensitive situation.

In some instances it may be best to employ an evaluator who is entirely removed from the program under study. The evaluator is presumably more objective if not related directly to the team and also may have a fresh point of view to bring to the evaluation. On the negative side, the evaluator may not have a complete understanding of the program or the time necessary to acquire the necessary background. Furthermore, he or she may not be available for followup on the recommendations stemming from the evaluation report.

The internal evaluator may not be so objective but is more likely to have the intimate knowledge of the program necessary to structuring an adequate evaluation. The internal evaluator is also assumed to have some commitment to the ongoing improvement of the team operation.

Accrediting agencies, government, and private funding agencies all make use of program reviews done by one's professional colleagues. One of the main problems with peer review is that peers do not always bring unbiased views to the review process and may be overly influenced by self-interest. Nevertheless, peer review is an important and much used method of evaluation.

Research

In addition to the need to evaluate the work of teams in particular institutions, there is also a need for general research concerning teams. Such research would be facilitated by the development of a theory of teams as indicated in Chapter 1. Certainly existing theory concerning groups and organizations may provide a framework for extending our knowledge of how teams function; however, as more and more data are amassed concerning teamwork, a more formal integrating construct is needed.

Briefly, a theory can be defined as a set of interrelated principles and definitions from which we derive specific hypotheses to test empirically. Such a theory has two basic functions:

1. to integrate existing knowledge
2. to suggest new relationships

and can be evaluated in terms of how well it fulfills those functions. The ultimate measure of a theory is not whether it is *true* (which we can never know), but whether it is *useful*. To the extent that a given theory organizes existing information and stimulates new research it may be regarded as a "good" theory.

As was pointed out earlier, there has been more rhetoric than research on the interdisciplinary team, and the research that has been conducted has been limited, spotty, and disorganized. The *team system* (Chapter 1) provides one framework that suggests directions of future research. The three major aspects of the team system are the *components,* the *processes,* and the *outcomes* of the team. These aspects consist of:

Components	Processes	Outcomes
Child	Goals	Child
Professional	Activities	Professional
Organization	Task	Organizational
	Maintenance	

Each aspect presents us with a myriad of possible variables for investigation. With so many potential relationships to investigate, it may be difficult for the researcher to decide where to invest time and energy. From the team schema we have presented, three types of relationships are apparent. (This does not mean there are not other kinds of relationships or ways of looking at team research—we are simply suggesting one way in which one might proceed.) These relationships suggest several types of research problems.

Research Relating Components to Outcomes

Research relating components to outcomes might focus, for example, on the impact of various organizational settings on the outcomes. Do children benefit more from the use of an interdisciplinary team than from alternative approaches? Is the service time shorter, does it cost less, is service more effective, and are the family and child more satisfied as a result of the team approach? Similarly, what outcomes are there for professionals? Do they learn more and thus become better practitioners? Do they waste more or less time? Is job satisfaction greater or less? Does the organization benefit—is there better communication, less litigation?

Research Relating Components to Processes

Here we are looking at relationships between variables associated with the components and team processes. Research is needed on the way in which the personal and professional attributes of team members either enhance or detract from the effective operation of the team. Do various alternative organizational structures facilitate or impede team processes? How do interprofessional perceptions affect team interactions? (An example of an approach to the study of interprofessional perceptions is shown in Appendix A.) Is it necessary for team members to "feel good" about the team for it to work well? Do certain types of leadership styles facilitate team goal setting?

Research Relating Processes to Outcomes

Here the processes are related to variables associated with outcomes. One research area could involve an examination of the patterns of team interaction and cost effectiveness. Another might look at the way in which both task and maintenance goals are formulated in relation to both the activity of the team and the team's effectiveness in meeting the needs of the client, the professions, and the organization.

There has to date been little empirical observation of teamwork (Wagner, 1977). One would hope that additional research will be undertaken in the near future. One method of research utilized by the authors made use of an instrument called the *Team Observation Protocol* (see Appendix B). Other ways of making such observations are reported by Feiger and Schmitt (1979) on observations of health care teams and Goldstein et al. (1980) on observations of IEP conferences.

The study of such questions is not without difficulty. As Nagi (1975) points out, there are a number of problems associated with studying teams, a prime one being the difficulty of defining and measuring quality of service. Associated with this are the problems of gaining access to data and of the possible resistance to research by team members who may view such studies as a threat.

A different type of problem is that a number of the people who have interest in the team as a research subject are strong *advocates* of the team approach. This may inhibit adequate research on the team, as reflected by the large proportion of nonresearch based publications.

Another type of problem is that many would define as teams only those that operate exclusively on democratic, egalitarian principles. But many teams as defined in Chapter 1 do not operate on such principles and are in fact authoritarian in nature. Thus the "value set" of the researcher may lead him or her to collect data only on teams that operate in a certain way, and this too may inhibit research.

Finally, we suggest that the interdisciplinary team presents a unique opportunity for research, in that the research effort itself should probably be interdisciplinary, borrowing from methodologies used in a number of fields.

THE FUTURE OF THE TEAM APPROACH

It is often easy to lose sight of the primary purpose of the team and become involved with organizational structure, interpersonal and interprofessional relationships, team development, and a myriad of other aspects that are characteristic of the system.

But it should be remembered that the interdisciplinary team in human service organizations owes its existence to the need for coordination. The team, therefore, should always be focused on the central issue of the child.

What will be the future of the team approach? There is, at present, no way to answer that question with certainty. However, it is highly probable that *teamwork* is likely to become *more* important in the years ahead. The movement toward specialization will accelerate, and the knowledge base of the professions will continue to expand (perhaps at a somewhat slower rate than in the immediate past). And increasing specialization means a continuing need for coordination, if the child is to receive high-quality care. Thus, to avoid the problems inherent in the fragmentation of services, some form of team approach will be demanded.

The Interprofessional Perception Scale

To examine how professionals view themselves, view other professions, and think other professions view them, a scale of interpersonal perceptions has been developed by the authors (Ducanis & Golin, 1978). The Interprofessional Perception Scale (IPS) is based upon the interpersonal perception method developed earlier by Laing, Phillipson, and Lee (1966). In an analysis of this method, Alperson (1975) concluded that the approach is adaptable to a variety of investigations, including group perceptions.

The interpersonal perception method includes several levels of perspective that each member of a dyadic relationship has of the other. These are termed:

- *Perspective,* i.e., what I say

- *Meta-perspective*, i.e., how I say you would answer the same question

- *Meta-meta-perspective*, i.e., what I say you would say that I said.

The IPS also involves three levels of response; it asks a professional to give an opinion of another profession (Level I), tell how members of that profession would respond (Level II), and finally tell how those professionals would say he or she responded (Level III). Thus, the IPS yields data regarding how a professional views another profession, whether he or she thinks that members of the other profession agree or disagree with that view, and whether they understand that perception. The scale can also be used to indicate how subjects see their *own* profession and whether they think other professionals agree with or understand that perception. Initially, the IPS was used by the authors to examine relations between health care professions, but it was later used with school personnel.

Since this approach can become quite complex, a hypothetical example may be helpful (see Figure A–1).

Figure A-1 Sample Response to IPS Item

Item	Level I		Level II		Level III	
	How would you answer?		How would they answer?		How would they say you answered?	
	True	False	True	False	True	False
Fully utilize the capability of your profession	[ ]	[x]	[x]	[ ]	[x]	[ ]

In this example, the respondent, a learning disability teacher, is asked to respond to the statement "persons in this profession (i.e., classroom teachers) fully utilize the capabilities of your profession" by answering True or False to three questions: How would you respond to the statement? How would classroom teachers respond to it? How would classroom teachers say you responded to it? The learning disability teacher responds False to the first question (Level I) and True to the second (Level II). That is, the learning disability teacher thinks that classroom teachers do not fully utilize the capabilities of learning disability teachers but that the classroom teachers think they do. The respondent's Level III answer is True; that is, the learning disability teacher thinks that classroom teachers think that the learning disability teachers think their capabilities are fully utilized. To summarize, the learning disability teacher thinks that classroom teachers do not utilize the skills of the learning disability teacher and that they think they do; they do not agree, in other words. Moreover, the learning disability teacher *perceives* a basic disagreement and thinks that the classroom teachers do not.

This configuration yields eight possible ways in which an item may be answered. A sample is shown in Figure A-2 (the data are taken from an earlier version of the IPS administered in this case to a group of nurses). The item stated that "the relations between nurses and physicians are very good." Figure A-2 shows that there were 38 individuals who responded to the item, 32 of them responding False to Level I and 6 responding True. Thus, most of the nurses who responded said that relations between nurses and physicians are not very good. If we continue to follow the responses of the 32 who answered False at Level I, we see that 21 of them say that physicians would indicate that relations are very good. In other words, two-thirds of the nurses who think relations are not good feel that physicians would perceive it differently. Inter-

Figure A–2 Illustration of Possible Patterns of Answers to an Item of the IPS

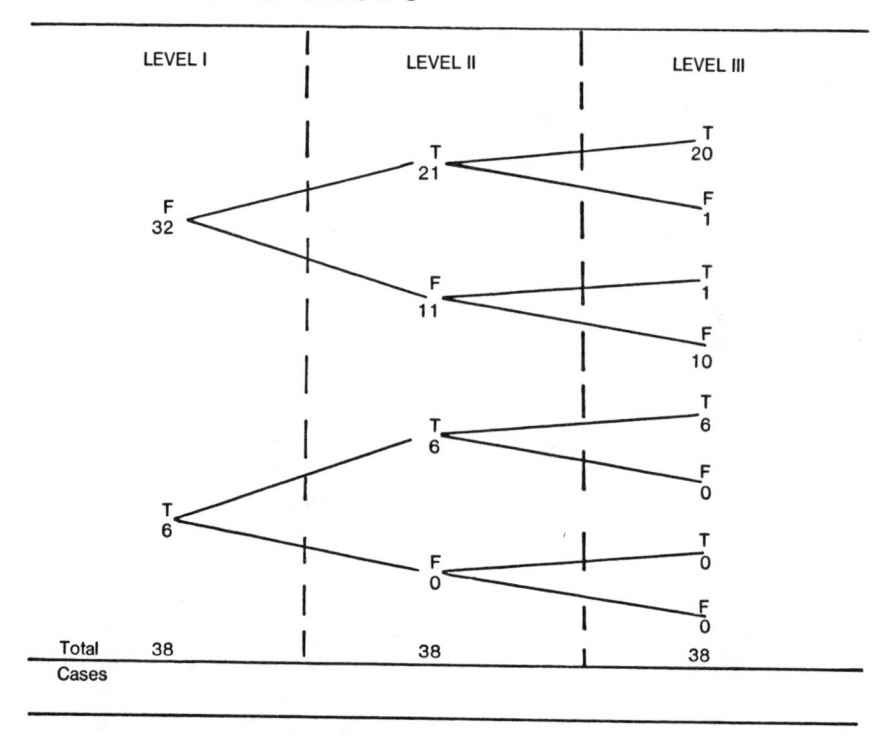

estingly enough, however, about one-third of those who think that relations are not good think that physicians would agree with them. Furthermore, 10 of these nurses also believe that a physician would think that nurses would say relations were not good.

This method of analysis, by itself or coupled with the corresponding pattern from another profession, can yield a great deal of data concerning the way in which professions view their interrelationships. In this instance, from one profession's point of view we can see: how the nurses picture the physicians, how the nurses think the physicians view themselves, and how the nurses think the physicians think the nurses perceive them. Thus Level I responses yield a direct view of how one profession perceives another, but Level II and III responses yield additional data on whether one profession thinks the other agrees or disagrees with that direct perception, and whether the other profession understands or misunderstands that perception.

If the eight possible patterns of answers are placed in a two-by-two contingency table, the possibilities for analysis become more apparent. Figure A–3 shows the distribution of the eight possible patterns. It may be seen that, independent of the direct perspective, one may perceive the other profession as either understanding or not understanding and as either agreeing or not agreeing with one's point of view.

These patterns may also be examined in conjunction with one another. For example, the perceptions of physical therapists and special education teachers may be compared. Thus it is possible to develop a view of the total pattern of perceptions between two or more professions.

Development of the IPS

On the basis of the results from a preliminary instrument, 15 items were identified for inclusion in a revised form. Instructions for the IPS may be found in Figure A–4. The IPS form used for *other professions* is found in Figure A–5, and Figure A–6 shows the form used for measuring perceptions of one's *own profession* and how it is thought to be perceived by others.

Content validity of the instrument is established by the direct nature of the questions posed. Reliability was established through a test-retest procedure over a three-week period, using the responses of 24 students in a graduate rehabilitation counseling program. Using scales for physicians, social workers, and "own profession," the reliabilities as measured by percent of exact agreement ranged from 74 percent to 86 percent for Level I responses, with a mean across professions of 80 percent. Level II measures showed a range of reliabilities of 74 percent to 81 percent, with a mean of 79 percent. Level III reliabilities were 72 percent to 80 percent, with a mean of 74 percent. Slightly lower reliabilities had been predicted for Level III in view of the complexity of the response (How would other professionals say you answered?).

Figure A–3 Possible Patterns of IPS Responses

	Perceived agreement	Perceived disagreement
Perceived understanding	T T T F F F	T F T F T F
Perceived misunderstanding	T T F F F T	T F F F T T

Figure A–4 Interprofessional Perception Scale—Instructions

All answers are confidential. *Do not sign this form.*

Respondent data: Profession _____

Age _____ Sex _____ Years Experience _____

Highest Degree or
   Certificate _____   Specialty
                                             (if applicable) _____

   This is a study of interprofessional perceptions. It is intended to get at some of the ways various professions view each other and how they think others view them.

   Please fill in the information at the top of this page, but *do not sign your name.*

   In answering the following items, do not spend too much time on any one statement. Your first impression is what we want. Please answer with as much candor as possible. Answer all three parts of each question as you proceed. Each page should take only about 5 minutes. *Please answer each item.*

   As you look at the following page, you will see that in Column 1 you should indicate whether you think the statement is true or false; in Column II you should indicate how you think the other professional would answer; and in Column III, how you think they would predict you would answer. Please place an X to indicate your answers.

   You may begin now.

Figure A–5 Interprofessional Perception Scale—Other Professions

Answer the following items in relation to this profession:

Physical Therapy

Persons in this profession:	How Would You Answer?		How Would They Answer?		How Would They Say That You Answered?	
	TRUE	FALSE	TRUE	FALSE	TRUE	FALSE
1. Are competent	☐	☐	☐	☐	☐	☐
2. Have very little autonomy	☐	☐	☐	☐	☐	☐
3. Understand the capabilities of your profession	☐	☐	☐	☐	☐	☐
4. Are highly concerned with the welfare of the patient	☐	☐	☐	☐	☐	☐
5. Sometimes encroach on your professional territory	☐	☐	☐	☐	☐	☐
6. Are highly ethical	☐	☐	☐	☐	☐	☐
7. Expect too much of your profession	☐	☐	☐	☐	☐	☐
8. Have a higher status than your profession	☐	☐	☐	☐	☐	☐
9. Are very defensive about their professional prerogatives	☐	☐	☐	☐	☐	☐
10. Trust your professional judgment	☐	☐	☐	☐	☐	☐
11. Seldom ask your professional advice	☐	☐	☐	☐	☐	☐
12. Fully utilize the capabilities of your profession	☐	☐	☐	☐	☐	☐
13. Do not cooperate well with your profession	☐	☐	☐	☐	☐	☐
14. Are well trained	☐	☐	☐	☐	☐	☐
15. Have good relations with your profession	☐	☐	☐	☐	☐	☐

Figure A–6 Interprofessional Perception Scale—Own Profession

Answer the following items in relation to <u>Your Own Profession</u>

Persons in this profession:	How Would You Answer?		How Would Other Health Professionals Answer?		How Would Other Health Professionals Say You Answered?	
	TRUE	FALSE	TRUE	FALSE	TRUE	FALSE
1. Are competent	☐	☐	☐	☐	☐	☐
2. Have very little autonomy	☐	☐	☐	☐	☐	☐
3. Understand the capabilities of other professions	☐	☐	☐	☐	☐	☐
4. Are highly concerned with the welfare of the patient	☐	☐	☐	☐	☐	☐
5. Sometimes encroach on other professional territories	☐	☐	☐	☐	☐	☐
6. Are highly ethical	☐	☐	☐	☐	☐	☐
7. Expect too much of other professions	☐	☐	☐	☐	☐	☐
8. Have a higher status than other professions	☐	☐	☐	☐	☐	☐
9. Are very defensive about their professional prerogatives	☐	☐	☐	☐	☐	☐
10. Trust others' professional judgments	☐	☐	☐	☐	☐	☐
11. Seldom ask others' professional advice	☐	☐	☐	☐	☐	☐
12. Fully utilize the capabilities of other professions	☐	☐	☐	☐	☐	☐
13. Do not cooperate well with other professions	☐	☐	☐	☐	☐	☐
14. Are well trained	☐	☐	☐	☐	☐	☐
15. Have good relations with other professions	☐	☐	☐	☐	☐	☐

Observing a Team Conference

One of the major problems in the study of teams is the lack of empirical data based on the systematic observation of team interaction. Most of the descriptive information presently available consists of reports by individual team participants who describe in rather general terms what their team does and how it is organized. There have been few attempts by outside observers to examine team functioning. Yet this kind of systematic observation is necessary if some of the major parameters of team functioning are to be identified.

In order to explore the variables involved in these interactions, a series of observations were made of case conferences by teams operating in a variety of organizational settings. Drawing upon the concepts of Flanders (1967, 1970), Hare (1976), Bales (1950a, 1950b, 1955), and others concerned with category systems for observing human interaction, the authors designed a recording method specifically suited to the observation of team decision-making processes. The Team Observation Protocol (TOP) evolved from a series of observations of progress, consultation, and disposition staffings in medical and psychiatric settings, schools, and rehabilitation centers. Less complex than some of the other category systems, the TOP can be used to describe what goes on in the team session, compare teams in various institutional settings, or help a team's efforts toward self-evaluation.

THE TEAM OBSERVATION PROTOCOL (TOP)

The TOP is used to categorize the major statements of team members, to identify who participates in the team discussion, what kinds of statements are made by the various professionals, and how a decision is reached by the team. Seven categories of statements are used: Client, Team, Questions, Information, Interpretation, Alternatives, and Decisions. The TOP does not attempt to collect verbatim recordings of participants' statements or to record nonverbal behavior.

Nonverbal expressions (nodding, frowning, pointing, touching, etc.) may be noted anecdotally, but there is no attempt to categorize them.

In recording the verbal activities of the team, the observer assigns each participant a code number and identifies statements by category. Responses are numbered in the sequence in which they occur, so it is possible to reconstruct the sequence of the statements if this is desirable. If only frequency data are required, checks rather than numbers may be used; however, numbering in sequence gives far more information with little extra effort. For example, the respondent may begin by sharing information about the client and conclude the statement by asking a question of another team member. This statement would be recorded once in each of the two categories. On the other hand, if the speaker's statement consisted of a long report of information about the client, this statement would be coded only once, even if it continued for five or ten minutes. Thus each statement is recorded every time there is a change of category or respondent. Since all the responses are numbered in sequence, the number of the last response reflects the total number of statements recorded during the session. The general recording rules are summarized in Table B–1.

Categories of the TOP

Table B–2 describes the seven statement categories. The TOP focuses greater attention on the cognitive, task-related aspects of team interaction than on affective, nonverbal elements. Only two categories are concerned with affective statements: Categories 1 and 2 include affective statements about the client and about other team members. The other five categories focus on the tasks in which the team is involved: sharing information, drawing interpretations or hypotheses from that information, exploring the various alternatives available to the team, and finally, deciding on a course of action. In most team conferences, much verbal activity falls into Category 3, Questions, as team members seek information and opinions during the decision-making process.

Table B–1 Recording Rules for the Team Observation Protocol

1. Each participant is identified by profession and sex and given a code number.
2. Only verbal statements are recorded.
3. Statements are recorded in numerical sequence (unless only frequency data are required).
4. Each statement is recorded by category and participant.
5. Each response is recorded only once regardless of length, unless there is a change in response category.
6. Each change in category is recorded as a new response.
7. Each change in respondent is recorded as a new response.

Table B–2 Category Descriptions of the Team Observation Protocol

Category	Description
1. Client	All affective statements (+ or −) regarding the client. Neutral statements about the client are coded in categories 3-7; category 1 includes only statements revealing an emotional reaction to the client, such as hostile or joking references to the client.
2. Team	All affective statements (+ or −) about the team or a team member. Neutral statements about the team would be coded in categories 3-7; category 1 includes emotional reactions to the team itself or to another team member. It includes joking, laughing, or hostile remarks.
3. Questions	All statements asking for information, suggestions, or opinions, or requesting reports.
4. Information	All statements giving factual information, dealing only with what is observed, without interpretation.
5. Interpretation	All statements which give an opinion or interpretation, going beyond empirical data to make inferences about what has been observed.
6. Alternatives	All statements which suggest alternatives, explore or compare possible courses of action.
7. Decisions	All statements which deal directly with the final decision — expressing, clarifying, or elaborating the decision reached.

Using the TOP

Figure B–1 illustrates the recording method and the categories of the TOP as used in a fictional case conference. To simplify the example, only the profession of the participants and the response categories are included, and only a limited number of statements are reported.

This hypothetical case represents a team decision concerning the placement of a second-grader with learning problems. Discussion is initiated by the principal, who asks for a report from the teacher concerning the child's classroom performance (Response 1). Following the teacher's report (2), the principal calls for a report from the school social worker (3), who replies with factual information regarding the child's family history (4) and inferences about the home situation (5). The principal asks a question (6), and the social worker responds

Figure B–1 Example of TOP Record

PARTICIPANTS	1. Client	2. Team	3. Questions	4. Information	5. Interpretation	6. Alternatives	7. Decisions	TOTAL
Physician			1-3 6-8		13	14	16-18	8
Nurse				2				1
Social Worker			12	4-7	5	15		5
Psychologist	17+			9	10	11		4
TOTAL	1+	0	5	4	3	3	2	18

with additional information (7). The psychologist's report is requested by the principal (8), and the psychologist describes the child's test performance (9), interprets the test scores (10), and suggests a course of action (11). The social worker asks a question (12). The principal replies (13), discussing the possibility of a resource room (14). The social worker also comments regarding the pros and cons of the resource room (15), and the principal states "Well, I think we should let the child try and see what happens" (16). The psychologist indicates a positive attitude about the child (17), and the principal concludes the discussion by reaffirming the decision (18).

Statements can be summarized by category and by participant (or by profession if several members of the same profession are present) and can be analyzed in a number of ways. For example, long staffings on a particular client can be broken into thirds or halves and the types of statements in each part compared. It may be found that the first third of the case conference will focus on questions and information statements, the middle third on interpretations, and the last third on alternatives and decisions. The numbering of responses facilitates the analysis of the interaction sequence. Although the example given in Figure B–1 is too brief for this kind of analysis, even a cursory examination of the data suggests that in this particular case the principal played an active leadership role in the decision process, while the teacher is quite passive. The principal begins and ends the discussion and asks most of the questions.

RESULTS OF TEAM OBSERVATIONS

Team conferences were observed in several settings, including medical rehabilitation units, alcohol/drug rehabilitation centers, residential schools for the developmentally disabled, and day schools. The team meetings were staffings of one or more clients, involving decisions about such matters as treatment, discharge, or home visits. Results of nine team observations are summarized in Table B–3. Since interest was focused on the decision process itself, recording was confined to the case presentations. Informal interactions before and after the team conference and between case presentations were not recorded in these observations. This probably accounts for the low percentage of responses about the team or team members (Category 2). Each case was recorded separately, from the introduction of the client to the concluding comment. The time spent on a single case varied from two or three minutes (usually when only a quick progress report was given on cases presented at the end of the meeting), to two or three hours (when the entire meeting was devoted to discussion of one client). The number of cases presented in a single session ranged from 1 to 15, and the length of the sessions varied from 42 to 159 minutes. The number of team members present at the discussion of any one case ranged from 3 to 20 (however, not every team member contributed to every case), and the number of members present at each of the nine team meetings ranged from 7 to 25.

Table B-3 Team Observation Protocol Summaries of Nine Teams

TEAM		1. CLIENT	2. TEAM	3. QUEST.	4. INFORM.	5. INTERP.	6. ALTERN.	7. DECIS.	TOTAL
1. Medical Rehabilitation 10 cases	N=	9	11	94	100	58	30	33	335
	%=	2.7	3.3	28.1	29.9	17.3	9.0	9.8	
2. Drug/Alcohol 4 cases	N=	30	10	42	74	47	24	10	237
	%=	12.7	4.2	17.7	31.2	19.8	10.1	4.2	
3. Medical Rehabilitation 12 cases	N=	17	0	108	126	85	45	22	403
	%=	4.2	0	26.8	31.3	21.1	11.2	5.5	
4. Medical Rehabilitation 15 cases	N=	3	2	74	89	60	27	9	264
	%=	1.1	0.7	28.0	33.7	22.7	10.2	3.4	
5. Residential School 1 case	N=	14	0	97	91	63	17	12	294
	%=	4.8	0	33.0	31.0	21.4	5.8	4.1	
6. Medical Rehabilitation 10 cases	N=	5	3	73	81	39	14	18	233
	%=	2.1	1.3	31.3	34.8	16.7	6.0	7.7	
7. Residential School 1 case	N=	6	0	30	40	45	4	3	128
	%=	4.7	0	23.4	31.3	35.2	3.1	2.3	
8. Residential School 1 case	N=	1	2	44	95	32	15	6	195
	%=	0.5	1.0	22.6	48.7	16.4	7.7	3.1	
9. School (Day) 1 case	N=	2	1	35	40	53	17	3	151
	%=	1.3	.7	23.2	26.5	35.1	11.3	2.0	
Total	N=	87	29	597	736	482	193	116	2240
	%=	3.9	1.3	26.7	32.9	21.5	8.6	5.2	

References

Abeson, A., & Zettel, J. The end of the quiet revolution: The Education for all Handicapped Children Act of 1975. *Exceptional Children*, 1977, *44*, 115–128.

Ackerly, S. The clinic team. *American Journal of Orthopsychiatry*, 1947, *17*, 191–195.

Allen, K. E., Holm, V. A., & Schiefelbusch, R. L. (Eds.). *Early intervention: A team approach*. Baltimore: University Park Press, 1978.

Alley, G. R., Deshler, D. D., & Mellard, D. Identification decisions: Who is the most consistent? *Learning Disability Quarterly*, 1979, *2*, 99–103.

Alperson, B. L. A Boolean analysis of interpersonal perception. *Human Relations*, 1975, *28*, 627–652.

Anderson, S. B., & Ball, S. *The profession and practice of program evaluation*. San Francisco: Jossey-Bass, 1978.

Anderson, S. B., Ball, S., & Murphy, R. T., & associates. *Encyclopedia of educational evaluation*. Washington, D.C.: Jossey-Bass, 1975.

Argyris, C. The incompleteness of social psychological theory: Examples from small group, cognitive consistency, and attribution research. *American Psychologist*, 1969, *24*, 893–908.

Armer, B., & Thomas, B. Attitudes toward interdisciplinary collaboration in pupil personnel services teams. *The Journal of School Psychology*, 1978, *16*, 167–176.

Baer, D. M. The behavioral analysis of trouble. In K. E. Allen, V. A. Holm, and R. Schiefelbusch (Eds.), *Early intervention: A team approach*. Baltimore: University Press, 1978.

Bailey, D. B., & Harbin, G. L. Nondiscriminatory evaluation. *Exceptional Children*, 1980, *46*, 590–596.

Bales, R. F. *Interaction process analysis: A method for the study of small groups*. Cambridge, Mass.: Addison-Wesley, 1950. (a)

Bales R. F. A set of categories for the analysis of small group interaction. *American Sociological Review*, 1950, *15*, 257–263. (b)

Bales, R. F. How people interact in conferences. *Scientific American*, 1955, *192*(3), 31–35.

Bales, R. F., & Slater, P. Role differentiation in small decision-making groups. In T. Parsons and R. Bales (Eds.), *Family socialization and interaction process*. Glencoe, Ill.: Free Press, 1955.

Banta, H. D., & Fox, R. C. Role strains of a health care team in a poverty community. *Social Science and Medicine*, 1972, *6*, 697–722.

Bartel, N., & Guskin, S. A handicap as a social phenomenon. In W. Cruickshank (Ed.), *Psychology of exceptional children and youth* (4th ed.). Englewood Cliffs, N.J.: Prentice-Hall, 1980.

Bateson, N. Familiarization, group discussion and risk-taking. *Journal of Experimental Social Psychology*, 1966, *2*, 119–129.

Bavelas, A. A mathematical model for group structures. *Applied Anthropology*, 1948, *7*, 16–30.

Beck, H. L. The advantages of a multi-purpose clinic for the mentally retarded. *American Journal of Mental Deficiency*, 1962, *66*, 789–794.

Becker, H. S. The nature of a profession. In H. Nelson (Ed.), *Education for the professions* (Part 2). Chicago: University of Chicago Press, 1962.

Becker, H. S. *Outsiders: Studies in the sociology of deviance*. New York: Free Press, 1963.

Beckhard, R. Organizational implications of team building: The larger picture. In H. Wise, R. Beckhard, I. Rubin, & A. L. Kyte (Eds.), *Making health teams work*. Cambridge, Mass.: Ballinger, 1974.

Bem, D. J., Wallach, M. A., & Kogan, N. Group decision-making under risk of aversive consequences. *Journal of Personality and Social Psychology*, 1965, *1*, 453–460.

Benne, K. D., & Sheats, P. Functional roles of group members. *Journal of Social Issues*, 1948, *4*, 41–49.

Bijou, S. W. Behavior modification in teaching the retarded child. In C. E. Thoresen (Ed.), *Behavior modification in education*. Chicago: University of Chicago Press, 1973.

Bitter, G. B. Family impact: Fallacies, feuds, and fundamentals. *The Volta Review*, 1976, *78*, 312–317.

Blackhard, K., Hazel, L., Livingston, S., Ryan, T., Soltman, S., & Stade, C. The interdisciplinary education team. In N. G. Haring (Ed.), *The experimental education training program, Vol. 2, Support Services*. Seattle: University of Washington, College of Education, 1977.

Blake, R., Shepard, H., & Morton, J. *Managing intergroup conflict in industry*. Houston: Gulf Publishing Company, 1964.

Blank, A. Effects of group and individual conditions on choice behavior. *Journal of Personality and Social Psychology*, 1968, *8*, 294–298.

Bloom, B. S. (Ed.), Taxonomy of educational objectives, Handbook 1, *Cognitive domain*. New York: David McKay Company, 1956.

Brill, N. *Teamwork: Working together in the human services*. Philadelphia: Lippincott, 1976.

Brown, L., & Reece, J. An interdisciplinary model for teacher education. *Journal of Teacher Education*, 1978, *29*(6), 51–52.

Brown, R. *Social psychology*. New York: Free Press, 1965.

Bucher, R., & Strauss, A. Professions in process. *American Journal of Sociology*, 1961, *66*, 325–344.

Burke, R. J. Methods of resolving interpersonal conflict. *Personnel Administration*, 1969, *32*, 48.

Caetano, A., & Kauffman, J. Reduction of rocking mannerisms in two blind children. *Education of the Visually Handicapped*, 1975, *7*, 101–105.

Carlins, E. B., & Raven, B. H. Group structure: Attraction, coalitions, communication, and power. In G. Lindzey & E. Aronson (Eds.), *Handbook of social psychology* (Rev. edition) Vol. 4. Reading, Mass.: Addison-Wesley, 1969.

Carter, L. On defining leadership. In M. Shiref & M. D. Wilson (Eds.), *Group relations at the crossroads*. New York: Harper & Row, 1953.

Cartwright, D. The nature of group cohesiveness. In D. Cartwright & A. Zander (Eds.), *Group dynamics: Research and theory* (3rd ed.). New York: Harper & Row, 1968.

Cartwright, D., & Zander, A. (Eds.). *Group dynamics: Research and theory* (3rd ed.). New York: Harper & Row, 1968.

Challela, M. The interdisciplinary team: A role definition in nursing. *Image*, 1979, *11*, 1, 9–15.

Clement, D. E., & Schiereck, J. J., Jr. Sex composition and group performance in a visual detection task. *Memory and Cognition*, 1973, *1*, 251–255.

Coe, R. *Sociology of Medicine*. New York: McGraw-Hill, 1970.

Cogan, M. L. Toward a definition of a profession. *Harvard Educational Review*, 1953, *23*, 33–50.

Connor, F. The past in prologue: Teacher preparation in special education. *Exceptional Children*, 1976, *42*, 366–377.

Corrigan, D. Political and moral contexts. *Journal of Teacher Education*, 1978, *29*(6), 10–15.

Crisler, J., & Settles, R. An integrated rehabilitation team effort in providing services for multi-disability clients. *Journal of Rehabilitation*, 1979, *45*(1), 34–38.

Cruickshank, W. (Ed.) *Psychology of exceptional children and youth* (4th ed.). Englewood Cliffs, N.J.: Prentice-Hall, 1980.

Dembinski, R., & Mauser, A. What parents of the learning disabled really want from professionals. *Journal of Learning Disabilities*, 1977, *10*(9), 49–55.

Deming, E. W. The logic of evaluation. In M. Guttentag & E. L. Struening (Eds.), *Handbook of evaluation research* (Vol I.) Beverly Hills: Sage Publications, 1975.

Diana v. State Board of Education, NOC 70-37, U.S. District Court, Northern District of California (1970).

Dion, K. L., Baron, R. S., & Miller, N. Why do groups make riskier decisions than individuals? In L. Berkowitz (Ed.), *Advances in social psychology* (Vol. 5). New York: Academic Press, 1970.

Dion, K. L., Miller, N., & Magnon, M. A. Group cohesiveness and social responsibility as determinants of the risky shift. Paper presented at the meeting of the American Psychological Association, Miami, Florida, September 1970.

Drucker, P. F. Managing the "third sector." *Wall Street Journal*, Oct. 3, 1978.

Ducanis, A. J., & Golin, A. K. *Interprofessional perceptions in the interdisciplinary health care team.* Paper presented at the meeting of the American Society of Allied Health Professions, Miami, Florida, November 1978.

Elmer, E., Bennett, H., Harway, N., Meyerson, E., Sankey, C., & Weithhorn, L. Child abuse training: A community-based interdisciplinary program. *Community Mental Health Journal*, 1978, *14*, 179–189.

Erikson, E. *Childhood and society* (2nd ed.). New York: Norton & Company, 1963.

Farber, B. Effects of a severely mentally retarded child on family integration. *Monograph of the Society for Research in Child Development*, 1959, *24*, No. 71.

Farber, B. Effects of a severely mentally retarded child on the family. In E. P. Trapp & P. Himmelstein (Eds.), *Readings on the exceptional child* (2nd ed.). New York: Appleton-Century-Crofts, 1972.

Feiger, S. M., & Schmitt, M. H. Collegiality in interdisciplinary health teams: Its measurement and its effects. *Social Science and Medicine*, 1979, *13A*, 217–229.

Fellendorf, G. W. Eduhealth: A term whose time has come. *The Volta Review*, 1975, *77*, 408–409.

Fenton, K., Yoshida, R., Maxwell, J., & Kaufman, M. Recognition of team goals: An essential step toward rational decision making. *Exceptional Children*, 1979, *45*, 638–644.

Fenton, K., Yoshida, R., Maxwell, J., & Kaufman, M. *Role expectations: Implications for multidisciplinary pupil programming.* No date. (ERIC Document Reproduction Service No. ED 157 231)

Ferguson, D. A., & Vidmar, N. Familiarization-induced risky and cautious shifts: A replication of sorts. Paper presented at the meeting of the Midwestern Psychological Association, Cincinnati, Ohio, 1970.

Fiedler, F. E. Personality and situational determinants of leadership effectiveness. In D. Cartwright & A. Zander (Eds.), *Group dynamics: Research and theory* (3rd ed.). New York: Harper & Row, 1968.

Flanders, J. P., & Thistlethwaite, D. L. Effects of familiarization and group discussion upon risk taking. *Journal of Personality and Social Psychology*, 1967, *5*, 91–97.

Flanders, N. A. Teacher influence in the classroom. In E. J. Amidon & J. B. Hough (Eds.), *Interaction analysis: Theory research and application.* Reading, Mass.: Addison-Wesley, 1967.

Flanders, N. A. *Analyzing teacher behavior.* Reading, Mass.: Addison-Wesley, 1970.

Flathouse, V. E. Multiply handicapped deaf children and Public Law 94–142. *Exceptional Children*, 1979, *45*, 560–565.

Flexner, A. Is social work a profession? In *Proceedings of the National Conference on Charities and Corrections*. Chicago: Hildemann Printing Company, 1915.

Fowle, C. M. The effect of the severely mentally retarded child on his family. *American Journal of Mental Deficiency*, 1968, *73*, 468–473.

Foxx, R. M., & Azrin, N. H. The elimination of autistic self-stimulatory behavior by overcorrection. *Journal of Applied Behavior Analysis*, 1973, *6*, 1–14.

Frank, L. K. Interprofessional communication. *American Journal of Public Health*, 1961, *51*, 1798–1804.

Freidson, E. *Patients' views of medical practice*. New York: Russell Sage Foundation, 1961.

Freidson, E. Disability as a social deviance. In M. B. Sussman (Ed.), *Sociology and rehabilitation*. Washington, D. C.: American Sociological Association, 1966.

French, J. R., Jr., & Raven, B. The bases of social power. In D. Cartwright (Ed.), *Studies in social power*. Ann Arbor, Michigan: Institute for Social Research, 1959.

Fry, R. E., Lech, B. A., & Rubin, I. Working with the primary care team. In *Making Health Teams Work*. Cambridge, Mass.: Ballinger, 1974.

Furth, H. G. *Thinking without language: Psychological implications of deafness*. New York: Free Press, 1966.

Gagne, R. *The conditions of learning* (3rd ed.). New York: Holt, Rinehart, & Winston, 1977.

Gallagher, E. B. Lines of reconstruction and extension in the Parsonian sociology of illness. *Social Science and Medicine*, 1976, *10*, 207–218.

Gallagher, J. J. *Ecology of exceptional children*. Washington, D.C.: Jossey-Bass, 1980.

Gamson, W. A. A theory of coalition formation. *American Sociological Review*, 1961, *26*, 373–382.

Gardner, W. I. *Learning and behavior characteristics of exceptional children and youth*. Boston: Allyn & Bacon, 1977.

Gath, A. Parents' reaction to Down's Syndrome. *Journal of the Division for Early Childhood*, 1979, *1*(1), 11–17.

Geigle-Bentz, F. L. Communication, democracy, leadership, roles and the team in the interdisciplinary health team approach. Unpublished doctoral dissertation, University of Pittsburgh, 1975.

Gibb, C. A. Leadership. In G. Lindzey & E. Aronson (Eds.), *The handbook of social psychology* (Rev. edition), Vol. 4. Reading, Mass.: Addison-Wesley, 1969.

Glaser, R. Instructional technology and the measurement of learning outcomes: Some questions. *American Psychologist*, 1963, *18*, 519–521.

Goldman, M. A comparison of individual and group performance for varying combinations of initial ability. *Journal of Personality and Social Psychology*, 1965, *1*, 210–216.

Goldstein, S., Strickland, B., Turnbull, A. P., & Curry, L. An observational analysis of the IEP conference. *Exceptional Children*, 1980, *46*, 278–286.

Golin, A. K., & Ducanis, A. J. Interdisciplinary implications of the ethical standards of the health professions. Paper presented at the meeting of the Association of Schools of the Allied Health Professions, Dallas, November 1977.

Golin, A. K., & Ducanis, A. J. Preparation for teamwork: A model for interdisciplinary education. *Teacher Education and Special Education*, in press.

Goode, W. J. Encroachment, charlatanism and the emerging profession: Psychology, sociology and medicine. *American Sociological Review*, 1960, *25*, 902–914.

Gordon, G. *Role theory and illness*. New Haven, Conn.: College and University Press, 1966.

Gorham, K. A. A lost generation of parents. *Exceptional Children*, 1975, *41*, 521–525.

Greenwood, E. Attributes of a profession. *Social Work*, 1957, *2*(3), 44–55.

Grossman, R. K. *Brothers and sisters of retarded children: An exploratory study*. Syracuse, N.Y.: Syracuse University Press, 1972.

Guttentag, M., & Struening, E. L. (Eds.) *Handbook of evaluation research*. Beverly Hills: Sage Publications, 1975.

Hackman, J. R. Group influence of individuals. In M. D. Dunnette (Eds.), *Handbook of industrial and organizational psychology*. Chicago: Rand McNally, 1975.

Hackman, J. R., & Morris, C. G. Group tasks, group interaction process, and group performance effectiveness: A review and proposed integration. In L. Berkowitz (Ed.), *Advances in social psychology*. New York: Academic Press, 1975.

Hare, A. P. *Handbook of small group research* (2nd ed.). New York: Free Press, 1976.

Haring, N. G. *Behavior of exceptional children* (2nd ed.). Columbus: Charles Merrill, 1978.

Haring, N. G. (Ed.). *The experimental education training program: An inservice program for personnel serving the severely handicapped*, Vol. 2, *Support Services*. Seattle: University of Washington, College of Education, 1977.

Haring, N. G., & Phillips, E. L. *Analysis and modification of classroom behavior*. Englewood Cliffs, N.J.: Prentice-Hall, 1972.

Harris, C. S. Two team systems: Toward definition. *Mental Retardation*, 1977, *15*(2), 9.

Hart, V. The use of many disciplines with the severely and profoundly handicapped. In E. Sontag, J. Smith, & N. Certo (Eds.), *Educational programming for the severely and profoundly handicapped*. Reston, Va.: Division on Mental Retardation, Council of Exceptional Children, 1977.

Haselkorn, F. Some dynamic aspects of interpersonal practice in rehabilitation. *Social Casework*, 1958, *39*, 396–400.

Hayden, A., & Gotts, E. Multiple staffing patterns. In J. Jordan, A. Hayden, M. Karnes, & M. Wood (Eds.), *Early childhood education for exceptional children*. Reston, Va.: Council of Exceptional Children, 1977.

Hayes, J. Annual goals and short term objectives. In S. Torres (Ed.), *A primer on individualized education programs for handicapped children*. Reston, Va.: The Foundation for Exceptional Children, 1977.

Heilman, M. E. Identification of certain competencies needed by health care personnel in order to function as a health care team. Unpublished doctoral dissertation, University of Pittsburgh, 1977.

Hewett, F. M. Teaching speech to an autistic child through operant conditioning. *American Journal of Orthopsychiatry*, 1965, *35*, 927–936.

Hewett, F. M. *The emotionally disturbed child in the classroom*. Boston: Allyn & Bacon, 1968.

Hewett, F. M. with Forness, S. R. *Education of exceptional learners* (2nd ed.). Boston: Allyn & Bacon, 1977.

Hobbs, N. Helping disturbed children: Psychological and ecological strategies. *American Psychologist*, 1966, *21*, 105–115.

Hobbs, N. *The futures of children*. Washington, D.C.: Jossey-Bass, 1975.

Hoff, M., Fenton, K., Yoshida, R., & Kaufman, M. Notice and consent: The school's responsibility to inform parents. *Journal of School Psychology*, 1978, *16*, 265–273.

Hoffman, L. R. Homogeneity of member personality and its effect on group problem-solving. *Journal of Abnormal and Social Psychology*, 1959, *58*, 27–32.

Hoffman, L. R., & Maier, N. R. F. Quality and acceptance of problem solutions by members of homogeneous and heterogeneous groups. *Journal of Abnormal and Social Psychology*, 1961, *62*, 401–407.

Hollander, E. Conformity, status and idiosyncracy credit. *Psychological Review*, 1958, *65*, 117–127.

Holm, V. A. Team issues. In K. E. Allen, V. A. Holm, & R. L. Schiefelbusch (Eds.), *Early intervention: A team approach*. Baltimore: University Park Press, 1978.

Horwitz, J. Dimensions of rehabilitation teamwork. *Rehabilitation Record*, 1969, *10*, 36–39.

Horwitz, J. *Team practice and the specialist: An introduction to interdisciplinary teamwork*. Springfield, Illinois: Charles Thomas, 1970.

Hughes, E. C. Professions. In K. S. Lynn (Ed.), *The professions in America*. Boston: Houghton Mifflin, 1965.

Hurwitz, J. I., Zander, A. F., & Hymovitch, B. Some effects of power on the relations among group members. In D. Cartwright & A. Zander (Eds.), *Group dynamics: Research and theory* (3rd ed.). New York: Harper & Row, 1968.

Hutchinson, D. *A model for transdisciplinary staff development: A monograph* (Technical Report No. 8). New York: United Cerebral Palsy Association, Inc., 1974.

Hutt, M. L., Menninger, W. C., & O'Keefe, D. E. The neuropsychiatric team in the United States Army. *Mental Health*, 1947, *31*, 103–119.

Inhelder, B. *The diagnosis of reasoning in the mentally retarded* (2nd ed.). New York: Chandler Publishing, 1968.

Jacobson, S. R. A study of interprofessional collaboration. *Nursing Outlook*, 1974, *22*, 751–755.

Jacques, M. *Rehabilitation counseling: Scope and services*. Boston: Houghton Mifflin, 1970.

Janis, I. L. *Victims of groupthink*. Boston: Houghton Mifflin, 1972.

Janis, I. L., & Mann, L. *Decision making*. New York: Free Press, 1977.

Joint Commission on Accreditation of Hospitals. *Standards for residential facilities for the mentally retarded*. Chicago: Author, 1971.

Jones, R. L. Protection in evaluation procedures criteria and recommendations. In *Developing criteria for evaluation of the protection in evaluation procedures provision of Public Law 94–142*. U.S. Office of Education, Bureau of Education for the Handicapped, 1978.

Kalish, H. Stimulus generalization. In M. Marx & M. Bunch (Eds.), *Fundamentals and applications of learning*. New York: Macmillan Company, 1977.

Kauffman, J., & Hallahan, D. The medical model and the science of special education. *Exceptional Children*, 1974, *41*, 97–102.

Kauffman, J. Where special education for disturbed children is going: A personal view. *Exceptional Children*, 1980, *46*, 522–527.

Kelley, H. H., & Thibaut, J. W. Group problem solving. In G. Lindzey & E. Aronson (Eds.), *Handbook of social psychology* (Rev. edition), Vol. 4. Reading, Mass.: Addison-Wesley, 1969.

Kennedy, E. P.L. 94–142 poses a 'lofty challenge.' *Journal of Teacher Education*, 1978, *29*(6), 7.

Kingdon, D. R. *Matrix organization: Managing information technologies*. London: Tavistock, 1973.

Klein, S. D. Brother to sister: Sister to brother. *The Exceptional Parent*, 1972, *2*(1), 10–15; (2), 26–27.

Kogan, N., & Wallach, M. A. *Risk-taking: A study in cognition and personality*. New York: Holt, 1964.

Krathwohl, D. R., Bloom, B., & Masia, B. *Taxonomy of educational objectives*, Handbook 2, *Affective domain*. New York: David McKay Company, 1964.

Krech, D., & Crutchfield, R. S. *Theory and problems of social psychology*. New York: McGraw-Hill, 1948.

Lacks, P., Landsbaum, J., & Stern, M. Workshop in communication for members of a psychiatric team. *Psychological Reports*, 1970, *26*, 423–430.

Laing, R. D., Phillipson, H., & Lee, A. R. *Interpersonal perception: A theory and a method of research*. New York: Harper & Row, 1966.

Larry P. v. Wilson Riles. NOC-71-2270 RFP, U.S. District Court, Northern District of California (June 21, 1972).

Laughlin, P. R., Branch, L. G., & Johnson, H. H. Individual versus triadic performance on a unidimensional complementary task as a function of initial ability level. *Journal of Personality and Social Psychology*, 1969, *12*, 144–150.

Leff, W. F., Raven, B. H., & Gunn, R. L. A preliminary investigation of social influence in the mental health professions. *American Psychologist*, 1964, *19*, 505. (Abstract)

Levine, S., & White, P. E. The community of health organizations. In H. Freeman, S. Levine, & L. Reeder (Eds.), *Handbook of medical sociology* (2nd ed.). Englewood Cliffs, N.J.: Prentice-Hall, 1972.

Lewis, C., & Resnick, B. Relative orientations of students of medicine and nursing to ambulatory patient care. *Journal of Medical Education*, 1966, *41*, 162–166.

Lieberman, L. Territoriality: Who does what to whom? *Journal of Learning Disabilities*, 1980, *13*(3), 15–17.

Losen, S., & Diament, B. Parent involvement in school planning. *The Exceptional Parent*, 1978, *8*(4), 19–22.

Lovaas, O. O., & Simmons, J. Q. Manipulation of self-destruction in three retarded children. *Journal of Applied Behavior Analysis*, 1969, *2*, 143–157.

Lovitt, T. C. Applied behavior analysis technique and curriculum research: Implications for instruction. In N. G. Haring & R. K. Schiefelbusch (Eds.), *Teaching special children*. New York: McGraw-Hill, 1976.

Lyon, C. Comprehensive medical evaluation of children with learning disabilities: Comparison of pediatricians' and teachers' perceptions. *Journal of Learning Disabilities*, 1980, *13*(3), 19–24.

Marquis, D. G. Individual responsibility and group decisions involving risk. *Industrial Management Review*, 1962, *3*, 8–23.

Martin, E. Education of the Handicapped Act and teacher education. *Journal of Teacher Education*, 1978, *29*(6), 8.

Martin, H. (Ed.). *The abused child: A multidisciplinary approach to development issues and treatment*. Cambridge, Mass.: Ballinger, 1976.

Martin, R. Expert & referent power: A framework for understanding and maximizing consultation effectiveness. *Journal of School Psychology*, 1978, *16*, 49–55.

McCormick, L., & Goldman, R. The transdisciplinary model: Implications for service delivery and personnel preparation for the severely and profoundly handicapped. *AAESPH Review*, 1979, *4*, 152–161.

Mercer, J. *Labeling the mentally retarded*. Berkeley: University of California Press, 1973.

Mercer, J. R. Psychological assessment and the rights of children. In N. Hobbs (Ed.), *Issues in the classification of children* (Vol. 1). Washington: Jossey-Bass, 1975.

Mercer, J. R. Protection in evaluation procedures. In *Developing criteria for evaluation of the protection in evaluation procedures provision of Public Law 94–142*. U.S. Office of Education, Bureau for the Education of the Handicapped, 1978.

Meyerson, L. Somatopsychology of physical disability. In W. Cruickshank (Ed.), *Psychology of exceptional children and youth* (3rd ed.). Englewood Cliffs, N.J.: Prentice-Hall, 1971.

Moran, M. *Assessment of the exceptional learner in the regular classroom*. Denver, Co.: Love Publishing Co., 1978.

Mordock, J. B. *The other children: An introduction to exceptionality*. New York: Harper & Row, 1975.

Mullins, J. *A teacher's guide to management of physically handicapped students*. Springfield, Ill.: Charles Thomas, 1979.

Myers, D. Enhancement of initial risk-taking tendencies in social situations. Unpublished doctoral dissertation, University of Iowa, 1967.

Myers, D., & Lamm, H. The group polarization phenomenon. *Psychological Bulletin*, 1976, *83*, 602–627.

Nadolsky, J., & Brewer, E. The staff conference and group decision-making: A preliminary investigation. *Rehabilitation Literature*, 1977, *38*, 242–249.

Nagi, S. Z. Team work in health care in the United States: A sociological perspective. *The Milbank Memorial Fund Quarterly, Health & Society*, 1975, *53*, 75–91.

National Education Association. *Journal of Proceedings and Addresses of the Thirty-Seventh Annual Meeting held at Washington, D.C.*, July 7–12, 1898.

Newland, T. E. Psychological assessment of exceptional children and youth. In W. Cruickshank (Ed.), *Psychology of exceptional children and youth* (4th ed.). Englewood Cliffs, N.J.: Prentice-Hall, 1980.

Nicolais, J. P. Policy development and strategy in the licensure of speech pathologists and audiologists. *American Journal of Occupational Therapy*, 1976, *30*, 20–26.

Nóll, V. H. *Introduction to educational measurement* (2nd ed.). Boston: Houghton Mifflin, 1965.

Parker, A. W. The team approach to primary health care. *Neighborhood Health Center Seminar Program, monograph series no. 3.* California: University Extension, Berkeley, 1972.

Parsons, T. *The social system.* Glencoe, Ill.: Free Press, 1951.(a)

Parsons, T. Illness and the role of the physician: A sociological perspective. *American Journal of Orthopsychiatry*, 1951, *21*, 452–460.(b)

Parsons, T. Some problems confronting sociology as a profession. *American Sociological Review*, 1959, *24*, 547–559.

Parsons, T. The sick role and the role of the physician reconsidered. *The Milbank Memorial Fund Quarterly, Health & Society*, 1975, *53*, 257–278.

Parsons, T., & Fox, R. Therapy and the modern urban family. *Journal of Social Issues*, 1952, *8*, 31–44.

Patterson, C. H. Is the team concept obsolete? *Journal of Rehabilitation*, 1959, *25*(2), 9–10; 27–28.

Perrow C. The analysis of goals in complex organizations. *American Sociological Review*, 1961, *26*, 854–866.

Piaget, J. *The language and thought of the child.* New York: Harcourt, Brace, 1926.

Piaget, J. *The origins of intelligence in children* (2nd ed.). New York: International Universities Press, 1952.

Piaget, J., & Inhelder, B. *The psychology of the child.* (H. Weaver, trans.). New York: Basic Books, 1969. (originally published, 1966)

Pruitt, D. G., & Teger, A. I. *Is there a shift toward risk in group discussion? If so, is it a group phenomenon? If so, what causes it?* Paper presented at the meeting of the American Psychological Association, Washington, D.C., Sept. 1967.

Pruitt, D. G., & Teger, A. I. The risky-shift in group betting. *Journal of Experimental Social Psychology*, 1969, *5*, 115–126.

Quick, M. Licensing of hearing clinicians and teachers of the hearing impaired. *The Volta Review*, 1976, *78*, 178–182.

Rae-Grant, Q. A., & Marcuse, D. The hazards of teamwork. *American Journal of Orthopsychiatry*, 1968, *38*, 4–8.

Rains, P. M., Kitsuse, J. I., Duster, T., & Freidson, E. The labeling approach to deviance. In N. Hobbs (Ed.), *Issues in the classification of children* (Vol. 1). Washington: Jossey-Bass, 1975.

Raiser, L., & Van Nagel, C. The loophole in Public Law 94–142. *Exceptional Children*, 1980, *46*, 516–520.

Reitan, H. T., & Shaw, M. E. Group membership, sex-composition of the group, and conformity behavior. *Journal of Social Psychology*, 1964, *64*, 45–51.

Renne, D., & Moore, J. *Transdisciplinary evaluation of children.* Salt Lake City, Utah: University of Utah, 1977. (ERIC Document Reproduction Service No. ED 150 799)

Reynolds, M. Basic issues in restructuring teacher education. *Journal of Teacher Education*, 1978, *29*(6), 25–29.

Reynolds, M., & Birch, J. *Teaching exceptional children in all America's schools.* Reston, Va: The Council for Exceptional Children, 1977.

Rhodes, W. C. The disturbing child: A problem of ecological management. *Exceptional Children*, 1967, *33*, 449–455.

Robbins, S. *Managing organizational conflict.* Englewood Cliffs: Prentice-Hall, 1974.

Robinson, N. M., & Robinson, H. B. *The mentally retarded child: A psychological approach* (2nd ed.). New York: McGraw-Hill, 1976.

Ross, A. O. *The exceptional child in the family.* New York: Grune & Stratton, 1964.

Rubin, I., & Beckhard, R. Factors influencing the effectiveness of health teams. *Milbank Memorial Quarterly*, 1972, *50*, 317–335.

Rubin, I., Plovnick, M., & Fry, R. *Improving the coordination of care: A program for health team development*. Cambridge, Mass.: Ballinger, 1975.

Salvia, J., & Ysseldyke, J. E. *Assessment in special and remedial education*. Boston: Houghton Mifflin Co., 1978.

Scheff, T. J. Decision rules, types of error, and their consequence in medical diagnosis. *Behavioral Sciences*, 1963, *8*, 97–107.

Schmitt, B. D. (Ed.). *The child protection team handbook*. New York: Garland STPM Press, 1978.

Scriven, M. The methodology of evaluation. In *Perspectives of curriculum evaluation*. AERA monograph series on Curriculum Evaluation, No. 1. Evanston: Rand McNally, 1967.

Segall, A. The sick role concept: Understanding illness behavior. *Journal of Health and Social Behavior*, 1976, *17*, 163–170.

Seligman, M. *Strategies for helping parents of exceptional children*. New York: Free Press, 1979.

Sells, C., & West, M. Interdisciplinary clinics for the developmentally disabled: Washington State's experience. *Mental Retardation*, 1976, *14*, 19–21.

Shaw, M. Communication networks. In L. Berkowitz (Ed.), *Advances in experimental social psychology* (Vol. 1). New York: Academic Press, 1964.

Shaw, M. E. *Group dynamics: The psychology of small group behavior* (2nd ed.). New York: McGraw-Hill, 1976.

Sirvis, B. Developing IEP's for physically handicapped students: A transdisciplinary viewpoint. *Teaching Exceptional Children*, 1978, *10*, 78–82.

Solnit, A., & Stark, M. Mourning and the birth of a defective child. In F. J. Menolascino (Ed.), *Psychiatric aspects of the diagnosis and treatment of mental retardation*. Seattle, Wash.: Special Child Publications, 1971.

Stainback, S., Stainback, W., & Maurer, S. Training teachers for the severely and profoundly handicapped: A new frontier. *Exceptional Children*, 1976, *42*, 203–209.

Steen, L. A. Computer chess: Mind versus machine. *Science News*, November 29, 1975, 345–350.

Steiner, I. D. *Group process and productivity*. New York: Academic Press, 1972.

Stoner, J. A. F. A comparison of individual and group decisions involving risk. Unpublished Masters thesis, School of Industrial Management: Massachusetts Institute of Technology, 1961.

Sussman, M. B. Occupational sociology and rehabilitation. In M. B. Sussman (Ed.), *Sociology and rehabilitation*. Washington, D.C.: American Sociological Association, 1966.

Swick, K. J., Flake-Hobson, C., & Raymond, G. The first step: Establishing parent-teacher communication in the IEP conference. *Teaching Exceptional Children*, 1980, *12*, 144–145.

Szasz, G. Educating for the health team. *Canadian Journal of Public Health*, 1970, *61*, 386–390.

Tarver, S. G. How special education has changed. In R. D. Kneedler & S. G. Tarver (Eds.), *Changing perspectives in special education*. Columbus: Charles E. Merrill, 1977.

Teger, A. I., & Pruitt, D. G. Components of group risk-taking. *Journal of Experimental Social Psychology*, 1967, *3*, 189–205.

Telford, C. W., & Sawrey, J. M. *The exceptional individual* (3rd ed.). Englewood Cliffs, N.J.: Prentice-Hall, 1977.

Thibaut, J. W., & Kelley, H. H. *The social psychology of groups*. New York: Wiley, 1959.

Thomas, E. D., & Marshall, M. J. Clinical evaluation and coordination of services: An ecological model. *Exceptional Children*, 1977, *44*, 16–22.

Tichy, M. *Health care teams: An annotated bibliography*. New York: Praeger Publishers, 1974.

Tichy, M. *Behavioral science techniques: An annotated bibliography for health professionals*. New York: Praeger Publishers, 1975.

Tichy, N. *Organization design for primary health care*. New York: Praeger Publishers, 1977.

Treiman, D. J. *Occupational prestige in comparative perspective*. New York: Academic Press, 1977.

Urban, J. Identification and management of hearing impairment. *The Volta Review*, 1975, *77*, 10–20.

Vogt, M., & Ducanis, A. Conflict and cooperation in the allied health professions. *Journal of Allied Health*, 1977, *6*(17), 23–30.

Vollmer, H. M., & Mills, D. L. (Eds.). *Professionalization*. Englewood Cliffs: Prentice-Hall, 1966.

Wagner, R. Rehabilitation team practice. *Rehabilitation Counseling Bulletin*, 1977, *21*, 206–217.

Walker, H. M., & Lev, J. *Statistical inference*. New York: Henry Holt, 1953.

Wallach, M. A., & Kogan, N. The rules of information, discussion, and consensus in group risk-taking. *Journal of Experimental Social Psychology*, 1965, *1*, 1–19.

Wallach, M. A., Kogan, N., & Bem, D. J. Diffusion of responsibility and level of risk taking in groups. *Journal of Abnormal and Social Psychology*, 1964, *68*, 263–274.

Wallach, M. A., Kogan, N., & Burt, R. Can group members recognize the effects of group discussion upon risk-taking? *Journal of Experimental Social Psychology*, 1965, *1*, 379–395.

Webster's third new international dictionary, unabridged. Springfield, Mass.: G. & C. Merriam Company, 1976.

Weiner, D., & Raths, O. Contributions of the mental-hygiene clinic team to clinic decisions. *American Journal of Orthopsychiatry*, 1959, *29*, 350–356.

Weinstein, A. S. Evaluation through medical records and related information systems. In M. Guttentag & E. L. Streuning (Eds.), *Handbook of evaluation research* (Vol. 1). Beverly Hills: Sage Publications, 1975.

Weisbord, M. R. Why organization development hasn't worked (so far) in medical centers. *Health Care Maintenance Review*, 1976, *1*(1), 17–28.

Weiss, C. Evaluation research in the political context. In M. Guttentag & E. L. Streuning (Eds.), *Handbook of evaluation research* (Vol. 1). Beverly Hills: Sage Publications, 1975.

Weitz, H. *Behavior change through guidance*. New York: Wiley & Sons, 1964.

Wendland, C J., & Crawford, C. C. *Team delivery of primary health care*. Los Angeles: Los Angeles County Medical Training System, 1976.

Whitehouse, F. A. Teamwork: A democracy of professions. *Exceptional Children*, 1951, *18*, 5–52.

Wiesen, A., Hartley, G., Richardson, C., & Roske, A. The retarded child as a reinforcing agent. *Journal of Experimental Child Psychology*, 1967, *5*, 109–113.

Wile, E. The team approach in a rehabilitation agency for the blind. *The New Outlook*, 1970, *64*(2), 33–37

Wilson, A J. Teamwork conference yields high dividends. *Journal of Rehabilitation*, 1962, *28*(2), 23–25.

Wilson, R. *The sociology of health*. New York: Random House, 1970.

Winter, M. The rehabilitation team: A catalyst to risky rehabilitation decisions? *Rehabilitation Counseling Bulletin*, 1976, *19*, 581–586.

Wise, H., Beckhard, R., Rubin, I., & Kyte, A. L. (Eds.). *Making health teams work*. Cambridge, Mass.: Ballinger, 1974.

Woodman, R., & Sherwood, J. The role of team development in organizational effectiveness: A critical review. *Psychological Bulletin*, 1980, *88*, 166–186.

Woodward, M. The application of Piaget's theory to research in mental deficiency. In N. R. Ellis (Ed.), *Handbook of mental deficiency*. New York: McGraw-Hill, 1963.

Wright, B. *Physical disability—A psychological approach*. New York: Harper & Row, 1960.

Wynne, M. D., & O'Connor, P *Exceptional children: A developmental view*. Lexington, Mass.: D. C. Heath & Co., 1979.

Yoshida, R. K., Fenton, K., Maxwell, J. P., & Kaufman, M. J. Group decision making in the planning team process: Myth or reality? *The Journal of School Psychology*, 1978, *16*, 237–245. (a)

Yoshida, R. K., Fenton, K., Kaufman, M., & Maxwell, J. P. Parental involvement in the special education pupil planning process: The school's perspective. *Journal of School Psychology*, 1978, *16*, 531–534.

Yoshida, R. K., Fenton, K., Maxwell, J. P., & Kaufman, M. J. Ripple effect: Communication of planning team decisions to program implementers. *Journal of School Psychology* 1978, *16*, 177–183. (b)

Ysseldyke, J. E., & Regan, R. R. Nondiscriminatory assessment: A formative model. *Exceptional Children*, 1980, *46*, 465–466.

Zander, A., Cohen, A., & Stotland, E. Power and relations among professions. In D. Cartwright (Ed.), Studies in social power. Ann Arbor, Michigan: Institute for Social Research, 1959.

Index

About the Authors

Anne K. Golin received her doctorate in clinical psychology at the University of Iowa. She holds the rank of Professor in the School of Education at the University of Pittsburgh, with a joint appointment in Rehabilitation Counseling and Special Education. Before going to the University of Pittsburgh, Dr. Golin served as a Field Assessment Officer for the Peace Corps Training Program at the University of Wisconsin-Milwaukee. Her primary academic interests are in psychology of exceptional children, the psychology of disability, mental health, and the interdisciplinary team. She has presented a number of papers at professional meetings, is a contributor to professional journals in psychology and rehabilitation, and has conducted workshops concerning the interdisciplinary team.

Alex J. Ducanis received his doctorate in educational administration from the University of Pittsburgh where he is now Director of the Higher Education Program and Professor of Higher Education and of the Health Related Professions. His academic interests are in research methodology, the American college and university, and the interdisciplinary team. He has published numerous research and scholarly papers and is a frequent contributor at professional meetings. Before returning to the University of Pittsburgh he served as Director of Institutional Research at the State University of New York at Binghamton and as Educational Research Associate in the New York State Education Department. He also served as the first Director of the Institute for Higher Education at the University of Pittsburgh.